COMMUNITY
THAT IS
CHRISTIAN

COMMUNITY
THAT IS
CHRISTIAN

2D. EDITION

JULIE A. GORMAN

Baker Books

A Division of Baker Book House Co
Grand Rapids, Michigan 49516

Published by Baker Books
a division of Baker Book House Company
P.O. Box 6287, Grand Rapids, MI 49516-6287

Previously published in 1993 by Victor Books

Printed in the United States of America

Library of Congress Cataloging-in-Publication Data

Gorman, Julie.
    Community that is Christian / Julie A. Gorman.
        p.   cm.
    Includes bibliographical references and index.
    ISBN 0-8010-9145-4 (pbk.)
       1. Church group work. 2. Small groups—Religious aspects—Christianity.
    I. Title.
    BV652.2 .G569 2002
    253´.7—dc21
                                              2002001968

For current information about all releases from Baker Book House, visit our web site:
http://www.bakerbooks.com

For Dianne,
who has lived out God's gift of community
by being spiritual companion and friend to me.

And for my students,
whose presence continually encourages me
to teach and live community.

CONTENTS

FOREWORD

Small groups emerged clearly in the latter part of the twentieth century as one of the most potent instruments available to the Christian church for growth, renewal, service, and outreach both in the United States and throughout the world. From the cell groups energizing the growth of the largest congregation in the world in Seoul, Korea, to the discipleship and Bible study groups of an inner city church in Philadelphia, Christian small groups provide important opportunities for evangelism and new member assimilation, for involvement with contemporary needs such as homelessness or world hunger, and for building relationships in an individualistic and often lonely culture. Over a decade ago, a national study led by Princeton University sociologist Robert Wuthnow documented the astonishing fact that approximately one in four adult Americans is involved in a small group that includes spiritual purposes. These trends have continued, and the largest percentage of these groups are church based.

Yet for all the importance of the small group movement, little of substance has been written for Christian leaders, whether lay or clergy, to help them better understand the sometimes complex dynamics and critical issues at work whenever people gather together in Christian small groups. This book performs that useful function from a solidly Christian, biblically grounded framework that will provide encouragement and insight for Christians seeking to begin or develop small groups in their church.

Author Julie Gorman brings solid qualifications to provide such a resource. As a pastor in several congregations and as a professor at Fuller Theological Seminary, she has taught thousands of Christians the art and science of building Christian community through small groups. She has not only studied the relevant research literature on small groups, but she has also visited, examined, and probed hundreds of church programs to gain increased knowledge of what makes groups work. She is a gifted teacher who demonstrates her commitment to equipping the people of God to know and do the will of God in the world. With her biblical understanding of discipleship, she provides practical help to beginners and experienced leaders alike. I have been privileged to work alongside her as a colleague and friend for many years. I am grateful for the work she has done to make her experience and learning available to an ever larger audience.

Roberta Hestenes
international minister, World Vision

CLOSE ENCOUNTERS
OF THE HUMAN KIND

> Community is what people say they are seeking when they join small groups. Yet the kind of community they create is quite different from the communities in which people have lived in the past. These communities are more fluid and more concerned with the emotional states of the individual.
>
> Wuthnow, 1994, p. 3

Small groups have come of age! They have found unprecedented acceptance and endorsement. Big business has come to recognize them as an essential component of good business. The world of education has realized it must produce graduates who are fluent in the skills of group dynamics and who have learned how to work in teams. Studies have shown the priority of small group experiences in enhancing the process of learning: Small groups increase involvement, improve achievement, and promote persistence and positive attitudes toward learning.

The population at large confirms this fascination with groups by their widespread participation in them. Research completed just before the turn of the century claims that approximately seventy-five million adult Americans are meeting regularly for some kind of small-group interaction and support—that's 40 percent of the adult population of the United States.

But while groups have become prolific, experiencing true community often remains the elusive gold ring. We say we want community, but we want it on the terms we create. "Having it our way" frequently means God's gift of community is skillfully adjusted to harmonize with cultural values. The rewards of individual freedoms, the power surge that comes from being self-improved and self-sufficient compete to reshape the gift into "lite" community that doesn't require too much nor add much weight to our lives. And thus the search for "being connected" goes on.

Wake Up!

This book is a call to believers to recognize and claim a community that is distinctively theirs by covenant and calling. If we are ever to think and act Christianly, we must take into account the heritage that is a part of our uniqueness as children of God. That heritage includes community. It is a gift from the One who created us and called us to be in his likeness. Such community can never be created by human devices but has already been designed by God and given to us. Our role, like that of the Israeli crossing into the Promised Land, is the taking of the land by choosing to plant the soles of our feet on the "given ground" to possess it.

This is a call to wake up to the fact that we can never realize the likeness of Christ by ourselves alone; we will never transform the world as individuals; we will never discover fullness of life in Christ if we stay solo. We are distinct as people of God because we were made to live in dependence on the head and interdependently with the diverse parts of the body. Community that is distinctively Christian will have group dynamic elements that are healthy. But it will embrace more. Community that is distinctively Christian will host the presence of God in the midst of it! It is God himself who makes community possible. His presence is catalytic to the experiencing of togetherness beyond human endeavor. As Palmer asserts, "Community is finally a religious phenomenon. There is nothing capable of binding together willful, broken human selves except some transcendent power" (Palmer, 1977, p. 18). This is why true community is experienced as "holy ground." Scott Peck writes,

> The wisdom of a true community often seems miraculous . . . and is more a matter of divine spirit and possible divine intervention. This is one of the reasons why the feeling of joy is such a frequent concomitant of the spirit of community. The members feel they have been temporarily—at least partially—transported out of a mundane world of ordinary preoccupations. For the moment it is as if heaven and earth had somehow met.
>
> Peck, 1987, p. 76

Community as Counterculture

Autonomy

As Americans we are proud that we can take care of ourselves. The Declaration of Independence is more than a political document. It is a personal manifesto. From our youth we have been taught such axioms as "Don't depend on anyone else," "Decide on your own," "If you don't look out for yourself, nobody will," "Stand on your own two feet." We have embraced freedom of choice as the highest virtue. We prize the license to move in and out of relationships based on our own decisions. The choice to have children, to stay married, and a host of other choices common today underscore this freedom. If the relationship does not fulfill us—whether friendship, group, church, marriage, or other—we can opt out.

Self-focus

"Rights language" is our native tongue. We make decisions based on our personal rights rather than on absolutes and virtues. People quit jobs, break rules, and abdicate responsibilities with no other explanation than "I felt (or didn't feel) like doing it." The drive for self-fulfillment reveals our preoccupation with personal autonomy and separateness. In our culture individualism is king and generates pride. Our heroes are those who made it on their own or survived to make it to the top of the heap by standing on others.

Personal Gain

We evaluate each relationship by "What can I get out of it?" "In general, Americans do not join groups for what they can contribute, but for what they can get out of them" (Dyrness, 1989, pp. 98–99). Even groups have "become for us a collection of individuals created by individuals for their own individual advantages" (Kraus, 1979, pp. 76–77).

As a result, the small group movement today is frequently seen as something to be used to another advantage (church growth or personal support system) or as an optional extra for social benefit. We are a nation preoccupied with taking care of ourselves, and such groups provide a self-help forum. They also provide someone to listen to us in a world that moves too fast and remains too independent to spend time caring about individuals.

Christian education with its emphasis on personal felt needs and individualized growth has contributed to this cultural cult of narcissism. Christianity in general has gravitated toward a privatized cultivation of the faith. The "free" church model with its emphasis on the voluntary association and commitment of individuals is founded on an individual's Christian experience. It is "me and Jesus," "my faith," "my God," "my relationship with him," "the church of my choice." The subjective question around which our faith revolves is "Have you come to know Jesus Christ as your personal Savior?" Personal piety is the benchmark by which we evaluate a person's faith. "Subjective criteria become the norm for reality and truth in religious profession. Spirituality is defined in terms of personality characteristics, belief patterns, and personal piety" (Kraus, 1979, p. 110).

While this personal emphasis has merit, it must always be in balance with the equally valuable corporate emphasis. In the Puritan era the development of a personal relationship with Christ, where it occurred at the expense of community, was identified as anti-Christian. Puritan Thomas Goodwin declared,

> To be proficient in "holy duties" is indeed more sweet to a man's own self, but to be proficient in our calling is more profitable to others—to the Church, the commonwealth, or the family—and so may glorify God more.
>
> quoted in Horton, 1991, p. 167

When scriptural interpretation is left to the individual, it often is shaped by that which supports the individual's lifestyle. When moral values are determined by the individual, they become relative, based on the feelings of one. When Christian graces are seen as an individual's achievements, their godly foundations are undermined by a sense of pride. When the corporate element is missing, we lose more than numbers; we become centered on self.

Results

Created to be an interdependent, integral part of community, individuals cannot abdicate this role without numerous consequences both to themselves and to the system that they comprise. Our culture exalts its freedom, choices, and personal achievements. But the people in our culture also live with loneliness, competition, and fear of not being accepted.

This sense of living in interconnectedness with people one didn't choose and who may not enhance one's personal achievements does not sit well with today's culture, even for many evangelical Christians. Self-realization, individual freedom, privacy, and autonomy have been bred into our being. We have identified such achievements and powers even with being Christian. Thus we can easily operate in the church with little change. We simply modify biblical frameworks to embrace our cultural philosophy. And "God helps those who help themselves" becomes a principle for Christian living. Pride is fostered in individualized spiritual growth, outdistancing the others who lack determination and perseverance. Groups become techniques for sharpening our own skills and coping with our own needs. Groups are to be embraced only when we feel comfortable, and they're to be ignored when we don't. Responsibility for others is nice as long as it doesn't interfere with our personal development and as long as we can choose those we're responsible for. Groups are fine as long as they know their boundaries and realize that the individual transcends the corporate. Each must determine what is best for him or her.

Can Christians who have been bombarded with cultural mores extolling American individualism be re-created to value the sanctity of the individual within an overarching sphere of community? That is the hope that has spawned this book. Can those who are born of God reframe their thinking in operational spheres that are opposed to this widely accepted individualism? Will we settle for a semblance of godliness in this area but deny the power of God to transform us into and through community?

Beware the Counterfeit

As possessors of a contrasting worldview, we struggle against another temptation in community. That temptation is to settle for a semblance of community by simply placing small groups on our church or classroom menu. Real community takes submission and commitment as well as intentionality and time. Simply calling a gathering a group or a committee does not make it into community. True community issues out of a realization that God has placed us and held us together as he wants. This connection is not because we are so likable or because we share in a common task or bring special abilities to the group. By calling us into this relationship in a group, God reveals himself in the world. Community becomes God's nurturing, caring, revealing, supportive means of displaying himself as a personal, relational being in our culture.

Living in community requires envisioning and cultivating responses of mutuality, service, and corporate responsibility. It implies receiving and pursuing increasing trust, self-disclosure, and interdependency.

There is no "lite" relational commitment for those who find it difficult to be in a group relationship. Likewise, our Christian classrooms must actually display distinctives that are different from the typical university classroom. Those distinctives must reveal God's priority on community. We cannot be content with counterfeits that bear the label but not the goods. "Let's form groups" is more than a methodology.

Life is *us* and not just *me*. We exist in webs of relationships. Whatever we become impacts our networks. This corporate connection has a reciprocal effect on us as individuals. We become as the networks affect us. (The impact on the body is the major reason for Ananias and Sapphira's judgment [Acts 5]). Because we are locked into this relational dance, no person exists outside of the system, unaffected by and isolated from others.

Every act of authentic self-disclosure makes one person's story a gift to the growth of another. When we genuinely understand another person's story, we grow as individuals and our spiritual nature is magnified. Therefore, every act of responsible challenge in the spirit of understanding is an invitation to an increase in stature. And when we engage in a nondefensive exploration in response to that challenge, we show our commitment to the larger dimensions of life (H. Miller, 1979).

We cannot play at community development. It is not an optional choice for those more relational by nature. It is not possible to set it aside to pursue private gain and seek God's blessings on our own. It is not enough simply to embrace the concept without allowing the reality of the needs and presence of others to affect our lifestyles. Dietrich Bonhoeffer speaks of people who love the idea of community more than the experience of community.

Community is a way of life. We don't like to think of being responsible for others. In our natural state we don't like being our brother's keeper. Nor do we want any other person having responsibility for us. Dependency is on the most-feared list today. Self-disclosure is reserved for the professionals whom we pay to listen. Vulnerability and weakness are dangerous. Commitment is binding and controlling. It is easy to settle for a counterfeit or substitute because of the cost to ourselves in pursuing real community.

Community: Work of God's Spirit

Groups are user-friendly. It is impossible to find a person who has never had any group experience. They have become "tools" in the hands of the experts. Our hunger for control causes us to analyze the functioning of groups and reduce such functioning to logic, combining principles with techniques in a system of group rules and rights. In so doing we think we can create community at will through the exercise of the right patterns. But community is more than control and implementation of group dynamic techniques.

The behavioral sciences of education, sociology, psychology, and anthropology contribute much insight to the descriptive workings of a group. Each presents information from the perspective of a limited system. Larry Crabb observes,

> In our demand that we be practical, we have nudged the Spirit aside and gone after objectives we can reach without Him. . . . Training classes for small group leaders often have more to do with techniques of leadership and handling conflict and drawing quiet people into the discussion than with spiritual dependence, spiritual character, and spiritual wisdom.
>
> Crabb, 1999, p. 126

Just as the new birth requires the "inner logic of the Spirit," which is beyond the outer logic of the mind, so the development of life together in community requires the unique touch of the transcendent One. Eugene Peterson comments, "When spiritual formation permits itself to be dominated by behavioral sciences, it is inevitably secularized and individualized with occasional prayerful nods upwards for help in self-actualization" (Peterson in Crabb, 1999, p. 126).

The person who operates out of a desire to practice the values that are in Christ will find himself or herself being group-dynamically effective, not on the basis of controlling a situation through a technique but out of an inner drive that is expressing the originator of community. Thus kingdom people who are walking in the truth naturally put into practice Spirit-directed skills of supporting, caring for, and building up others in the body relationship.

"Equipping" by its very nature is not just teaching skills but holistically growing people up in Christ's way of living and loving so that the whole body ends up increasing in maturity in him. The building of community will never be achieved by the perfection of better techniques but by the development of spiritually attuned people who realize and respond to the interconnected system of relationships into which they have been placed by God himself. Community is developed not only by insight into relational skills but also primarily by cultivation of a heart that knows and loves God and his people. Thus this book is actually a call for Christian formation as essential to living in community.

There is nothing sinful about methodology and research. The following pages contain principles from research and development of groups over the years. Such studies often illustrate the rules under which the Creator operates. But community as God envisioned it can never be reduced to dynamics and skills. We can teach expressions and cultivations of caring, but we can't give members hearts that care, especially when it might cost them comfort to express that caring. We can help members understand principles and priorities of commitment, but we cannot generate commitment within them, a commitment that takes precedence over their own self-interests. We can acquaint people with the value and skills involved in esteem-building in one another, but that does not guarantee that those people will promote someone else's well-being at their own expense. Implanting the mind of Christ is the Spirit's work. We borrow from research and development anything that does not contradict our theological superstructure. But when it comes to community, to whom shall we go? Not to the latest guru. Peter's words remain true, "You alone have the words of life." To live community is to live Christ's life and to follow his call.

> Community life is not a creation of human will but an obedient response to the reality of our being united. Many people who have lived together for years and whose love for one another has been tested more than once know that the decisive experience in their life was not that they were able to hold together but they were held together. That, in fact, we are a community not because we like each other or have a common task or project but because we are called together by God.
>
> Nouwen in Vanier, 1989, p. 45

Conceptual Design

This book is prepared for pastors, congregational leaders, and all who seek to explore and to implement community in their congregations. It is a text for those who equip people who will or who presently lead small groups, and it contains plan design and instructions for setting up a ministry of groups. It is intended to stimulate and inform the people of God as they facilitate community and work in covenant relationships with others. It is an interactive manual for transformation of community living in home, school, church, or marketplace.

Part I frames the big picture of community. It includes chapters on the biblical evidence of corporate togetherness and belonging, a chapter on the major mind-set that undermines community—individualism—and how that philosophical framework pervades and shapes our thinking today. The third chapter in Part I targets relational conditions in society that foster a deep-seated hunger for groups today.

Part II uses two chapters to sketch desirable goals and to describe true community and the process of transformation that enables a changed people. Chapter 6 is the gateway to group development, which comprises Part III of the book.

Topics dealt with in Part III include principles important to the beginning of a group, self-disclosure that causes a group to bond, contribution of individual uniquenesses to the formation of a group, communication facilitating, and response to conflict in community settings. There is also a chapter on turning points, which mark the growth cycles of groups.

Part IV finishes the book with a focus on two major realms of small group development: leadership and the ministry of small groups in a church setting.

Where relevant to the topic addressed, cultural and gender distinctives are included at the end of a chapter to maintain awareness of the treatment of this subject when modified by diversity. Gender specifics are dealt with under "In a Different Voice" and cultural uniqueness under "Through Others' Eyes."

As you begin this journey through *Community That Is Christian,* why not invite a friend with like-minded interest to read another copy so you can discuss and shape your ideas in community, and so you can enjoy community-building along the way.

PART I

THE BIG PICTURE
OF COMMUNITY

1

BIBLICAL FOUNDATIONS OF COMMUNITY

The most conspicuous weakness of evangelical Protestant theology has been its lack of understanding and witness to authentic community as the fulfillment of the believer's personal relation to God.

Kraus, 1979, p. 109

Christians should be concerned about community because it traces its origins directly back to God. The essence of community finds its roots deep in biblical-theological soil. Without God there would be no community. Some people equate community with small groups and claim that the act of instituting small groups is biblical.

There is a difference between small groups and community. Do we find small groups used as a methodology in Scripture? Yes. Does that make the methodology of grouping a few people together for some purpose biblical? Not necessarily. Boats were used in Scripture for various purposes, but we do not consider boats biblical. Small groups may become a means to an end. They can provide for the experiencing of community. Some people spend hundreds, even thousands, of hours in groups. But they may experience glimpses of community in only three or four of those groups or perhaps not at all. While community is God's intended purpose for when his people get together, it is not automatically present, nor can it be created on demand. Community takes time, commonality of commitment, and an openness to the formation of the Spirit. Groups may or may not become wombs for this birth of community among members.

When groups are viewed simply as a technique or program, they lose their essence. One author writes, "Most of the current small group activity in the church is not organic but technical and curricular. Churches do groups because they work" (Icenogle, 1994, p. 11). Within the perspective and purpose of community, small groups can become sirens that beckon us to return to the nature of what God created us to be.

God created and calls us to oneness. When we pursue that we move from a collection of players to a winning team; from instruments labeled woodwinds, strings, percussion, and brass to an orchestra that produces the sounds of music; from artist, color, shapes, canvass, paint, and subject to masterpiece. No one would think to claim that the canvass, the instruments, or the positions were the sought-after end. When we are together in community (harmoniously combined in oneness), we reflect our Creator.

Richard Halverson declares that Jesus Christ, by putting us in his body, determined that we would need each other as much as we need him (Halverson, *Perspective*). And the only way our corporate body can function is by being tuned to him. A. W. Tozer wisely observed that one hundred pianos are never more closely tuned to each other than when they are tuned to the same tuning fork.

Relating is at the heart of knowing God. Relating is also at the heart of becoming the people of God. Our faith journey is one we make together. Community is the context for our growth, and it is a distinctively Christian concept.

God Is Person

Because God is a person he is capable of having relationships. He is not an inanimate object, a force, a principle, or an impersonal dynamic. God is a person enjoying and pursuing relationships. He has awareness of himself and can communicate. The entire account of Scripture is a record of his commitment to developing relationships with others. Think of how different your perspective would be if God were a power or machine and not a person. Because God is personal, he opens up to us a world of relational possibilities. He personifies meaning by making it personal: "I am the truth." "I am the resurrection." "I am the life." And

```
***********************************
*      PASADENA CITY COLLEGE       *
*           BOOKSTORE              *
*         (626)585-7378            *
***********************************
SALE
01-18-05 10:19
  REG#7  TRAN#4735  CSHR#141


PENS/PENCILS/HIGHLIGHTER
413                              0.79
SUBTOTAL                        $0.79
TAX 8.250%                       0.07
TOTAL                           $0.86
Cash                             1.00
CHANGE DUE                      $0.14

*     Thank You For Shopping At    *
*           PCC Bookstore          *
*   Please Refer to Posted Refund  *
*          Policy for Returns      *
***********************************
```

SALE
01-18-05 10:19
REG07 TRAN4795 CSHR141

PENS/PENCIL SATION UNITER
413   0.79
SUBTOTAL $0.79
TAX 8.25%   0.07
TOTAL $0.86
Cash   1.00
CHANGE DUE $0.14

the way we know the meaning of any of these is by connecting with the Person of God.

God Is Person in Community

Christian believers can see some of the striking implications of social Trinity theory. First, the confession that we are created in the image of God begins to resonate with new overtones. In our fellowship and koinonia, in such homely endeavors as telling one another the truth or in doing such honest work as will help those in need—"above all in that love which binds everything together in perfect harmony"—we show not only that we have become members one of another, but also that we as restored community, we-in-the-plural, have become a remarkable image of God.

Plantinga, 1988, p. 27

Community is rooted in the very nature of God's personhood and, therefore, existed before creation. "Community finds its essence and definition deep within the being of God. . . . It is grounded in his nature and reflects his true identity as a plurality of persons in oneness of being" (Bilezikian, 1997, pp. 16, 43).

The doctrine of the Trinity has been called a contrived doctrine. In other words, nowhere in Scripture is the doctrine of the Trinity specifically spelled out compared to the way that the doctrine of God's holiness is declared. The Scriptures plainly state, "God is holy." Nevertheless, the Word of God firmly indicates that while being three separate persons, God is also one. We encounter the distinct Persons of Father, Son, and Spirit, often in the roles each plays. Bilezikian cites Genesis 1: "The Father generating creation, the Spirit hovering over it as protector, overseer and sanctifier of what God had made, and the Word which the Father speaks as executor of the will of the Speaker, an agent of creation" (Bilezikian, 1997, p. 17). Each Person acts differently, having distinct jobs to do, but they are essentially One.

Ray Anderson comments about the creation of humankind as it relates to God's personhood:

There is at least an intentional correspondence . . . between the intrinsic plurality of human being as constituted male and female and the being of God in whose likeness and image this plurality exists. . . . Quite clearly the imago is not totally present in the form of individual humanity but more completely as co-humanity. It is thus quite natural and expected that God himself is also a "we."

Anderson, 1982, p. 73

God's Image Portrays Community

While each of the Persons in the Godhead is unique, they represent interrelationship par excellence. Moltmann says it this way:

> The three divine persons are not there simply for themselves. They are there in that they are there for one another. They are persons in social relationship. The Father can be called Father only in relationship with the Son; the Son can be called Son only in relationship with the Father. The Spirit is the breath of the one who speaks. The breath goes out from the Father in the eternal moment in which the Father speaks the Word, which in another relationship is called the Son. . . . Being-a-person *(Personsein)* means "being in relationship."
>
> Moltmann-Wendel & Moltmann, 1983, p. 97

It is from observing Scripture's record of the words, actions, and attitudes communicated by one of the Persons in the Godhead to another in the Godhead that we glimpse the standard for what oneness is in community. Consider the following:

- There is reciprocal interdependence: The Father gave the Son (John 3:16), who in turn revealed the Father. "I have revealed you to those whom you gave me out of the world" (John 17:6a).
- What belongs to one belongs to the other: The Father gave the Son the people whom he enlightened, and the Son saw them as the Father's people. "I have revealed you to those whom you gave me out of the world. They were yours; you gave them to me and they have obeyed your word" (John 17:6). "All I have is yours, and all you have is mine. And glory has come to me through them" (John 17:10).
- What the Son had to give was given him by the Father: "Now they know that everything you have given me comes from you" (John 17:7).
- One portrayed the other: "Anyone who has seen me has seen the Father" (John 14:9).
- Each honored the will of the other: "Don't you believe that I am in the Father, and that the Father is in me? The words I say to you are not just my own. Rather, it is the Father, living in me, who is doing his work" (John 14:10). "For the very work that the Father has given me to finish, and which I am doing, testifies that the Father has sent me" (John 5:36). "My food . . . is to do the will of him who sent me and to finish his work" (John 4:34).

- Each showed deference to and dependence on the other: "These words you hear are not my own; they belong to the Father who sent me" (John 14:24). "What I have heard from him I tell the world" (John 8:26). "I do nothing on my own but speak just what the Father has taught me" (John 8:28). "I am telling you what I have seen in the Father's presence" (John 8:38). "The Son can do nothing by himself; he can do only what he sees his Father doing" (John 5:19). "By myself I can do nothing; I judge only as I hear" (John 5:30). "He [Spirit of truth] will not speak on his own; he will speak only what he hears" (John 16:13).
- One sought to please the other: "I seek not to please myself but him who sent me" (John 5:30). "I always do what pleases him" (John 8:29).
- One gave glory to the other: "Father. . . . Glorify your Son, that your Son may glorify you" (John 17:1). "He (Spirit) will bring glory to me by taking from what is mine and making it known to you" (John 16:14).
- One obeys the other: "I will send him [the Counselor] to you" (John 16:7).

What is therefore remarkable is that the social Trinity, shorn of certain angularities and excesses, is probably the most biblically faithful and theologically redolent theory now available.

Plantinga, 1988, p. 24

The self-sufficiency and personal independence that characterize our present evaluation of success are totally foreign to the Godhead that exists in interdependent oneness of community. This interconnectedness and exaltation of the other contributes to the glory of God.

think about this:

- What characteristics of true community are revealed through these expressions of oneness in the Godhead itself? When God calls us to community he wants us to . . .

God Made Us in His Image as Persons in Community

God created us as "persons." *Personhood* is only known in relation to others. Our identity as relational beings is carved out of interpersonal relating. Because God knew and experienced community, he made his creatures capable of the same. The creature must be separate but with a drive to relate. It is through encounter with others that the self exists "in the image and likeness of God" (Anderson, 1982, p. 74). Adam was created with the capacity and necessity for relating to God. The Divine made a creature with whom he could interact. Like an artist stepping back to admire his work, God surveyed what he had made and it was good (Gen. 1:31). The creature was what God wanted.

Made in his image we reflect our Creator. Made as persons we are made for relationship—with our Creator and with one another.

> Community as God ordained it was not an incidental concern of his nor did it happen haphazardly as the serendipitously creative result of a transcendental cosmic brainstorm. Community is deeply grounded in the nature of God. It flows from who God is. Because he is community, he creates community. It is his gift of himself to humans.
>
> Bilezikian, 1997, p. 27

As bearers of his image we hunger for community to fulfill that image. Even the books in our bookstores today reveal the never-ending desire for intimacy with another. Bilezikian captures the essence of this imprinted drive:

> Each one of us hides an awful secret. Buried deep within every human soul throbs a muted pain that never goes away. It is a lifelong yearning for the one love that will never be found, the languishing in our inner selves for an all-consuming intensity of intimacy that we know will never be fulfilled, a heart-need to surrender all that we are to a bond that will never fail. . . .
>
> The silent churning at the core of our beings is the tormenting need to know and to be known, to understand and to be understood, to possess and to be possessed, to belong unconditionally and forever without fear of loss, betrayal, or rejection. . . .
>
> Our mourning is for the closeness that was ours by right of creation. Our grief is for the gift lost in the turmoil of rebellion. And now, whenever there is hope, our hope is for paradise regained, for human destiny remade in the redemptive restoration of community, the only certainty of oneness for here and for eternity.
>
> Bilezikian, 1997, pp. 15–16

We can expect to see in the creature a reflection of the divine interdependency found in the community of the Godhead. As Anderson observes, "the image is not totally present in the form of individual humanity but more completely as co-humanity" (Anderson, 1982, p. 73). Thus God pronounced "aloneness" not good and made for Adam another "adam" that was "bone of his bone," an equal one who would complete the community design that God had in mind. God had created two who together as male and female reflected his own differentiated being. Now Adam would know community with co-humanity and with God as a "we." They were dependent on God yet displayed his glory; separate beings, yet they enjoyed oneness in community, doing the work assigned by the other and finding fulfillment in carrying out this role.

The record of Adam from the beginning until now reflects God's design that we enjoy him in relationship and that we know community with one another. Our God-hunger can be muffled, but it can never be drowned out. Our relational need to know and be loved by others was etched into the very image of God within us. Therefore, community is never optional—it is necessary for being what God designed us to be.

The pattern in the Garden was not happenstance. Community with the Creator was primary, but being in community with others of like kind was required for the Creator to be satisfied that the created being had become what he desired. God has made the two inseparable. John summarized: "Whoever loves God must also love his [her] brother" (1 John 4:21). "Connection with the King causes interconnectedness between all those connected with the King. . . . Jesus' relation to God as His father becomes the paradigm for universal interconnectedness" (Lee & Cowan, 1986, p. 148). God is relational, and he cultivates that hunger for another in us.

Whatever system God touches has the marks of relationship on it whether humankind in general, the nation of Israel, salvation, revelation, or the church. And this relational imprint bears both dimensions of being in relationship with God and in relationship with others.

Fractured Community: The Fall

Community was broken because one part sought to become the other. And the serpent tempted, "You will be like God" (Gen. 3:5). Independence was desired over dependency. Oneness was changed into separation, a separation that would transform every part of humanity's existence. Physical death meant separation of inner person from the body. Spiritual death was separation of the image-bearers from God, breaking the relationship. The image-bearers were separated from each other, knowing shame, hiding themselves from each other. "Shame is a wound felt from the inside, dividing us both from ourselves and from one another" (Kaufman in Bradshaw, 1988, p. 2).

The image of God in human beings was not totally destroyed, but it was fatally fractured. Adam passed on this tarnished reflection to his children. "[Adam] had a son in his own likeness, in his own image; and he named him Seth" (Gen. 5:3). The children bore Adam's damaged image. But the shadow of restored relationship hovers over the devastating curse of judgment. There is the promise of an Offspring who would crush the serpent's head (Gen. 3:15). Bonhoeffer speaks about the restoration of community and its relation to God's image in us:

> Since this community is destroyed by moral failure, clearly it has moral character originally, and is part of the divine image in man in the narrator's view. Divine and human community are in some way part of the original moral and spiritual life of man and that means part also of his future life (restored in Christ). . . . This points us to the church.
>
> Bonhoeffer, 1963, pp. 42–43

After the fall there could have been a cessation of community with humankind doomed eternally to hunger for relationships that could never be experienced. But isolation and alienation were never part of God's plan.

God would not let his intention of community be destroyed. The image was still there and God was still God. The Old Testament is a record of God's continued pursuit of relationship with his creatures in this fallen state. The call of the Lord God that rang among the trees continues, "[Adam,] where are you?" (Gen. 3:9).

Keeping the Vision Alive

God kept the image of community before his people through covenant and command. G. Ernest Wright observes that according to the Old Testament, the formation of community is God's central act (Wright, 1954).

Covenant

A major way God cultivated this relationship with the creatures he had designed was in the making of covenants. These promise-making acts involved one party binding himself in an act of commitment to another party or parties. Conditions of the treaty were spelled out in the covenant itself. Thus "covenant is the intentionality and responsibility of being together in relationship" (Icenogle, 1994, p. 11).

Promises were made to Abraham, Noah, Moses, David, and others—promises that extended to heirs years later. Though a covenant was originally made with a particular individual, many would participate in the covenant as members of corporate Israel. Thus to be a member of Israel was to possess the covenant and the opportunity to know the Promise Keeper. This placement created the concept of individual-in-community. Likewise the awareness of the individual's personal responsibility to God did not foster greater individualism but actually brought greater understanding of the kind of community where the Spirit bonds people together into one (Kraus, 1979). The meaning of one's personal significance is tied to the fact that one is a part of the corporate unit.

In the same manner in the New Testament community of the body of Christ, "there is no more possibility of there being a personal identity in Christ apart from the brother than there is of loving Christ without loving the brother (1 John 4:20)" (Kraus, 1979, p. 92). Our awareness of who we are as new persons in Christ Jesus is shaped by the identification we have with the body of Christ.

Command

God's rules for how Israel is to function include clear commands to operate out of a concern for community. The image-bearer is always individual-in-community—the action of the one affects all and vice versa. God mandates for his children to remain dependent on and connected with him and to sustain an interdependency with "brothers."

Israelites were commanded to show mercy by canceling debts made with a "brother": "Every creditor shall cancel the loan he has made to his fellow Israelite. He shall not require payment from his fellow Israelite or brother, because the LORD's time for canceling debts has been proclaimed" (Deut. 15:2).

They were called to care for their covenant relations: "If there is a poor man among your brothers in any of the towns of the land that the LORD your God is giving you, do not be hardhearted or tightfisted toward your poor brother" (Deut. 15:7).

Each was to return land and give up slaves: "If a fellow Hebrew, a man or a woman, is sold to you and he serves you six years, in the seventh year you must let him go free. And when you release him, do not send him away empty-handed. Supply him liberally from your flock, your threshing floor and your winepress" (Deut. 15:12–14).

This deep sense of connectedness is part of what it means to be of the Hebrew race. It runs through generations. And the whole tribe or people was affected by the experience of one of their number. Thus when Abraham was blessed, Lot also experienced the blessing. Jacob's blessing spilled over to Laban. Likewise Achan with his covetousness caused the defeat of the whole people in the attack on Ai. God sees them collectively. "Israel has sinned. . . . That is why the Israelites cannot stand against their enemies" (Josh. 7:11–12). Achan is Israel. To be an Israelite means you are not an individual with a separate destiny but an individual with a corporate destiny (Lee & Cowan, 1986).

The Israelite came to love that connectedness with community. In a time of solitary exile the psalmist recalls with longing, "How I used to go *with the multitude,* leading the procession to the house of God, with shouts of joy and thanksgiving *among the festive throng*" (Ps. 42:4, italics added). To be in community with covenant people who join in worship of the God of the covenant was the greatest blessing an Israelite could experience. Individual fulfillment, Kraus suggests, comes through allying oneself with the life and purposes of the covenant group (Kraus, 1979).

Likewise, an individual's worst fate in Israel would be to experience being cut off from God's people (Kraus, 1979). Judgment of the severest nature was to be severed from the group—to be sent outside the camp:

> Judaism had fostered an intense sense of interrelatedness and community. It developed what might be called a "corporate personality." A man was so intensely related to his brother that it was his duty to avenge his brother (2 Sam. 14:7). He accepted punishment for his brother's sin (2 Sam. 21:1–14). Innocent persons were punished if the head of a household sinned, as seen in the case of Achan (Josh. 7:24). Because a man was regarded as so nearly identical with his brother, levirate marriage was practiced (Deut. 25:5). A parent exercised the right of absolute disposal of a child, all illustrated by Abraham and Isaac (Gen. 22:1), or Jephthah and his daughter (Judg. 11:29), or Reuben offering his sons as hostages (Gen. 42:37).
>
> Miller, 1958, pp. 34–35

Israel's commitment was bifocal. Ruth in aligning herself with Naomi declared, "Your people will be my people and your God my God" (Ruth 1:16). To commit to one meant commitment to the other. The Jews were called to solidarity with God and with one another.

The last book of the Old Testament, Malachi, contains an ever-recurring theme: God's faithfulness to this pursuit of relational community. "'I the LORD do not change. So you, O descendants of Jacob, are not destroyed. . . . Return to me, and I will return to you,' says the LORD Almighty" (Mal. 3:6–7). The Old Testament closes with the promise of One who will bring restoration to a broken community. "See, I will send you the prophet Elijah before that great and dreadful day of the LORD comes. He will *turn the hearts of the fathers to their children, and the hearts of the children to their fathers"* (Mal. 4:5–6, italics added). The Old Testament ends on a ray of hope for renewed community—with our Maker and with one another.

Jesus Renewed the Divine Image of Community

A new command I give you: Love one another.

John 13:34

The coming of Jesus renewed the perspective of God on individuals and community. When the time had fully come, God sent his Son, born as an image-bearer. While the first Adam bore his image, the second Adam was the exact representation of his being—he was the radiance of God's glory, glory as the only begotten of the Father. The Father sent the Person of the Son into our world that we might know restored authentic relationship. The Son came that we might know God.

Jesus didn't just talk about relating to God, he personified it. He didn't allow truth to remain cold and conceptual. He lived it. When Martha in grief recited the cold objective truth, "I know he [my brother] will rise again in the resurrection at the last day," Jesus turned the truth into personal reality—"I am the resurrection and the life" (John 11:24–25). Anyone who knew Jesus well knew that truth relationally. He, as a person, was that truth. One cannot have relationship with a concept, but one can relate to a person. Because God is love, wisdom, holiness, and power, we can relate in ways not possible if we simply view God as only knowing, explaining, illustrating, defining, or revealing these qualities. Because he personifies these things, we not only can understand them, we intimately embrace them in relating to him. As we "know" him, we also "know" them. What all the words of the Law and the first Testament could not convey, God communicated in the personal relationship of the Son.

Interpersonal relations among humankind were changed too. As Kraus notes, the incarnation did not result in a new book of theology or a new code of ethics. It resulted in a new community, not a new principle or idea but a new order (Kraus, 1979). People whom society devalued and disdained to have in community (women, children, slaves, sinners, widows, etc.) were given new valuation by Jesus. They were seen as made in the image of a loving Creator who would redeem not only their self-image but, more significantly, their God-image and God-relationship.

y: Defined, Proclaimed, Constructed, and

Community Defined

The command to love God was joined by the priority of loving your neighbor as yourself—this was the Law—summarized in relationships. "The Law tells us what the repaired image of God should look like, and it summarizes that repaired image in terms of loving relationships with God and men" (Miller, 1979, p. 40). There is no relational system Jesus did not touch. "Jesus' direct and profound experience of God as his father . . . and Jesus' simultaneous recognition that the consequences of that relationship inundate all other relationships everywhere and all the time" created conditions for major transformation in personal encounters. The parenthood of God transforms our relationships, reconstructing our human systems (Lee & Cowan, 1986, pp. 146, 150).

It is impossible to divorce the proclamation of the gospel from its impact on personal relationships. The natural family is engulfed by the eternal family. Responding to the subtle pressure of his mother and brothers who would take charge of him, Jesus establishes new connections. "Here are my mother and my brothers! Whoever does God's will is my brother and sister and mother" (Mark 3:34–35). Neighborliness is redefined. Need, not value systems, now determines neighbor. As Lee and Cowan observe, "Need puts us in each other's backyard!" (Lee & Cowan, 1986, p. 149). The specialness normally reserved for our friends is now to be lavished on our enemies. Domination and hierarchical systems are out. To be leader, one must serve (Mark 10:41–45). Patriarchal rule is renounced (Matt. 23:8–10). We are brothers and sisters, family to each other (Lee & Cowan, 1986, pp. 150–51). The husband-wife relationship is compared to a new paradigm, Christ and the church (Eph. 5:22–32). The father-child association is laced with mutual respect and understanding (Eph. 6:1–4). Slaves and masters are cautioned to condition their responses as though they were before the face of God. The disdained and the guilty are perceived through nonjudgmental filters. And the natural boundaries of nationality, gender, age, and economic status must no longer be divisive.

"So there is no piece of the relational web, whether minisystem or megasystem, that is untouched by Jesus' experience of what God's relationship with us creates among us" (Lee & Cowan, 1986, p. 149). A relational revolution was taking place.

Community Proclaimed

Jesus proclaimed a gospel of community, a gospel that has at its very essence relationships. Leonardo Boff in his book, *Ecclesiogenesis: The Base Communities Reinvent the Church,* states:

> Jesus' whole preaching may be seen as an effort to awaken the strength of these community aspects. In the horizontal dimension Jesus called human beings to mutual respect, generosity, a communion of sisters and brothers, and simplicity in relationships. Vertically he sought to open the human being to a sincere filial relationship with God, to the artlessness of simple prayer, and to generous love for God.
>
> Boff, 1986, p. 7

A cursory glance at the content of Jesus' teaching reveals numerous examples of this.

Observe the content of the parables. They reflect either our relational life with God or our relational life together among ourselves (Lee & Cowan, 1986). These two points were at the heart of Jesus' teaching.

Community Constructed

Jesus not only proclaimed community, he constructed it. "Jesus did not select the Twelve as founders of future churches. *Jesus established the Twelve as a community; as messianic, eschatological church.* The apostles are not to be understood first and foremost as individuals but precisely as the *Twelve,* as messianic community gathered around Jesus and his Spirit" (Boff, 1986, p. 28).

Ralph T. Morton's *The Twelve Together* is so named because Morton saw the disciples' life together as the basis of their training; the disciples must be seen as a body not merely a collection of individuals. The impact of being together with one another and with him was that they came to view themselves collectively as a body—his body, the church (Morton, *The Twelve Together*).

So important is the creation of this community in the eyes of Morton that he claims the story of the Gospels is not so much the unfolding history of the experience of Jesus but a history of the formation of the corporate identity of the disciples as they found life with Jesus (Morton, *The Twelve Together*). The Gospels show truth and life as seen through the eyes of the community. Howard Snyder puts this in shocking perspective. Judging from the Gospel records, he says, "Jesus Christ actually gave more time to preparing a community of disciples than to proclaiming the good news" (Snyder, 1975, p. 74).

Some of the disciples' most profound lessons evolved out of their being in community with one another. Christ's command to "wash one another's feet" (John 13:14) has more impact when one realizes that the disciples sometimes saw each other as competitors for position with Jesus. They knew each other's flaws and blind spots because they lived together. It would be far easier to serve a stranger, someone they didn't know so much about.

As the community of disciples plays a part in Jesus' ministry, it becomes his body in action. And the major part is played not by the disciples as individuals but by these men as a corporate unit (Morton, *The Twelve Together*). Being in community enabled them to learn how much they needed the others and what they could contribute to the building up of the whole. Jesus was setting up a model for the church, a model that taught them dependency on one another, a model they would operate under in the Book of Acts.

> It gives one a pleasant surprise to think of Simon the zealot and Matthew the publican, men coming from so opposite quarters, meeting together in close fellowship in the little band of twelve. In the persons of these two disciples extremes meet—the tax-gatherer and the tax-hater; the unpatriotic Jew, who degraded himself by becoming a servant of the alien ruler; and the Jewish patriot, who chafed under the foreign yoke, and sighed for emancipation. This union of opposites was not accidental, but was designed by Jesus as a prophecy of the future.
>
> Bruce, 1971, pp. 35–36

By calling them into community Jesus gave the disciples opportunity to remold old habit patterns and establish new ones. He constructed for them a model they could remember, recognizing that their life together with him would be the basis of their witness when he was gone. The Law was written, read, and interpreted. The gospel was lived, modeled, and proclaimed in a community context.

As the Twelve came to know Jesus and to embrace his values of mutuality among one another, they also embraced his model of relating to the Father. He talked about knowing the Father, and it was evident that he did. When he used the word "know," it was in the Hebrew sense of intimate interaction, experiencing the Father the way they knew him. In knowing him, they also came to know each other in such a personal, corporate way that they would be called his body, a term of oneness.

Creating that oneness was key. Richard Halverson writes, "Jesus' profoundest death wish was the unity of his disciples" (Halverson, 1972, p. 53).

Community Entrusted

It was to the community of witnesses and not to individuals as such that the messianic mission was given. The community is central to representing the incarnation of Christ. "According to Luke, the disciples were actually instructed to withhold verbal witness to the resurrection until the new community of the Spirit was formed as the authenticating context for their message (Luke 24:48–49)" (Kraus, 1979, p. 23). It was in the forming of this community that meaning came to their mission and message. The community of believers actually became the means of establishing the validity and authority of an individual's witness.

They portrayed in actuality what believers verbally described. Thus they became a "community of interpretation," embodying in relationships the meaning of the gospel announcement. By their very lifestyle they interpreted scriptural meaning (Kraus, 1979). Even today Scripture is interpreted primarily by how the gospel is lived more than by principles of interpretation.

A study of Acts reveals that community was fundamental to, not optional for, early Christians. In passages where the apostles deal with responsiveness to God, there is equal emphasis on the relationship to his family. The writer of Ephesians commends them for "faith in the Lord Jesus and love for all the saints" (Eph. 1:15). Each epistle echoes this dual emphasis of relationship with God and living out the gospel with brothers and sisters in the faith. Hebrews speaks of offering a "sacrifice of praise" to God and a "sacrifice" of "doing good and sharing with others." Both of these are listed as pleasing God (Heb. 13:15–16).[1]

---

1. There is regular interchange between these two foci. The Epistles abound with Paul's recognition of the presence of these two elements. "We always thank God . . . because we have heard of *your faith in Christ Jesus* and of the *love* you have *for all the saints*" (Col. 1:3–4, italics added). To the Ephesians, "For this reason, ever since I heard about *your faith in the Lord Jesus* and *your love for all the saints*, I have not stopped giving thanks for you" (Eph. 1:15–16, italics added). "We ought always to thank God for you, brothers, and rightly so, because *your faith is growing* more and more, and the *love* every one of you has *for each other is increasing*" (2 Thess. 1:3, italics added). "In view of God's mercy . . . offer your bodies as living sacrifices, *holy and pleasing to God*—which is your spiritual worship. . . . Just as each of us has one body with many members, and these members do not all have the same function, so in Christ we who are many form one body, and *each member belongs to all the others*" (Rom. 12:1, 4–5, italics added). "Let us be thankful, and so worship God acceptably with reverence and awe. . . . *Keep on loving each other* as brothers" (Heb. 12:28–13:1, the chapter break not being in the original letter, italics added). Note the dual sacrifices of Hebrews 13:15–16, "Through Jesus . . . let us continually offer to God a sacrifice of praise—the fruit of lips *that confess his name*. And do not forget *to do good* and *to share with others*, for with such sacrifices God is pleased" (italics added).

Those who came after Jesus, to whom the spreading of the gospel was committed, continued throughout the rest of the New Testament this dual priority on preaching, teaching, and living communion with God and interdependent relatedness within the community of believers. Where we find one, the other is not far behind. Banks notes this dual connection in Paul's writings:

> For Paul the gospel bound men and women to one another as well as to God. Acceptance by Christ necessitated acceptance of those whom he had already welcomed (Rom. 15:7); reconciliation with God entailed reconciliation with others that exhibited the character of the gospel preaching (Phil. 4:2–3); union in the Spirit involved union with one another, for the Spirit was primarily a shared, not individual experience. The gospel is not a purely personal matter. It has a social dimension. It is a communal affair.
>
> Banks, 1988, p. 33

Community Will Be Realized

> Whenever individualism tended to break down the community, Paul seems to have reminded his readers that God had called them into a "fellowship" (1 Cor. 10:16). Where the "strong" within the community wanted to ignore the "weak" Paul reminded them that God had called them into a Christian community (Rom. 14:1–15:13).
>
> Thompson, 1977, p. 15

All emphasis on community has its end in eschatology, the cessation of earthly living and the being "caught up together with the Lord." The hope of the Christian has at its core the "withness" between believer and God. We speak of those who have gone through death as with the Lord. There is also "withness" in being his "bride." We anticipate oneness with believers from all time and from every tribe and nation as we celebrate the Lamb. Jesus is even now "preparing a place for us," but the place is made desirable because it is in the Father's house, dwelling with him forever. Today we are in rehearsal. But there is coming a day when we will be eternally in his presence.

Community was and is kingdom living in the making. We are never closer to the heart of God than when we respond corporately to him and

---

Often the two community emphases are bound into one as in Hebrews 6:10, "God . . . will not forget your *work and the love you have shown him* as you have *helped his people* and continue to help them" (italics added).

his Word as his corporate people who reflect his glory. He chooses to be glorified in his church and in his Son (Eph. 3:21). As his community we amplify the voice of God in declaring the gospel as good news for all (Peterson, 1980).

> The authentic religious heritage of Judaism and Christianity is primarily a communal and not an individualistic one. It shows how we are to be *together* in the world, not just how to be good individuals. It reminds us that "who is my neighbor?" is our most fundamental kind of question. It is the "way we have learned from Christ."
>
> Lee & Cowan, 1986, pp. 120–21

Firestarters

What Are Firestarters?

A light drizzle falls on the earth outside my window. Cool damp days like this call for a blazing fire in the fireplace. The cheerful orange and yellow flames brighten the grayness of the landscape and add a warmth that is more than physical. From October through April the curls of smoke escape out of our chimney, testifying nightly to blazing warmth within.

I was a dyed-in-the-wool tinder-and-match firestarter. There was something about the challenge of "doing it with one match." However, I often returned in a short time to find my fire struggling to survive, gasping for a really good catch to cause it to take off and ignite the big one. Then I discovered a two-inch by six-inch brick of combustible material that, when ignited, blazed forth with energy enough to envelop everything around it in flames. I found that the use of such a device produced a hotter fire in a much shorter time and in its burning reached out to ignite surrounding materials of combustible quality. This little brick that creates heat and warmth is called a "firestarter."

In helping people become proficient in leading and responding in small groups, I usually begin by teaching them some new content or axiom of truth that's applicable to a small group setting. However, I've noticed that learners really come alive when first placed in a small group setting and given a dilemma to resolve or a scenario with which to identify. It is then that their learning is most full of energy and most likely connected to application of new truth in real life situations. Those initial real life settings propel them into learning more quickly and with greater connection to life.

What follows in many chapters are examples of these vignettes or experiences that are meant to teach and to enable participants to experience truth. Like firestarters, they move participants quickly into the heat of issues and active involvement that connect content with affective feelings so motivation is present. They are meant to start a conflagration amid learners who then can continue a longer term burn as they examine their responses and learn from them. Some scenarios may be used to establish principles, some to try out application of known truth, some to identify with people in their particular circumstances.

Firestarters are not meant to be used as the sole learning material. They are to be used to create questions and further insights in the learners. They will help issues catch on fire and move quickly into the heart of learning that is personally transforming. They will raise concerns that will pull in participants on a thinking and feeling level and will give them material to move below the surface of group discussion. Firestarters are for busy people, for people hungry to experience greater learning in group process. Firestarters are for teachers who want to increase the degree of learning so that learners personally identify with content.

So grab a firestarter and light that match!

1. Select a parable (e.g., Prodigal Son, Good Samaritan) and examine it closely to determine what it proclaims about relational life with God or with others.

2. The concept of togetherness that was fostered in the early church is highly significant. It is graphically depicted in the "one another" passages found in the Epistles. Examine some of these listed below and select three for which you will illustrate ways these could be lived out corporately in today's church.

- giving honor to one another (Rom. 12:10)
- living harmoniously with one another (Rom. 12:16)
- admonishing one another (Rom. 15:14)
- waiting for each other (1 Cor. 11:33)
- demonstrating equal care for one another (1 Cor. 12:25)
- serving one another (Gal. 5:13)
- bearing burdens of each other (Gal. 6:2)
- giving comfort to one another (1 Thess. 5:11)
- building up each other (1 Thess. 5:11)
- maintaining peace with each other (1 Thess. 5:13)
- doing good to one another (1 Thess. 5:15)

- lovingly bearing with each other (Eph. 4:2)
- being subject to each other (Eph. 5:21)
- forgiving one another (Col. 3:13)
- confessing to and praying for each other (James 5:16)
- exhibiting hospitality to each other (1 Peter 4:9)

3. Create a sermon or teaching experience based on one of the points noted in this chapter. Which illustrations cause the emphasis to come alive? What responses will you call for from the people as they seek to "live" on the basis of this truth being a reality in their everyday lives?

2

CHALLENGE TO COMMUNITY
Individualism

He can no longer have God for his Father,
who has not the Church for his mother.

Cyprian

Recall the last movie or television program you viewed. Was the emphasis on individual self-fulfillment or a group effort? What freedoms or rights were extolled? Identify a popular ad today. Does it appeal to a self-centered or a corporate value? Glance at a newspaper. How is autonomy highlighted?

In what ways do you see your life, your attitudes, your values, your responses, and your theology affected by individualism?

While the concept of community is deeply rooted in biblical soil, we live in the land of the self-made individualist. "Meism" is nurtured as a cardinal virtue. Self-centered individualism is considered an essential right of being a person. This is the principal language of our time.

Individualism's Identity

"For My Benefit"

It is not surprising that we view people and society as things to be used for our individual satisfaction and growth. It goes without question that the individual takes priority over the group. This mentality threads through our approach to all strata of relationship-building. "Will this person enhance my being?" "Is this a worthwhile relationship?" "Will I get anything from belonging to this group?"

Friendship today is viewed as important for meeting one's personal needs. Dyrness notes that even the vocabulary we use indicates the priority of the isolated individual in choosing to develop relationships. "We 'make' friends, we 'work' on our relationships" (Dyrness, 1989, p. 103). The optional nature of such connectedness is obvious. Allan Bloom in his sweeping synopsis of the student world depicts young people today as self-centered in relationships, where the underlying tone is freedom and few obligations. Personal, momentary gratification is not experienced as love and is often not characterized by any sense of moral commitment to one another—it is a relationship with no rigid strings of attachment (Bloom, 1987).

Marriage is also viewed as a chance to enhance one's personal growth and to have one's individual needs cared for. The personal fulfillment requirements now placed on a marriage are many. The union is seen as a contract for convenience. The freedom to move in and out of this contract is a matter of individual choice. The option to have children, to stay married, and a host of other choices common today have created "a new atmosphere for marriage and a new meaning for family life" (Bellah, Madsen, Sullivan, Swidler, & Tipton, 1987, p. 110). If a relationship does not fulfill us—whether friendship, group, church, marriage, or other—it can be easily discarded. "I'm not having my needs met" is justification for moving on and not looking back. In a throwaway world we have the "notion that relationships are 'things' to be selected and rejected at our convenience" (Gaede, 1985, p. 140).

The family itself is seen as the nursery for producing self-reliant, independent individuals who are deemed successful when they deny their need of the relationship. Bellah's interviews for his book *Habits of the Heart* reveal the family as reinforcing the priority of separateness. "The idea we have of ourselves as individuals on our own, who earn everything we get, accept no handouts or gifts, and free ourselves from our families of origin turns out, ironically enough, to be one of the things that holds us together" (Bellah et al., 1985, p. 62).

The currently highlighted awareness of codependency fosters in its wake a phobia against any kind of dependency on a relationship being a sign of frailty and a cause for alarm. Self-sufficiency and preservation are goals that drive us.

"I'm in Charge"

The passion for self-fulfillment at any cost has accentuated our need for personal autonomy and separateness. We can decide on our own. Nobody tells us what to do. We can also drop out of things if that is what is required to ensure our freedom. This condition has become so prevalent that we have given the category a label, "midlife crisis," though the response is not limited to the midlife era exclusively. Individuals leave spouses, children, and responsibilities behind in pursuit of "freedom." In formerly unprecedented moves, the individual exercises his or her "right" to do whatever he or she wants, whenever he or she wants, without concern for the effect of his or her actions (Miller, 1979). In like manner people today quit jobs, break moral rules, and abdicate responsibilities with no more explanation than the self-focused, "I felt like doing it." Rare is the family untouched by one of these scenarios of autonomy.

"I Have a Right to . . ."

"Rights language" is becoming our native tongue. Moral decisions are increasingly made on the basis of rights rather than on absolutes and virtues (MacIntyre, 1984). Dyrness summarizes MacIntyre's views in this way: "What is demanded by the individual has come to replace virtue language—the good practiced by the person" (Dyrness, 1989, p. 97). It is interesting to note that the concept of personal rights as we know it did not even have a means of expression in Hebrew, Greek, Latin, Arabic, or Old English before the Middle Ages, or Japanese before the mid-nineteenth century. Individual rights were invented to lend support to autonomy (MacIntyre, 1984).

Kraus claims we now equate freedom with individual independence. Likewise, "'civil rights' means the individual's right to 'life, liberty, and the pursuit of happiness'" (Kraus, 1979, p. 76). America has a low ratio of citizens per lawyer to preserve these "rights." Bloom, in *The Closing of the American Mind*, states, "In modern political regimes, where rights precede duties, freedom definitely has primacy over community, family, and even nature" (Bloom, 1987, p. 113).

Competitive Edge

Competition is a handmaid to individualism, and competition in America is as normative as baseball and apple pie. Many would list free enterprise as having made America what it is today. We have grown up feeling that we are responsible for our success and we must take every opportunity to stay ahead of the competition. Our proverbs reflect this sense of responsibility for our own destiny: "He who hesitates is lost." "Strike while the iron is hot." "The early bird catches the worm."

This attitude has invaded Christendom as well. We pride ourselves on being "better Christians" than others. Though we sing "saved by grace," we quickly lapse into a do-it-yourself kind of Christian living. Wuthnow labels the present state of spiritual growth as "hard work." Self-help books on the subject abound (Wuthnow, 1994). Success in the world and church comes from taking advantage of every opportunity. We think "that the person who really deserves our respect is the one who started with nothing and made himself important with no one else's help" (Miller, 1987, p. 66). In our American culture, we admire those who are not dependent on others.

> On Capitol Hill individualism is rampant. There are 535 political parties in Congress, the same number as members.
>
>   Naisbitt & Aburdene, 1990, p. 302

Evidence in Groups

Such strong identification with individualism is bound to pervade our groups. Kraus claims that "the group has become for us a collection of individuals created by individuals for their own individual advantages" (Kraus, 1979, pp. 76–77). It becomes difficult to put others first when an individualistic, competitive spirit suggests this offering may give him or her the advantage, power, and status over you. We are enculturated into building our own kingdoms, and we take greater pride in personal achievement than in group enterprise. We fear letting another know our weakness because it could be used against us. "Dying to self" is basically un-American.

Current scenarios are a far cry from the community depicted in the biblical vision given by God. The present individualism is also far removed from the conditions envisioned by those who came to the New World. In 1630 John Winthrop, first governor of the Massachusetts Bay Colony, enjoined his fellow colonists, "We must delight in each other, make others' conditions our own, rejoice together, mourn together, labor and suffer together, always having before our eyes our community as members of the same body" (Winthrop, 1965, p. 92).

What Is Individualism?

Individualism as pictured above is a distortion of the biblical view of the sacredness of the person. It is a perversion of God's intentions in fashioning us as unique created beings, no two alike. The person, as designed by God, is no threat to the building of community.

Bellah and associates note two crucial distinctions in understanding individualism. The first is a "belief in the inherent dignity, indeed the sacredness, of the individual." The second identifying mark is "a belief that the individual has a primary reality whereas society is a second-order, derived or artificial construct" (Bellah et al., 1985, p. 334). This latter view basically asserts that individuals with their self-interests come first and have priority. Relationships are formed voluntarily to maximize that self-interest. In plain language, "I will relate to you if it does something for me." The individual is superior and controls the relationship to his or her own end. Such self-centeredness makes the individual responsible only to and for himself or herself.

Kraus draws a similar distinction, labeling one perspective "individuality" and the second "individualism." Speaking from an Old Testament framework, he claims individuality calls

> attention to the individual as a responsible person in community, while the latter [individualism] exalts the independence of the individual and his private rights. Individuality is affirmed in the form and content of the covenant; individualism is considered a matter of alienation and pride.
>
> Kraus, 1979, pp. 84–85

This latter perspective is the essence of sin—being individually independent and self-sufficient from God and from others. Adam wanted to gratify himself and be self-sufficient—to "be as God," as the tempter put it.

Dyrness argues that the "basic content of autonomous individualism is not biblical. We are not made to be individuals . . . we are created in and for relationship" (Dyrness, 1989, p. 101). And it is in relationship that we reflect his image as he is in relationship in the Godhead.

Common Themes

Self-fulfillment, autonomy, rights, freedom, self-centeredness—these are the facets of negative individualism and the factors that mitigate against community. Individualism puts self at the center of a person's world—everything revolves around the nurturing, exalting, and gratifying of that self. Personal success at the cost of all else, satisfaction of needs and drives, standing up for one's rights, getting one's due—these are the expressions of a self-driven culture.

Autonomy refers to self-directing freedom and moral independence. Inherent in autonomy is the idea of self-sufficiency and personal responsibility. But individualism distorts this self-assumed responsibility to the point of abdicating any responsibility for others. Autonomy sees the self as superior to and isolated from others, and it emphasizes freedom from conformity to anything outside self. It abhors restrictions and self-denial and prides itself in "being one's own person." In its distortion of rights it denies rights to others and operates as if no one else exists, taking no responsibility for the fall out of actions and decisions made by the single-focused self. "That's not my problem" is the expression of one who has removed himself or herself emotionally from the group and cares only for what concerns him or her.

The Other Side of Individualism

Though it aims for freedom, self-fulfillment, and self-sufficiency, individualism has not brought all it promised. It is not the idealized state once portrayed as the end of all being. "The American individualism so characteristic of the contemporary United States generates a pervasive loneliness and anxiety" (Lee & Cowan, 1986, p. 63). Daniel Yankelovich in researching American society found that "a me-first, satisfy-all-my-desires attitude leads to relationships that are superficial, transitory, and ultimately unsatisfying." One of his surveys showed that "70 percent of Americans now recognize that while they have many acquaintances they have few close friends—and they experience this as a serious void in their lives. Moreover, two out of five (41 percent) state they have fewer close friends than they did in the recent past" (Yankelovich, 1982, p. 248). This awareness is an echo of the need for community that God put within the heart of those who were created in his image.

M. Scott Peck states the reality with which we are faced:

> We can never be completely whole in and of ourselves. . . . There is a point beyond which our sense of self-determination not only becomes inaccurate and prideful but increasingly self-defeating. . . . We are inevitably social creatures who desperately need each other not merely for sustenance, not merely for company, but for any meaning to our lives whatsoever.

> Peck, 1987, pp. 54–55

Valuing Individual Differences

While the Bible clearly speaks against self-centered, self-sufficient individualism, it is not against individuality. Self-gratification and autonomy as defined by our culture are not fostered by God. Our individuality, on the other hand, is not created or achieved by us but is a gift from God (Dyrness, 1989). The Bible is full of encouragements to grow and to value people as individuals, uniquely created as one of a kind.

Coming individually to know Jesus means being introduced into community. None remains isolated. God creatively recognizes both individual and community by introducing the concept of the individual in community. Kraus sees this as unique to Yahweh and his covenant relationship (Kraus, 1979). In balance, both the individual's relationship to God and the corporate relationship to God are seen as fulfilling his plan. The person's individuality is not only preserved but enhanced in the midst of the group. It is the group that brings self-awareness and a sense of identity to the individual: "I am of the group, but I am uniquely my own person." The individual is not lost or engulfed by his or her solidarity with the group as envisioned by communism.

> A communist society is collective: it sees itself as made up of many individuals who are essentially interchangeable units. . . . The church, however, is not *collective* by nature, but is *corporate*. The parts are not identical but are "members . . . of the body" of Christ (1 Cor. 12:12–30). Each "organ" is unique and retains its individuality, but all function together as one body. The individual is not lost in the corporate identity of the church, but is freed to function as who he really is, for as each individual functions in the body, he will bear the vertical and horizontal relationships of the image of God.
>
> H. Miller, 1979, p. 67

When the people of God function together, it is as a living organism. When his people come together, Christ has promised to be there among them in a way that he is not present for the individual alone. He dwells in us individually, but when we come together corporately we reflect the image of God (H. Miller, 1979). What we have together is greater than the sum of the individual parts. No one loses individuality in this coming together, but rather one discovers and esteems individual unique qualities as they are revealed in the web of relationships. The apostle explained this pictorially in 1 Corinthians 12. The ear is for hearing because no other organ is designed for that purpose, but the ear alone would be useless because the other functions would be missing. It is being bound together in one body that creates the true value of the individual parts. Competition, autonomy, and claims to self-sufficiency are unthinkable when seen in this perspective. While "individually members of" the body of Christ (1 Cor. 12:27), we are also "all baptized into one body" (1 Cor. 12:13).

The Infection of Evangelicalism

> Gradually, the idea of a covenant community gave way to a vision of collected individuals. Faith was not so much a mutual conviction regarding creedal statements and a consequent common experience, but an individual experience—more to the point, a decision which each person could understand in his own way.
>
> Horton, 1991, pp. 166–67

When the blatant concepts of individualism are examined in the light of biblical standards, they are seen to be clearly opposed to the character formation desired by God. However, in subtle ways individualism has become acceptable and normative for evangelical Christianity. Steven Lukes defines religious individualism in its purest form as

> the view that the individual believer does not need intermediaries, that he has the primary responsibility for his own spiritual destiny, that he has the right and the duty to come to his own relationship with his God in his own way and by his own effort.
>
> Lukes, 1973, p. 94

While much of this statement strikes a responsive chord in the soul of evangelicals, our theology and praxis, colored by our cultural context, tend to diminish the emphasis on individual in community and foster attitudes of aloneness and personal interpretation that act apart from others.

Theological Frameworks

Barton W. Stone was a frontier preacher who lived from 1772 to 1844 in Kentucky. Stone's rugged individualism led him to reject traditional ideas about the importance and role of the institutional church. His views led him to leave the Presbyterian church. Stone epitomized the way many evangelicals in America viewed the church. In true frontier individualism, the cry became, "Every man for himself, and God for us all!" Such rugged individualism pervaded not only politics but also the realm of faith.

Is this not what life is all about, one man facing up to his responsibility on his own two feet and not trying to hide in the crowd or permit another man to mediate between himself and God? Just as the ideal American of an earlier day stood alone in taming the frontier and in modern times achieves dignity and worth through individual endeavor in, say, industry or sports, so the American Christian must face God alone and come to terms with Him on his own.

Woodbridge, Noll, & Hatch, 1979, p. 164

Centuries earlier Luther, in reaction to abuses of the Catholic church, launched a rebellion whose energizing force was an emphasis on "inner light," the priesthood of the believer, and justification by faith alone. Calvin added to this individualistic bent "ruthless self-examination" and concentration on an individual's personal achievement. The true believer became egocentric and perfectionistic (Lukes, 1973, p. 95). Such emphases resulted in a preoccupation with individual progress and personal sanctification. All of this separated a believer from others and isolated growth to the individual sphere. It also nurtured an attitude of private rather than community concern.

Much of our theological thinking today is based on the presupposition of an autonomous individual person who is prior to, and thus superior to, a group of believers. Thus the individual-in-community concept was moved off center to give precedence to the personal development of the individual (Kraus, 1979). Social dimensions were considered suspect, tending toward liberalism.

Conversion is limited to the realm of the soul, a "rational change in belief patterns called faith." The salvation experience is not necessarily viewed as incorporating reconciliation with fellow individuals. "Saved individuals will, or should, be more loving, honest, and altruistic, but conversion does not change the fundamental patterns of individual-group relations" (Kraus, 1979, pp. 106–7). This kind of thinking, that salvation does not result in a conversion of the whole person, prevents us from seeing human relationships as being redeemed.

We may expect in the church a new degree of cooperation and mutual caring; and we may hope that the saved individuals will compete fairly and with at least a modicum of compassion in the worldly order. But by theological definition, salvation does not introduce us to a fundamentally new order of relationships in which the private principal is superseded by commonalty as the basic operational assumption. Private gain, even in the religious sphere, remains the primary motivator.

Kraus, 1979, p. 107

And we accept this valuing of the individual over the group instead of embracing God's more equitable order of individual-in-community. In cultural individualism our thinking about groups and relationships will always be colored by what this does for the individual. The church's development will always be viewed as secondary to personal gain.

Religious Practice

Our "free" church paradigm is premised on voluntary association and commitment of individuals, based on the individual's Christian experience. Again, the individual is the controlling factor. Private personal experience and choice are the operative factors. A private faith is a natural corollary. Faith is a personal matter, of no business to others. The spiritual growth of a believer is off limits to others in the body of Christ. Prayer, practice of the disciplines for growth, change in lifestyle—these are not to be intruded upon by others, nor even inquired after. Wesley's methodical societies were radical in their corporate responsibility and regularized accountability for one another's growth. By today's standards, the early church was meddling and overstepping its bounds when it dealt corporately with sin and took seriously every weakness.

Personal piety is a matter of one's own individual choice and is evaluated by internal motives rather than a community. It is natural that this kind of thinking would arise out of a private rational faith that depended on the subjective question, "Have you come to know Jesus Christ as your personal Savior?" The individual's word on this was taken to be gospel truth because such a transaction was between an individual and his or her God. This is a far cry from our Puritan roots in which one's calling involved serving others more than self.

Even the development of a person's relationship with Christ, when it came at the expense of that community, was considered to be anti-social and thus anti-Christian. Puritan Thomas Goodwin is quoted as saying, "To be proficient in 'holy duties' is indeed more sweet to a man's own self, but to be proficient in our calling is more profitable to others—to the Church, the commonwealth, or the family—and so may glorify God more" (Horton, 1991, p. 167). "Subjective criteria become the norm for reality and truth in religious profession. Spirituality is defined in terms of personality characteristics, belief patterns, and personal piety" (Kraus, 1979, p. 110).

Love today is easier to extol as a theological concept and psychological feeling than as an action and a moral commitment to relationships regardless of how one feels or reasons. Evangelicalism has been concerned with the number of these interior decisions more than with the outworking of faith in community. Groups remain at the discretion of the individual, a voluntary association of individuals who group together for self-fulfillment and the good life (Kraus, 1979). Prayer remains inherently individualistic, praying for one's own needs and development.

Doctrines Viewed Individualistically

That individualistic thinking dominates our perspective is evident when doctrines are considered. For example, the doctrine of creation portrays the autonomous individual as prior to the social group when in actuality the family stands at the zenith of God's creative efforts. The autonomous, nonsufficient man was the only "not good" aspect of God's creative force and was remedied by the formation of Eve, which satisfied both Adam and God. When the doctrine of sin is considered, we automatically think of "my sin," not corporate sins in which we all participate. Salvation is also seen as very individualistic. On our own, we see ourselves making a personal, internal commitment that results in a privatized conversion.

Another doctrine that's viewed individualistically is sanctification. More often than not it is viewed, not as a work of the Spirit through the individual in community but as "what I do to promote my own spiritual growth." Corporate sanctification is abdicated as being too binding and too much beyond our control.

Doctrines of the sacraments are usually focused on an individual's relationship to God more so than on the strengthening, affirmation, and meaning these acts bring to the corporate unit of the church.

Worship and witness are also conceived as personal and individual, whereas Scripture often pictures these as collective and needing the body for fullest impact.

Divine guidance is pictured as an inner-directed impulse. Redrawn from a corporate dimension there is wisdom from the Spirit that comes through the body for our motivation and direction. Our perspective on eschatology more often than not is visualized as the individual being rescued from this planet and finally receiving the rewards for personal efforts accomplished while in the flesh. While this theme is certainly biblical, there is equal emphasis on the "bride" as a corporate whole presented without spot or wrinkle to the Bridegroom for his delight.

Moral Rightness

In the realm of ethics and morality, how a person determines right and wrong can become a very individualistic decision. Lukes comments that "ethical individualism can be seen as the philosophical consequence of taking the idea of autonomy seriously and carrying it to its logical conclusion" (Lukes, 1973, p. 101). If I am not affected by others and am allowed to determine my own course of action as based on my own choices of what seems right to me, then feelings are more likely to influence my choice. The "oughts" of outside sources, obligations, and moral standards are set aside as ethics for a society. Free thinking and free behavior become the rule of thumb for the individual.

A name often associated with religious individualism is Søren Kierkegaard, the first existentialist who interpreted Christianity as a personal, private, inward faith in opposition to the conformism and worldliness of the Lutheran church. It was Kierkegaard, ever the champion of the individual, who desired that his tombstone be inscribed with "That Individual" (Lukes, 1973).

This isolated inner-life conception, while righting wrongs of misconceived and misused corporate emphases, led to further offenses in new directions. "The rise of ethical individualism clearly has much to do with the decline of Christianity as an all-pervading basis for moral certainty" (Lukes, 1973, p. 102). When the source of moral values is the individual, biblical absolutes are ignored. And the church that promotes biblical values is seen as one voice among many offering choices to the individual who autonomously makes up his or her own mind. Interpretation of Scripture, left to the individual, often becomes that which supports the individual's lifestyle, which perpetuates moral relativism, something that is in vogue today.

Individualism, American Style

American culture's ideals and values foster individualism as a way of thinking and living. It is almost a symbol of national identification (Lukes, 1973). According to a survey by Frank Acuff, America ranks first in individualism, followed by Australia, Great Britain, and Canada. The least individualistic countries are Singapore, Taiwan, and (least of all) Venezuela.

In the campaign of 1928, Herbert Hoover coined the phrase "rugged individualism," which has since become a source of national pride. But long before the phrase became popular, individualism was at home in the cultural mores of the United States. Bellah and associates describe it as the core of what it means to be an American (Bellah et al., 1985). Self-realization, individual freedom, privacy, and autonomy have long been embraced by poets, pioneers, politicians, psychologists, entrepreneurs, and ecclesiastical bodies. Our whole system of free enterprise expresses this individualism.

The culture of America is particularly fertile ground for the development of individualism. To even question the virtues of individualism seems almost anti-American. Personal dignity and freedoms are a matter of national pride. Personal autonomy is schooled into us from the cradle on. "The ultimate ethical rule is simply that individuals should be able to pursue whatever they find rewarding, constrained only by the requirement that they not interfere with the 'value systems' of others" (Bellah et al., 1985, p. 6). In other words, my value systems are my own and nobody else's business. We grow up thinking of ourselves as independent agents, free of encumbrances. Being a person means you choose for yourself.

Advertising cultivates this image. You determine what is best for you. Personal gratification and success are laudable ends. Classic phrases that have made advertising history reflect this inalienable right of the customer: "Go for the gusto." "Have it your way." "You deserve the best."

Our heroes are those who have made it on their own. They represent the self-contained person who has achieved success by virtue of his or her own outstanding ability, single-mindedness, and freedom from obligation and encumbrances. We glorify entrepreneurship and achievers who stand out from the crowd. We put sports figures, rock stars, presidents, and CEOs into the limelight, ignoring the teams that helped them to succeed. Their feats are attributed to what they did to foster their own success. If they made it, they did it by their own virtue, ability, and fortitude. "Pulling yourself up by your own bootstraps" is an ethic to be emulated. We inspire our children with *The Little Engine That Could.* Each of these values contains enough admirable aspects to cause them to be desirable. After all, a person should learn to take responsibility for self, be motivated to live above the mediocre, and make use of natural abilities and opportunities. While these are legitimate, just as valuable are ideals that focus on responsibility and sensitivity to others.

How do we define what is "good" today? "I have my rights" is at the opposite end of the spectrum from "I have responsibility." This first kind of thinking results in treating others and groups as stepping-stones to personal growth. "A major problem with a preoccupation with my individual development is that it provides no intrinsic value 'for you,' except as an environment for my growth" (Dyrness, 1989, p. 98). Groups are used—whether friendships or family—to facilitate individual development. When they cease to provide this in the way the individual desires, they are discarded. To justify our abdication of responsibility, we rationalize with "rights language." Groups often become little more than collections of individuals bent on their own ends. This prompts competition and protectionism or a holding back of commitment. Personal goals cannot be sacrificed for group growth.

> The great unifying theme at the conclusion of the twentieth century is the triumph of the individual.
>
> Naisbitt & Aburdene, 1990, p. 298

Even before Hoover introduced the phrase "rugged individualism," our leaders have used individualism for their own ends. Teddy Roosevelt epitomized this free spirit for many Americans. American individualism encompasses such traditional values as natural rights and free enterprise, giving ethical priority to productive justice, which declares that each person has a right to what he or she works for or produces. Is this Christian? How does one also address the corporate concern in the Scriptures that my excesses must not impoverish others? Nor my confort be at the expense of justice? Furthermore free enterprise is sustained and encouraged by competition. While competition and "king of the hill" mentality are accepted as normal for our society, is this concept really Christian? What does it do for those who lack the ability to compete? To those who fail to win? To those who win? Is this the meaning of "rugged" when placed with individualism?

These are not easy questions to answer. They find arguments of misuse on both sides. And they are steeped in time-honored, accepted values that have shaped our ways of doing business, giving grades, and granting honors. Scripture does not deny the individuality and uniqueness of every person. But the call is to excellence by challenging one to compete with his/her previous record, not with one another. The latter frequently prompts negative attitudes and tends to undermine the corporate unity of the body, a condition dear to the heart of God and imperative for our impact on a society that often operates by different standards.

Not only our pioneers and politicians but also our poets have enculturated us to think individualism is the highest gain. Ralph Waldo Emerson's treatise on self-reliance shows how immersed the poets of America were in this tradition. Speaking of being economically responsible for ourselves, he writes, "Do not tell me . . . of my obligation to put all poor men in good situations. Are they my poor?" (quoted in Lukes, 1973, pp. 30–31). Walt Whitman exulted in "Song of Myself" the glorious freedom he felt in expressing who he was in uninhibited fashion, "I celebrate myself, and sing myself." Thoreau lived out this individualism at Walden Pond. James Bryce observes that throughout American history, "individualism, the love of enterprise, and pride in personal freedom, have been deemed by Americans not only their choicest, but their peculiar and exclusive possessions" (quoted in Lukes, 1973, p. 31).

Individualism and Small Groups

Wuthnow sees the small group movement as reflective of America's love of independence. Groups attract people fed up with institutions, people who want to help themselves. They tend to draw people together by voluntary association, a very American value. Finally, by nature they reject received wisdom as it has been embodied in formal packages and lean toward pragmatic approaches to solving their problems. "Thus, the movement makes faith more relevant but also risks turning belief into something that people can manipulate for their own selfish purposes" (Wuthnow, 1994, pp. 4–5). Culture is forging an image of small groups, and this, in turn, is redefining community for Americans.

All of this contributes to tensions in the small group ethic, vacillations and paradoxes we will explore in future chapters. There is the dilemma of "wanting social support and community, yet resisting too much infringement on personal space." The challenge is finding a balance between spiritual support and spiritual openness or the deep-seated disjunction of modern culture, of being caught between a highly pragmatic, materialistic culture that celebrates possessions, status, and social achievement, on the one hand, and the deeper human needs for acceptance, happiness, and justification of shortcomings when measured against such high social standards, on the other.

Talking about failure is difficult though unrealized dreams, inadequacy, disappointments, failures, and breakups are real issues. "So accommodating is the religious culture that faith itself for ordinary Americans is unlikely to interfere very dramatically with their views regarding work, social status, earning money, or desire for happiness." Enjoying life is more important (Roof, 1999, p. 127).

"Commitment is viewed negatively because it limits our ability to feel independent and free, to experience new things, to change our minds on the spur of the moment and to focus upon self-gratification rather than helping others" (Barna, 1990, pp. 34–35).

Peck looks at the psychological results and notes that independence requires wholeness but wholeness requires our needing each other to find any meaning to our lives (Peck, 1987). We experience the most holistic sense of significance when we give to others what we are and when we need and receive from them who and what they are. Paul in his apostolic treatise on gifts stated the same truth centuries before. "If the whole body were an eye, where would the sense of hearing be?" (1 Cor. 12:17).

Again it is the individual in community that most reflects the balance necessary for fulfillment. Deborah Tannen capsulizes this twofold need:

> We need to get close to each other to have a sense of community, to feel we're not alone in the world. But we need to keep our distance from each other to preserve our independence, so others don't impose on or engulf us. This duality reflects the human condition. We are individual and social creatures. We need other people to survive, but we want to survive as individuals.
>
> Tannen, 1986, p. 31

Our individualistic tendencies can cause us to move from group to group, trying to meet the self-centered needs that drive us to get involved. Groups can become perfunctory exercises that we periodically try, but we may never succeed in knowing real community. Many have substituted group membership for the experience of community and their feelings about groups have turned sour or humdrum. We hunger for community, encounters with others that cause us to reach out, to self-disclose, to commit. These occasions bring a feeling of wholeness, of belonging, of valued distinctiveness, and of relatedness to others. Individualism can drive us to experience community in order to survive.

Through Others' Eyes

Perspective on Community

How does culture affect our view? "Culture is a learned system of knowledge, behavior, attitudes, beliefs, values, and norms that is shared by a group of people" (Beebe & Masterson, 2000, p. 153). As such culture plays a major role in developing rules and learned behavior. Individuals in a culture tend to take for granted the worldview embraced by their culture. They operate out of it and only become conscious that it exists when another worldview presents a different reality or when their worldview fails to operate.

Ethnocentrism is a tendency to place one's own group at the center of reality and to evaluate and interpret all other situations according to the norms and values of one's own culture. It becomes judgmental. "We do it right. You do it differently. You must be wrong." The "in" group's ways seem logical, and thus appear to be superior. The cultural exclusivist asks, "What does this cultural activity mean to me? How can it be said or done so that it is meaningful to me? How can others see life as I see it? How can I make the other person be more like me?" (Mayers, 1974, p. 241). The culturally open observer asks, "What is the person with whom I am communicating like? What can I say or what can I do to know that there is complete understanding on the part of the other?" (Mayers, 1974, p. 242).

Interpretation in small groups is always colored by the perceptions of the culture. While no attempt is made to stereotype particular ethnic groups, nations, or genders, this section at the end of each chapter will highlight some of the more evident differences in regard to interpretation or application of the topic.

A major division used in culture theory is that of individualistic and collectivistic cultures. Individualistic cultures tend to accent the goals of an individual more than those of a group because such cultures value uniqueness. On the other hand, collectivistic cultures emphasize group goals more than individual goals to demonstrate the high priority placed on harmony and solidarity. While North Americans may be high in individualism and thus frustrated by having to work in groups, cultures in other countries often prefer group work because it leans toward supporting one another and improving outcomes. Latin Americans would be an example of such (Triandis, Brislin, & Hui, 1988). Likewise the Japanese depend on groups to achieve agreement and a sense of commitment among their workers (Cathcart & Cathcart, 1988). This suggests that group work assigned in a classroom will be welcomed by some more than others because of basic values ingrained in the culture, and the development of spiritual community will face varied hurdles dependent on the makeup of the group.

In a Different Voice

In general, in the United States the male is enculturated toward greater independence than the female. Studies of early childhood have shown that little boys even in preschool years tend to play individually and more competitively while little girls tend to gather others around them in their play. "Let's play house. You be the baby and I'll be the mommy." Small group research has contributed evidence that women disclose more in a small group than in any other configuration while men find a small group the more difficult context, preferring to disclose one-on-one. A casual survey of small groups in a church will usually record more women in such than men, who prefer roles that allow them to exercise individuality and control more than affiliation.

Firestarters

Look over the doctrines listed below. In which is your natural inclination to interpret the doctrine individually? What new insights do you gain when you begin to think corporately and contemplate corporate responses?

- Sanctification—growing in likeness to God   Salvation
- Sin—immoral acts of commission/omission   Prayer—Worship
- Judgment—evaluation and punishment   Divine Guidance
- Eschatology—last days, rapture   Discernment
- Word of God—writing, interpreting   Eternity

3

THE TODAY SHOW
Twenty-First-Century Community

Every time somebody got voted off the island, I thought, "Thank you! You just earned me another $15,000."

Gervase Peterson, *Survivor: The Australian Outback*

It became a sacred icon of its time. For two decades before the end of the century the nostalgic strains of *Cheers* proclaimed one of television's most popular and long-standing sitcoms. The words that opened every show reminded listeners that everybody needs a place to belong and someone to care, a place where "everybody knows your name."

The characters that formed the *Cheers* crew were a less-than-desirable bunch, from an eccentric postman to a neurotic psychologist. None of them was the kind of person deliberately chosen to be in a church small group. Yet, together, these socially marginal people found a place and acceptance in a Boston bar. The media reveals the hope that hides in every human heart, that somebody knows and accepts me no matter how different or abnormal I may appear.

Charles Swindoll writes:

> The neighborhood bar is possibly the best counterfeit there is to the fellowship Christ wants to give His church. It's an imitation, dispensing liquor instead of grace, escape rather than reality, but it is a permissive, accepting, and inclusive fellowship. It is unshockable. It is democratic. You can tell people secrets and they usually don't tell others or even want to. The bar flourishes not because most people are alcoholics, but because God has put into the human heart the desire to know and be known, to love and be loved.
>
> Swindoll, 1983, p. 128

The Current State of Community

At the turn of the century the television programs highest in the ratings feature winning for yourself at any cost, the lone competitor winning it all, even at the expense of destroying colleagues *(Survivor, Who Wants to Be a Millionaire? Big Brother, Temptation Island, The Weakest Link)*. In each of these programs the "group" was used to prove the supremacy of the singular winner. A *Survivor* contestant is quoted in *TV Guide:* "The players are . . . constantly plotting about how to win the whole thing. They're asking themselves, 'Which one can I win against?' . . . And this is the point in the game where it can actually pay to be a jerk, if you're an a——, people want to keep you around because they think that they can beat you in the final vote" (*TV Guide*, April 7–13, 2001, p. 195).

In the twenty-first century networks are still in existence, but there is a brutality inherent in coaxing out the survival of the fittest. The realism of "Am I my brother's keeper?" is now a fascination that drives us to face the worst about our natures. In his survey of the American small group movement, sociologist Robert Wuthnow frankly states, "Individualism . . . once meant being responsible for ourselves and our neighbors. But we have replaced this traditional concept with a more radical individualism that looks out for number one at the expense of everyone else" (Wuthnow, 1994, p. 35). Individualism means not just independence with a choice to care for our neighbors. Now we have no compunctions about destroying them. For many people this is an everyday reality as they walk into the office, enter the classroom, or drive down the freeway. We are immune to everything but staying on top. Quoting Gervase Peterson from *Survivor*, "Immunity. That's the watchword from here on out. Winning the immunity challenges is the only way to guarantee that you're going to survive another three days and possibly win" (*TV Guide*, 2001, p. 195).

We exist in an impersonal world where the law of the jungle makes us leery and alert. While this is going on in our external world, buried deep within each person, there is the reminder of another longing. Bilezikian identifies this wishful sadness.

> Our mourning is for the closeness that was ours by right of creation. Our grief is for the gift lost in the turmoil of rebellion. And now, whenever there is hope, our hope is for paradise regained. For human destiny remade in the redemptive restoration of community, the only certainty of oneness for here and for eternity.
>
> Bilezikian, 1997, p. 16

While we adapt to the survival of the fittest, we have a faint "memory" of a better scenario in which we can bask in the safe intimacy of loving and being loved without threat of loss.

And so we find small groups still attractive today. But these are refashioned networks of communication. They are designed to fit our current needs. Wuthnow suggests that the success of the small group movement is due in large part to fitting in with the trends already fashioning our present scene. The adaptability of the group format adds "fuel to the fires of cultural change that have already been lit" (Wuthnow, 1994, pp. 21, 24). A small group format does not demand a "form of community that can be gained only at great social or personal cost. Instead, it provides a kind of social interaction that busy, rootless people can grasp without making significant adjustments in their lifestyles" (Wuthnow, 1994, p. 25).

This popularized experience supports and enables what one author labels as among the major cultural realignments in U. S. history. In the eighteenth century, realignment in the world of religion arose from the abolishing of the state church, thus allowing denominations to flourish. In the nineteenth century, the major shift was toward diversity, democracy, and congregational autonomy, ushering in the acceptance of Catholicism and Judaism along with Protestantism. The present stress on variety and choice and the need for competitive programming makes these modular group communities, which offer flexibility and fluidity, not only attractive but essential. And the popularity of the small group movement is reshaping the religious world (Wuthnow, 1994).

Redefining Community

These desirable factors of small groups—adaptability, flexibility, fluidity—are in reality the dynamics responsible for redefining the very image of community. As we mix our cultural standards with our personal needs, we are creating a new form of community that is quite foreign to the image projected in Scripture. The kind of community that is generated by groups today is often radically different from that kind of community characterizing families, tribes, ethnic groups, and neighborhoods throughout the majority of human history (Wuthnow, 1994).

Our current fashioning of the image of community has been influenced by such factors as the absolute supremacy and control of the individual when it comes to being present, participating, and deciding. For this autonomous individual the major goals are personal happiness and success as determined by personal evaluation. Wuthnow discovered that in groups today, "The social contract binding members together asserts only the weakest of obligations. Come if you have time. Talk if you feel like it. Respect everyone's opinion. Never criticize. Leave quietly if you become dissatisfied" (Wuthnow, 1994, p. 6). The group becomes one more tool to help the individual achieve what he or she has already determined, thus providing opportunity for the individual to focus on self in the presence of other members. We use groups for our own ends. This is in contrast to the picture of community drawn in chapter 1 as biblical community.

Redefining Spirituality

Even more startling is the impact this process is having on our view of the sacred. Because our community is designed to reflect the image of God, what affects one naturally affects the other. Our view of God colors our view of what God's people are to be together and what we become together influences our experience of God.

How are small groups changing our view of the sacred? Research data indicates that in becoming portable support systems that are under our control, groups may simply salve our consciences and reinforce what we want to hear. Because of our lack of commitment and sense of autonomy, we can walk out if the group doesn't perform the way we want it to.

By emphasizing self-help and practical results in coping with present issues, the sacred may be reduced to helping one feel better about things as they are rather than challenging one to make sacrifices and to experience pain in order to know God's truth in the midst of those circumstances. Right and wrong are often defined by the group rather than by doctrines. As such, "Spirituality no longer is true or good because it meets absolute standards of truth or goodness but because it helps us get along" (Wuthnow, 1994, pp. 18–19). A small group can focus on the immediacy of adapting

> to the demands of everyday life rather than providing a sense of tran-
> scendence that casts a new perspective on everyday life. It also makes the
> individual the measure of all things. . . . Spirituality no longer is true or
> good because it meets absolute standards of truth or goodness but because
> it helps us get along. We are the judge of its worth. If it helps us find a
> vacant parking space, we know that our spirituality is on the right track.
>
> Wuthnow, 1994, p. 18

In encouraging people to talk about their faith, groups become one of the most potent means of shaping (both positively and negatively) a person's theology.

The present yearning for the spiritual and the breakdown of natural sources of community go hand in hand. Lacking the support of belonging and purpose that goes beyond the individual and characterizes community, people have turned inward and sought connection with a Higher Being, a relatedness, a sense of intimacy with a divine other. We need this connection to feel that we matter, that there is purpose in our being, that someone will be there for us when we need. And this need is heightened by certain factors in today's society.

The natural networks of community no longer provide the elements of care and personal support to sustain us in an impersonal, high-pressure world. Four of these areas that reflect this change are family structure, neighborhood and friendship ecosystems, workplace and classroom situations, societal conditions.

Family Structure

Divorce continues to affect almost one in every two marriages, shaking the most natural setting for establishment of a caring community. Of the two people who seemingly care the most for a child, one is likely to leave before that child turns eighteen. "Trends indicate that of all the children born in 1990, six out of ten will live in a single-parent household for some period of time before they reach the age of 18" (Barna, 1990, pp. 67–68). *Newsweek* announced that 70% of adults in the United States now believe that couples who fail to get along in marriages where there are young children should not feel obligated to stay together just for the sake of the children (*Newsweek*, quoted in Barna, 1988, p. 18). Such reinterpretation of commitment is certain to affect the security and values of people left in the relationship.

Allan Bloom reflects, "Of course, many families are unhappy. But that is irrelevant. The important lesson that the family taught was the existence of the only unbreakable bond, for better or for worse, between human beings" (Bloom, 1987, p. 119). Few people know the security of a stable family network where commitment is made and kept regardless of circumstances. The generation that is shuffled back and forth between Dad's family and Mom's family questions if there is a place of belonging, if people can be trusted to care, and if getting close is going to mean being hurt. For these folks, a small group can be a place to begin to learn caring and to learn how to develop commitment. And a Christian small group can interpret the sacred through its community.

Tom Beaudoin, writing about and as a Gen Xer, speaks about the results of family disintegration on his generation:

> Xers not only personally learned about the fragility of commitment but were also forced into a premature—and untutored—adulthood. The ease with which my friends could talk about divorce, sex, and other adult issues astounded me. Their childhood experiences of poverty, latchkey independence, and divorced and "blended" families . . . led to an immersion in popular culture as both substitute parent and surrogate minister.
>
> Jesus . . . offered the ultimate blended family, perfect for the generation that grew up with more than half of marriages ending in divorce and with frequent remarriages. By following Jesus, a new family formed, one to which Christian Xers could have cleaved. . . . Xers can be particularly poised to claim this familial theology as their own.
>
> Beaudoin, 1998, pp. 8, 86

Referring to the next generation, the Millennials, Howe and Strauss observe, "More Millennials are growing up with single parents than was true of Gen Xers. . . . Since 1980, the entire growth in single parenthood has come from two entirely new categories: single fathers and, especially, *never-married* moms" (Howe & Strauss, 2000, pp. 124, 126). "Likewise, more Millennials are growing up with two working parents, and more are relegated, for more hours of the day, to the supervision of third parties" (Howe & Strauss, 2000, p. 126).

This second phenomenon is engendered by the condition of survival replacing relationships. Major energy goes into the securing of income to make possible the continued existence of the family. This leaves little energy left over to meet the needs of the family and to cultivate relationships. One interviewer of hundreds of kids observes that "what Millennials really want is for moms and dads to be less tired and stressed

. . . or to make more money," thus reflecting parental priorities (Howe & Strauss, 2000, p. 135).

Children are often left to their own devices, creating a new breed called "latchkey children," so called because of the door key they wear around their necks. Surprisingly, a Census Bureau survey revealed that the highest percentage of these children come from white higher-income households where the mother is educated and in a white-collar occupation (Louv, 1990).

As each person becomes more responsible for self and for fulfilling his or her own needs, relationships become more a catch-as-catch-can experience. Life is programmed, productive, and performance-based rather than relational. It takes time and effort to build intimacy. And time is something we don't have. Neither do we have much intimacy.

That former bastion of relationship-building, the family meal, has been replaced by fast foods and pull-from-the-freezer, pop-in-the-microwave, time-saving meals that enable us to keep on schedule while adding one more item to our accomplishments. Sitting down to relax over a meal with conversational sharing and developing relationships has been replaced with TV viewing over the TV tray.

By each person doing his or her own thing, individual priorities may be fulfilled but not necessarily community priorities. Vacations tend to be shorter and are less likely to incorporate all the household members. Most homes now provide more than one television set so family members can watch separate programs in different parts of the house (Barna, 1990). Computers are personal and likely to consume the individual for hours in a separate location. The latest generation has known nothing but this state of affairs. We are an information generation that finds it increasingly difficult to communicate with one another.

VCRs, walkmans, boom boxes, and other nonrelational machines occupy much of the family's relational time. Richard Louv in his provocative book, *Childhood's Future*, reflects on this substitution: "I came to believe . . . that much of the reason so many of us today spend so much time in the company of machines is because the true company of people is becoming harder to come by" (Louv, 1990, p. 127). Social worker Judy Frank targets the same need: "What we hear over and over from the kids is, 'I want someone to play it with me.' We see kids who are hungry for personal interaction, somebody to really sit and play with them. Playing with a machine, no matter how brilliant its responses, still leaves a child essentially alone" (Sussman, 1988). On the home front we are creating individuals who grow up believing this is the norm and who miss out on the richness of enjoying personal relationships, someone to listen, to help them process issues, and to deliver the human touch. Somewhere that need must be met.

Neighborhood/Friendship Ecosystems

The changes in family relationships send individuals outside of the home for personal and relational gratification. One of the most popular sources available today is the on-line chat room. Thousands of people open up to virtual strangers because they are there and listening, and one can opt out of relationship easily by the click of a mouse. Gen Xer Beaudoin sees cyberspace as an opportune natural communal and religious connection for his generation.

> Technology enables intimate discussion about spirituality. . . . This is perfect for Xers, who have grown up with such a tense relationship to formal communities of faith and who are so well suited to nonfamilial, ad hoc communities. . . . Cyberspace affords opportunities for intimate faith discussion without necessitating face-to-face communication. . . . In this way, Xers challenge religious institutions to rethink the definition of community. . . . Religious institutions have an opportunity to use this virtual space to build community when ministering to Xers.
>
> Beaudoin, 1998, pp. 88, 90

Is virtual community enough? Does it meet the need for someone to count on, someone to care? Because many Xers were robbed of personal relationships when growing up, is this virtual relating sufficient to satisfy their hunger?

Many neighbors don't bother getting acquainted because high mobility will soon scramble the mix of people and the effort required in getting acquainted will be lost. Former boundaries that solidified neighborhoods are gone, and so is the ethnic identification that caused people to be open to others who resided in the same locale. While individuals once gained a distinct public sense of identity by living in a particular neighborhood, attending a certain school or parish, they now appear to exist in anonymity (Wuthnow, 1998).

The same factors that mitigate against the building of community in the family today are present and operative in neighborhood and friendship community-building. It is normal to view others as threats to our achievement, our privacy, our holding on to what we have. The stress of maintaining autonomy, protecting schedule and lifestyle, coping with change and pressure from other facets of our lives causes us to be militant about not letting others into our personal lives and not wanting to be involved in theirs. Maintaining anonymity protects us. Externally, the increasing presence of home protection devices, fences, and rising insurance rates remind us that nobody expects to be his or her neighbor's keeper, and we expect the worst from others and need to be protected from them.

Many Americans have turned to intentional association with others of like minds or like maladies. Self-help, self-fulfillment, self-enhancement groups joined for support and recovery breed relationships of a utilitarian nature, usually focused around one facet of a person's life. Some have found the greatest sense of community with those who share their weakness. Vulnerability and banding together to enable growth and achievement in each other becomes for many the major source of intimacy available to them. These are the people they could call on in the middle of the night.

These groups, with their focus on self-gratification, in some ways increase the tension between individualism and community. According to one source between 8 and 10 million people belong to at least 500,000 of these self-help groups (Wuthnow, 1994). We are a nation that seeks support so that we might survive as individuals.

> Small groups nurture our self-esteem, . . . because the other people in the group take us seriously. They listen, they accept, they empathize, they support. They give us all the things we never find in everyday life. Why? Because they are not everyday life. They are not the source of our employment. We don't share bank accounts. We don't bear mutual responsibility for the welfare of our children. We don't go to bed with them at night. But the people we share with in groups are nevertheless significant enough that we value what they say. Their caring means a lot.
>
> Wuthnow, 1994, p. 187

Mobility

Both neighborhoods and circles of friends are seen as transitory for modern Americans. Knowing that on the average one in five Americans moves every year, why pay the price to get to know someone you will soon be leaving? Pilgrims on the move tend not to put down deep roots. Pilgrims must be ready to move on, a factor that breeds autonomy. People you know now are not likely to be people you hang around with in the future. This realization causes a temporariness in our relations. Charles Swindoll shares the confession of the wife of an executive: "To decrease the pain of saying 'good-bye' to our neighbors, we no longer say 'hello'" (Swindoll, 1983, p. 20).

Crowded

Overpopulation has produced interesting emotions. On the one hand, the constant stimulation of too many people produces in us a need for solitude. We shrink from having to interact with "one more person." We stare straight ahead at the closed elevator door while people crush in upon us. The television, which we can shut off at will, seems like a friendlier companion than a live person who requires involvement and may demand more than we feel we can give. And many people will join a large church or a large "small group" to fulfill both the need for community and to protect themselves from others.

On the other hand there is a loneliness in the depersonalization forced upon us by the bigness of our society. We are given numbers to represent us. Our mail comes to "Resident." To our employer we are often known by our position. We find we are not credible unless we present the required forms of identification. Globalization and our awareness of the magnitude of people living on this planet cause our sense of significance to shrink. "The time required to double the world's population has dropped from 1,000,000 years to 200 years, to 80 years until now. At the present accelerated rate of population growth, the earth's population will double in 35 years" (Luft, 1984, p. 151).

Functional Connections

We live with what one author calls "functional relationships." These relationships exist totally as a means to an end, a way for us to get something we need. We have no relationship with the grocery clerk, gas station attendant, toll booth operator, or bank teller other than as a means to help us achieve our ends. They could be machines. We become used to using people, to interacting without the personal, to expect nothing more than results. Each nonperson has no purpose but to be instrumental in satisfying our need. We therefore don't get involved in their lives as individuals. We are isolated from the fact that the service station attendant's marriage is breaking up, or the bank teller just lost her mother to cancer. TV coverage of personal tragedies serves only to arouse interest in us. We cannot care for so many people so we compensate by viewing them in anonymity. If we don't know, we cannot care, and thus we are not responsible.

This lack of knowing and bonding has opened the door for increase in vandalism and crime in neighborhoods. The Neighborhood Watch program is an attempt to help neighbors get to know one another and thus to assume responsibility for watching what happens to a "real person's" property. It attempts to construct community based on mutual concern so that mutual benefits may occur.

In protecting our individual privacy we have lost our bond of community. In trying to get ahead we have lost our sense of connectedness. In keeping our distance we have lost the warmth of intimacy. The present understanding of neighbor and friend seldom provides the longed-for community. Small group leaders must accept the fact that the church family often is seen in the same way as the neighborhood/friend system—quick and expedient, and easily left behind when another more pertinent means comes along.

think about this:

- How does the above express or explain your present or past situations of friendship, group membership, neighbor connections?

Workplace/Classroom Situations

In many ways this sphere of our existence has helped generate what the two previously discussed areas have become in terms of community, because it now has priority over both family and friendship. Work dominates where we live and how much time we spend with family and friends. When work says move to another city, most people don't think twice about what this will do to relationships and sources of community they have committed to and depended on. The current career does little if anything to foster a sense of care, commitment, and corporate responsibility. The individual is usually viewed as dispensable, competitive, interchangeable, and sooner or later a liability. Community in the workplace is an endangered species.

It is difficult to foster the growth of another when you know that such development may cause that individual to get the job advancement you're after. Students face the same issues when class grading is done on the curve. One premed classroom reported students giving each other fraudulent exam papers in order to increase their own chances of getting into med school with the right answers.

With an eye to their own personal success, workers want to relate to those above them, those who can grant them favors and build influence. The number of people vying for a limited number of jobs causes competition, which makes us protective and isolated.

For hundreds of thousands of workers, work is their identity. It is the reason for their value, and they realize that for them to succeed, they must do nothing that shows weakness or dependence or that would compromise their personal advancement. Caring for others can get in the way of objectivity in decision-making. Students groan when asked to work on group projects, fearing the lesser ability of another will lower their score.

Learners in a classroom are frequently viewed as minds and mouths instead of being valued as whole persons whose lives outside the classroom are probably shaping them more than inside the classroom. Workers also reflect the fact that the company has little or no commitment to them as individuals. They function as a cog in the machine. Each knows that if a person becomes nonproductive, sick, or old, he or she is disposable. It is with shock that longtime higher management employees have received their walking papers because of mergers and streamlining for increased productivity. Coworkers simply step in and fill the gap without missing a step.

The situation at work and in the classroom has moved from being a place of mutual effort to one of individualized competition where help given is seen as suspicious and help needed is viewed as weakness. It's each for himself or herself, alone against the others. They don't want to hear your problems; they have their own. They don't want to celebrate your victories; they wish they were the victor. In academia we come to realize "that what most counts is what I learn, what I know, what my grades are. . . . We learn at an early age that whatever intellectual abilities we have are ours and should be exploited for our own benefit. Why should I use my gifts and abilities to help anyone else learn?" (Kenneson, 1999, 143). This perspective invades other areas of our lives.

> Many high school coaches . . . find it next to impossible to get players focused on working together rather than for individual honors. "Why should I work together if doing so means someone other than me might be named MVP?" Similarly, many marriage partners find it difficult to view their spouses as partners, so accustomed are they to viewing other people as competitors. If one spouse receives an honor or a promotion, does the other feel a sense of satisfaction knowing that he or she helped to make this possible? Or does the other spouse feel slighted, believing that the honor or promotion was earned at his or her "expense"?
>
> Kenneson, 1999, pp. 143–44

The result of all this autonomy is that the workplace and the classroom are no longer safe places for finding and cultivating community.

Societal Conditions

The Fragmented Life

In interviews with neighbors or classmates who knew the perpetrator of a horrendous crime, interviewees are frequently heard to say, "But he was such a nice guy. We never would have guessed that he would be capable of doing this." Even parents claim ignorance of their own children's sense of values. Life is broken up into many separate parts. Nobody knows you whole. Some see you as pressured parent, others as testy office secretary, angry driver, or intense workout partner, and still others as traditional church member. Each of these roles fits into its own separate world. You can put on and take off various roles depending on which sphere you are in.

High mobility makes it possible to take up existence in a setting where no one has known you in the past. Children live far from parents. Those you went to school with have long been left behind. Relocation in business or change in marriage status means beginning again. There is little if any sense of continuity with the past. Indeed many adults see these times as starting over, cutting ties with the past and ties with former community. Life is a loose string of acquaintances, a disconnected series of roles that do not overlap. Social roles today tend to be so splintered that most people are known in only one role, which can lead to increased freedom but also to increased insecurity and loneliness.

think about this:

- In what ways does your life appear as disconnected parts where the elements of one segment are unknown to the others?

Rapid Change

Another factor motivating search for community is the insecurity and anxiety caused by accelerated change. Already mentioned is the accelerated rate of population growth that causes a doubling of the earth's population in the brief span of thirty-five years and increased ease of mobility that allows us to relocate on a temporary or permanent basis in entirely new settings. Millions are whisked into workplace settings miles from their homes, retreating back in the evenings or on weekends. "Fully 30 percent of the U.S. workforce is now opting for what economists call 'nontraditional' employment—including contract work, self-employment, and temp jobs" (Howe & Strauss, 2000, p. 131). Many employees are separated from their boss and coworkers miles away, linked only by computer. Distance learning allows students to take classes in their homes during whatever time is convenient. Their only connection with classmates is via e-mail. "Electronic communication is a medium through which a growing amount of human exchange occurs.

Consequently, people find that many of their emotional and support needs go increasingly unmet" (Roof, 1999, p. 163).

Only a few years are now required for the innovative cycle between the origination of an idea and its application, a process that used to take as much as a millennium. We are bombarded with information that causes continuous change in our lifestyle and thinking. In only four and a half centuries the increase in publication of new books has gone from one thousand a year to one thousand a day. Scientific literature is currently being produced at the rate of some 20 million pages per year (Luft, 1984). Innovations caused by the computer alone affect each person every day.

We are dwarfed by the amount of change that engulfs us and requires us to readjust. We have become "change junkies." We must have constant change. It is a fix to dull our feelings. The constant state of flux in which we live gives birth to a sense of rootlessness and insignificance. What can we substitute for the personal relationships found in community? Machines lack emotion and care. Things are designed for obsolescence. Time spins by, another ever-present reminder that we are the victims of relentless change. What moorings can we clutch to bring some security and control?

The Good Life

Americans grow up convinced that they have a right to happiness. Most of the Third World would never make this claim. To them, survival is success. But for us, the good life is an inalienable right, and we pursue it with gusto. Should anyone thwart that happiness, we are quick to scream injustice. All types of actions are justified on the basis of not being happy. We leave marriages, we drop out of classes, we resign from jobs, we change churches, we transfer to another group. Comfort is increasingly a norm we feel we are owed even though we joke about "no pain, no gain." And so we buy—to make us feel good—the latest, most updated, most powerful that will surely satisfy us (for the moment). It is how we construct who we are.

Philip Cushman speaks about this new definition of self: "The new cultural terrain was now oriented to purchasing and consuming rather than to moral striving; to individual transcendence rather than to community salvation; to isolated relationships rather than to community activism; to an individualistic mysticism rather than to political change." And what has emerged is the "self-contained individual . . . a self that experiences a significant absence of community, tradition, and shared meaning" (Cushman, 1995, pp. 78–79). It was in the Garden that God declared "It is not good for Adam to be alone." God's evaluation of the good life is relationship together, "the body of Christ," the church relating to her God and his bride.

Through Others' Eyes

The United States is a multicultural nation, very likely the most diverse nation on earth. This offers the potential for immense richness and integration and for numerous misunderstandings and divisions. Most new immigrants are from Asia and Latin America. At the turn of the century Hispanic Americans totaled 22% and Asian Americans, 4%, with African Americans making up 13% of the total population. Added together these total almost 30% of our population with a predicted over 40% in the next two decades (*Chronicle of Higher Education*, 1999). Some cities are home to greater concentrations. Los Angeles, in 1996, included 1 million (29%) Hispanic Americans in its 3.5 million population. San Francisco (750,000) housed more than 250,000 (39%) Asian Americans. Cincinnati and St. Louis had 40% African American population (Carpenter, 1996). The Los Angeles Unified School District includes students who speak 108 different languages. Any view of community-building must take into consideration such factors of diversity that will bring into the mix high numbers of occasions for adaptation and special awareness.

What might be some of these areas of diversity that could cause a group to be affected? How have you experienced such in a small group? How has your cultural background influenced a perspective, conviction, or value you bring to a small group experience?

Firestarters

1. Scan the front page of a newspaper or the table of contents found in a current issue of a newsmagazine. What additional societal factors mentioned there affect the need for or shape of community today?

2. How does the latest issue of your favorite magazine or an evening of TV viewing give insight into the values affecting the acknowledgment and cultivation (or lack thereof) of community today?

3. How has your own life been affected by the issues presented in this chapter? List the issue in your own words and then document your experience.

4. A review of Boomer spirituality shows the paradox individualized comfort presents when combined with what we realize we need. "American Boomers want community, but on strictly individual terms. They want human closeness without feeling cramped or obligated. They want a personal God who doesn't ask much personally.... They want a faith that's fulfilling, practical, earthy, tolerant, transcendent, fun, empowering, morally serious without being morally demanding, a faith that restores wonder and deepens intimacy, and they want it not to cost too much or take up a lot of time" (Buchanan, 2000, p. 9).

*What implications do you see growing
out of each of these Boomer values?*

Boomer Values	How Groups Are Affected
Short-term involvement	
Not motivated by duty, blind loyalty	
"I am my own authority"	
Say what they think—confrontation vs. politeness	
Look for what helps them	
Have high expectations	
Refuse to do what is meaningless to them	
Want practical action, not theory	

PART II

TRUE COMMUNITY

4

THE REAL THING
True Community

I am cast upon a horrible, desolate island, void of all hope of recovery. I am singled out and separated, as it were, from all the world, to be miserable.

Daniel Defoe

The man stumbled around in shock. He had just gone through a monumental life-changing experience! He, alone, had lived! And that was the issue. He was alone: "I am divided from mankind, a solitary; one banished from human society. I have no soul to speak to or to relieve me."

Shipwrecked and cast upon the shore of a tropical island, Robinson Crusoe had natural food in abundance, an unlimited stay in an island paradise where the climate was ideal and the natives were peaceful. He was supplied with tools for working, weapons for defense, and seeds to plant. His situation seemed pleasant if not ideal. He was the lone survivor of the disaster. Yet he was morose and dispirited. He felt his aloneness and cursed his solitary life. He was devoid of human community, and life seemed bleak without it.

The woman knew she had just experienced an unheard-of, life-changing reality that would be hard to accept. Who would believe it?

She stood alone. Who would share her amazement, her awesome wonder, her increasing perfusion of questions? Who would join her in the process of waiting? And then she remembered—Elizabeth! The messenger had mentioned Elizabeth! And she was not alone anymore. Henri Nouwen continues,

> Elizabeth and Mary came together and enabled each other to wait. Mary's visit made Elizabeth aware of what she was waiting for. . . . These two women created space for each other to wait. They affirmed for each other that something was happening that was worth waiting for. I think that is the model of the Christian community. It is a community of support, celebration, and affirmation in which we can lift up what has already begun in us. The visit of Elizabeth and Mary is one of the Bible's most beautiful expressions of what it means to form community, to be together, gathered around a promise, affirming that something is really happening.
>
> The whole meaning of the Christian community lies in offering a space in which we wait for that which we have already seen. Christian community is the place where we keep the flame alive among us and take it seriously, so that it can grow and become stronger in us.
>
> Nouwen, 1987, p. 11

This is God's gracious heritage to his children—a common love, a common hope, a common expectation, a common realization that we can share together as we wait for his appearing. He has not left us alone. He has made himself present where "two or three of us are gathered together in his name." We are those who know a shared life in him. Luci Shaw has captured this mutual encounter of life together:

> Salutation
> Framed in light,
> Mary sings through the doorway.
> Elizabeth's six month joy
> jumps, a palpable greeting,
> a hidden first encounter
> between son and Son.
> And my heart turns over
> when I meet Jesus
> in you.
> quoted in L'Engle & Shaw, 1997, p. 169

But spiritual community, enjoying like-minded companionship with the family of God, is often difficult and as elusive as the proverbial "gold ring." By "moving in with Christ" we get "family," but they seem far from perfect and there are times when our promised togetherness seems far from reality. Cynicism, anger, even despair crowd out our hope of unity. Eugene Peterson writes, "Americans are good at forming clubs and gathering crowds. But clubs and crowds, even when—especially when—they are religious clubs and crowds, are not communities. The formation of community is the intricate, patient, painful work of the Holy Spirit. We cannot buy or make community; we can only offer ourselves to become community" (Peterson in Crabb, 1999, p. viii).

Whenever the Spirit of God is involved we can expect that the focus will be on Christ—in community, on Christ being formed in us individually and together. This requires dissatisfaction with anything less and willingness to be remade in the likeness of the One who is the source and focus of our relationship. This will bring us face-to-face with our inborn, enculturated, and distorted individualism. My life, our life together, must go through the process of re-formation when we meet Jesus in our midst. Spiritual community requires a reformation!

The questions present themselves: Can we trust the Spirit? How badly do we want to know community? Are we willing to let others play a part in our growing up in Christ Jesus? Are we willing to become what he offers as the "real thing"? Will we become what God has designed us to be? What's the price of not saying "yes"?

True Community

Trust

True community is more than being together. It requires trust. Today, especially, we find it difficult to trust. We warn our children about strangers. We create reams of paper contracts to shore up our mistrust of people. We keep our cards close to our chest because openness can be used against us. Experience is a good teacher. We have learned our lesson well. Depression-era parents enjoined, "trust no one but the family," but the collapse of the family has left us with no one to trust. Marriage partners find trust betrayed. Employees find agreements disregarded. Children experience promises not kept. Christians struggle in this area: "God I trust—but not people!" The older one becomes, the more one realizes one cannot even trust oneself.

Trust is a core component of community. So are we doomed never to know it? No, because God is trustworthy. By committing our lives to him we can live above the circumstances. Our dependence on God is the only thing that causes us to become more trustworthy. The more we acknowledge his sovereign goodness and power in our midst, the more we can commit to him the situations in our group. That kind of trust in

God can bring our growth and togetherness out of any situation. By allowing God's hand to be at work in our lives, we also promote the holiness of the group as a whole and as individuals in the group. Weaknesses and failures become stepping-stones to growth. Instead of trying to control or change ourselves and others, we begin to see ourselves and others for what God is creating in us and them and that leads to accepting and empowering while experiencing the same.

Larry Crabb suggests four characteristics of spiritual community: 1) celebrating people as created and forgiven by God; 2) visioning what another is becoming and trusting God to accomplish such; 3) discerning happenings as climates for growth; 4) empowering others to fully become what God is desiring for them to be (Crabb, 1999, pp. 136–41).

A person does not develop trust in others simply by being in a group where members study together, pray together, and share a common group leader. Trust involves intentional openness to God and each other.

Time and Effort

Cultivating this kind of group focus requires time. Our instant-minded culture may be frustrated with the impossibility of quick community. We find ourselves hoping for a quick "community fitness exercise," expecting that a weekly regimen of a two-hour group workout, a type of relational aerobics, will automatically produce a community.

True community will most likely be shaped by reality and sacrifice. Real community is the place where ego dies. That means such patterns as "our determination to fully trust no one must die and an eager willingness to receive what is best from others and to give what is best from within ourselves must take its place" (Crabb, 1999, p. 47). All of this goes back to a spiritual formation understanding of change, acts accomplished only by responding to the Spirit who prompts such. Community is not a commodity—a technique or product of methodology—it is a creation of the Spirit. Emphasis is not on urging people to improve in creating community but to consciously place themselves under conditions in which spiritual community flourishes.

The role of the church is to proclaim and enable true community. As Christians we cannot be satisfied with the provision and quality of small groups as people experience them in the world. The church is where we learn what true community is as God conceived it. Believers cannot settle for group times that only scratch the surface of people's lives. Our getting together must be depicted as more. The church's prophetic role is to offer the unique opportunity for an unsurpassable quality of relatedness that is uniquely Christian. Where else can people know that kind of unshakable commitment? Where else can they experience that kind of trust that grows out of faith in the *God who dwells in the people he has claimed?*

The church cannot simply put people in groups to accomplish ecclesiastical ends. Community with others in God's family is our heritage. Such community is a setting for discovering biblical insights that are impossible to know in an ordinary group setting. Christians must internalize and proffer a vision of community that the image of God in each of us responds to. There ought to be a sense in these body-of-Christ networks that we have come home. We have found the family for which we have longed.

Natural Hindrances to Community-Building

Our naturally learned ways of responding to people can unconsciously undermine the climate that fosters openness. One of these is preconceived expectations, created out of our fear of the unknown. To fill the void of the not-yet-experienced, we set up expectations that are usually false. While these projections become security for us, they soon slip into the role of tyrants as we try to make this group experience conform to our expectations, and as we seek to force others into our preconceived molds. We are often trapped into fulfilling role expectations we have placed on ourselves, e.g., "I expect I'll have to get them organized." When measuring up to expectations is the goal, it becomes difficult—if not impossible—to really hear or experience anything outside the preconceived notion.

Another hazard is judgment based on limited, brief, and/or distorted experiences, i.e., labeling or prejudice. These too must be brought to our attention and given up for community to develop. As long as we continue to see others through the pigeonholes of "conservative," "emotional," or "nitpicker" we keep them at a distance and lock them into behavior patterns. All we see reinforces our evaluation and keeps us from openness. It is the opposite of "envisioning" mentioned above. Christians have their own sets of labels that prevent bonding—"super spiritual," "liberal thinker," "charismatic," etc.

Third, community requires us to give up our rigidities that make us think we alone know the right way, have the correct solution, or have experienced the truth. Feeling this superiority, we begin to view ourselves as the saviors, fixers, and healers of others' maladies. If they have a problem, we can solve it. If they have a pain, we can make it better. If they disagree, we can convert them to better thinking. Such intention is motivated by a need to eliminate "your pain so I feel better," to change "your ideas so mine aren't threatened," to take care of "your problem so I can become savior."

In true community, people care and come alongside, realizing that their presence or "thereness" brings greater strength than quick solutions. We often puzzle over Christ's role of "withness" when he could eliminate the discomfort. "When you pass through the waters, I will be *with* you" (Isa. 43:2, italics added); "Even though I walk through the valley of the shadow of death, I will fear no evil, for you are *with* me" (Ps. 23:4, italics added); "Go and make disciples. . . . And surely I am *with* you always" (Matt. 28:19–20, italics added). True community involves being present with another.

Openness to being in community means we must be willing to give up our self-centered need to control and manipulate. This does not advocate a total absence of planning; rather it is openness to being influenced and willingness to sacrifice one's need to always be in control so that others may go through what is necessary for them to build interdependence with one another. This may mean that both members and leader will come face-to-face with their own inadequacies and shortcomings. Such may drive the group to God. Leaders can enable, but not control, group attitudes, progress, and insights. Closely aligned with this sacrifice is the need for approval. Letting members and groups take responsibility for their own actions may not be popular. For those of us who are born rescuers, this is a painful sacrifice for the sake of evolving community (Peck, 1987).

True community is built on the sacrifices of old resentments and angers, on facing insecurities and fears, and on giving up preoccupations. Again, only the Spirit of God can reveal and motivate these barriers to openness. "Unless a kernel of wheat falls to the ground and dies, it remains only a single seed. But if it dies, it produces many seeds" (John 12:24). "Whoever wants to become great among you must be your servant" (Matt. 20:26). "Whoever wants to save his life will lose it, but whoever loses his life for me will save it" (Luke 9:24). Community is not cheaply bought. Dietrich Bonhoeffer said there are people who love the *idea* of community but not necessarily the more *costly experience* of community.

It is the Spirit of God that prompts our willingness to be open. This freedom to listen to the Spirit's promptings grows out of a trust in God's ability to transform us and the construction of a safe environment where such a change can take place. When moving on from old patterns to new, we crave structures that protect us as we make this leap. Henri

Nouwen admits, "We all need a place safe enough to embrace our brokenness, our failure, and our inability to cope, and, in the midst of torment, a place to again discover life." We need "a safe place to hit bottom" (Nouwen in Crabb, 1999, p. 161).

This is where community is such an asset. "A central task of community is to create a place that is safe enough for the walls to be torn down, safe enough for each of us to own and reveal our brokenness. Only then can the power of connecting do its job. Only then can community be used of God to restore our souls" (Crabb, 1999, p. 11). Feeling secure can be even more difficult in a system where Christians evaluate according to rules and regulations. It is easy in such a system to feel rejected on the basis of actions, and this rejection is taken as rejection of the person, not the act. Our need for this kind of healing openness goes along with our hunger to be known by God and leads us to God who alone can forgive and empower us to become the kind of people who dwell in community. Crabb voices our need:

> You yearn for a safe place, a community of friends who are hungry for God, who know what it means to sense the Spirit moving within them as they speak with you. You long for brothers and sisters who are intent not on figuring out how to improve your life, but on being with you wherever your journey leads. You want to know and be known in conversations that aren't really about you or anyone else but Christ.
>
> Crabb, 1999, p. 19

Escapes from Community

Because community requires this facing of self and turning to God, it is easier to escape into numerous substitute states than to embrace the building of community as God designed. It is easier simply to attend a group and remain the same. Inevitably the development of community will require a dying to self, and we avoid this with any alternative that presents itself. What are these off-ramps that lead us away from community-building?

Good Manners

In the early stages of a group we avoid the honesty of community-building by taking flight into politeness, denying who we really are. This produces a form of pseudocommunity where differences are treated as nonexistent and "peace at all costs" is the rule of the day.

Blame

This stage of affability becomes strained after several occasions together and so we move to blame—another is at fault for our feeling this way. Scapegoating places our stored-up frustrations and distresses on the shoulders of one who can be blamed for those uncomfortable feelings. This may be a leader or a group member, but such people are targeted as the focus of our irritations and dissatisfactions with the group and our inability to be all that we expected to be in this gathering.

Organization

Subgrouping and other forms of organization are chosen to serve as outlets for our pent-up frustrations over not achieving what we hunger for. "We're not getting anywhere. Let's divide into two groups and come up with some answers" tries to escape having to work through feelings and insights in the process of community-building. "Let's vote on it" is another trapdoor that releases groups to move on without dealing with differences.

Needy Members

Sometimes we miss community-building opportunities by ignoring the pain of others or of ourselves. By denying the pain, we can move on and cover the agenda. In actuality, community can be forged by exploring painful areas together. Likewise when we fruitlessly attempt to change others or fix their conditions, we often forfeit community-building experiences that cause us to come alongside and hear and support. Wanting others to be and think like us is the opposite of community. Community embraces a variety of viewpoints, abilities, and experiences. It is energized by uniqueness and acceptance.

Factions

Liaisons and resulting exclusions are another means of resisting community-building. Pairing, whether romantic or otherwise, can interfere with a group's development as a whole. Whenever some are excluded or ignored as nonexistent, community is undermined. Facing these alliances directly may help to relieve their exclusivity. "Group in the corner, we all want to share the benefits of your insights" or "I'm guessing we're all curious about the joke you two seem to be sharing. Why don't you let us all in so none of us feels excluded."

Abdicating Responsibility

Refusing to take responsibility forces a leader or strong members to carry more than their share (Peck, 1987). Such action destroys the mutuality so necessary to community. "It's not my responsibility" becomes easy avoidance. This state of dependency is a codependency where the weak have learned to manipulate the strong. Dependency must not be allowed to replace the interdependency of community. It creates uncommitted, uninvolved, ungrateful members and overworked, overprotective, over-controlling leaders who have become victims of the group and often end up bitter and disillusioned. Biblically speaking, all strengths are given for the good of the body, for the strengthening of the church, for the common good. The only dependency for believers is on God himself.

Why Small Groups?

Robert Wuthnow's survey of group members shows that groups are viewed as places where each individual comes to think about himself or herself. Groups primarily service individuals. They have become portable support systems that help us get through our week. And that commitment is not strong enough to last through differences; members recognize that they can move on to another group who will affirm that they as "customer" are always right. "Members are . . . more likely to ask what the group can do for them than what they can do for the group" (Wuthnow, 1994, pp. 14–15).

Scripture speaks of a "form of godliness" that denies the power of the real thing. In many ways, we have a form of togetherness in groups that by its very nature disallows the reality of what God created us to enjoy in community. The easiest form of untruth to accept is one that looks like truth in some ways and promises to provide what only the true reality can create.

In our human attempts to understand and thus motivate (control) a person's response to becoming a part of a small group, we have documented some important findings. Among the most notable of these is a theory called FIRO (Fundamental Interpersonal Relations Orientation) (Schutz, 1958). This theory measures three basic psychological drives that groups seem to satisfy. The first is *inclusion*. We have an inherent need to be a part of a group and accepted by others. Second, we have both the need to influence others and to be influenced by others. This need is categorized as *power*. As such this drive is not necessarily negative but can be demonstrated in exercising responsibility, in organizing and initiating, in attempting to persuade others. People may join groups to implement positive ways of meeting such need and in so doing care for others. The third FIRO need is that of openness to care or *affection*. We want to like others and to be liked by them. Groups enable us to express this positive desire (Forsyth, 1999).

These three are measured in both the need to express the behavior and the need to receive the behavior from others. In regard to inclusion, we like to invite others to join with us and we like others to invite or include us when they do things. Regarding power, we like to take responsibility for doing things, and we enjoy having others take charge of doing what needs to be done. In regard to affection, we work at building close relationships with others and we enjoy people demonstrating friendliness toward us.

These insights can be very helpful in designing a group and in identifying various expressions of needs in a group. The difference in community is that the emphasis on God and others helps keep these needs in balance and doesn't use others to make us feel good.

Each expression of these psychological needs is capable of distortion because of our sinful natures. Thus, inclusion can cause acceptance to become so distorted that it resorts to any behavior to remain acceptable. Street gangs are an example of this need run amuck, leading to unlawful behavior and unacceptable rationalization for the sake of belonging. Power can be the drive that promotes domination and disrespect or can lead to victimization—such utter dependency that the boundaries of the person are destroyed. Affection distorted can lead to insatiable search or to hedonistic capitulation where we use another to meet our own needs for feeling loved and cared for.

A community can acknowledge such distortions as sin, and because they are committed to being together to express the nature of God, they can work through and find forgiveness and enabling power in the realization of the Spirit's role and each member's limitations. Attitudes and behaviors do not have to undermine communication and commitment.

There are many other reasons people join groups and are willing to be together for community. Groups enable our living out the roles we have been given in the body of Christ. Emotionally they allow for self-disclosure and caring.

In a spiritual community, people reach deep places in each other's hearts that are not often or easily reached. . . . They openly express love and reveal fear, even though they feel so unaccustomed to that level of intimacy. When members of a spiritual community reach a sacred place of vulnerability and authenticity, something is released. . . . An appetite for holy things is stirred. For just a moment, the longing to know God becomes intense, stronger than all other passions, worth whatever price must be paid for it. . . . Togetherness in Christ encourages movement toward Christ.

Crabb, 1999, p. 22

This is a powerful reason for desiring community: True community, orchestrated by God, eventuates in our moving toward Christ.

Distinctive!

Community issues out of mutual allegiance to a Higher Being whose cause is greater than our individualized goals. It is in being attuned to the same focus that the members become bonded to one another. Community is not achieved by focusing on the development of community for its own sake. Community is like joy, a by-product, a consequence of being open to what is beyond ourselves. It is not an end in itself. It always brings us back to a source greater than itself that enables its creation. It does not call attention to itself but produces praise for the One who chose to create it as one of his good gifts for those he loves.

Whenever your heart has resonated with or experienced a longing for this community as described in this chapter, it is a confirmation of your having been made in God's image and being drawn to his likeness. Community can be a place where you can experience the joy of fellowship and it can become an environment for your transformation and spiritual growth.

"There is no life that is not in community. And no community not lived in praise of God" (Eliot, 1952, p. 101).

Firestarters

1. Someone has observed that the fastest growing small groups in America are in the inner city. They are known as gangs. Their rapid growth is due in large part to the conditions of community they replicate but without the centrality and power of God that true community entails. Consider what about gang behavior reflects an innate desire for community. Make a list of characteristics that appeal to the gang member's inner longing for community. Then compare your list with the list below.

Community as Expressed in Gangs

- Experiencing acceptance and belonging

- Sense of family with other members
- Sense of belonging to something greater than the collected individuals
- United for the group purpose/cause
- Encouraged to use individual "giftedness" for benefit of gang membership and expansion of gang territory
- Passionate for cause
- Sharing strengths and service brings sense of self-esteem, worth from all
- Most coveted assets: group impact and group reputation
- Personal identity is that of the group
- Lifestyle of "evangelism" recruit, expand territory
- Joyful sacrifice of the one for the benefit of all
- Loyal even to death

2. Look over the following statements about community. Which seems to be of special importance to you and why? How is this characteristic of community in contrast with the average small group experience today—even in churches?

- Community says we belong because we are chosen by God.
- Community is a relationship that is given because of who we are, not what we have done.
- Community is the result of shared commitment to a higher allegiance.
- Community is essential to our being in Christ.
- Because of community, I don't have to impress you. I can just be me.
- In community I don't have to "have it all together." I can be vulnerable, real.
- In a community mind-set it is good to say, "I need you," because together we accomplish more than we do alone.
- In community I don't have to be everything. I contribute who I am and that is enough.
- A community framework makes it safe to risk and grow and make mistakes because I am supported and I belong no matter what.
- In community what is important to you is important to me. Yours are as valuable as mine.

- Community frees me from judging you. I have a greater concern to nurture and strengthen you. I don't need to fix you.
- In community I lend you my strengths and carry your weaknesses as you do mine.

To discover which psychological needs appear to be most important in your involvement in a group respond to the following questions.

Think about a small group of three to five people you are or have been involved with. What are or were the costs? Rewards?

On a scale of 1 to 5 (1 = low, 5 = high) rate yourself on the following:

- my need to demonstrate affection to others in the group
- my need to receive affection from others
- my need to be included when members gather informally in "after group sessions," parties, informal social events such as going out for a cup of coffee
- my openness to include other members in my leisure time activities
- my need to be in charge of situations in the group
- my willingness to allow others to be in charge of situations in the group

How do you think one of the group members would rate you on the above?

What verbal and nonverbal acts do you use:

- to show affection to the group
- when you receive affection from others in the group
- to make sure you are included in "after group" sessions, parties, informal social events
- to include other members in your leisure activities
- to take charge of situations
- to motivate others to take charge of situations

Adapted from Verderber & Verderber, 1986

5

AND NOW FOR A CHANGE
Transformation in Groups

> The important thing is this: to be willing at any moment to sacrifice who we are for what we can become.
>
> Charles Du Bois

In the culture in which we live, groups are seen as an effectively democratic way of involving all, permitting a diversity of opinion, and getting things done. But God's intentions for groups of his people are much greater. And this is an area where the distinctions of spiritual community show up. God intends spiritual formation, and groups become Spirit-energized agents for change.

As Christians, we must not buy into a lesser view of groups that simply reflects the world around us. Simon Chan, in championing the cultivation of spirituality, warns,

> Recent thinking about the church stresses the need for small groups. But most of these groups reinforce a "feel good" spirituality through group dynamics. They hardly challenge individuals to make deeper commitments to objective and absolute norms apart from themselves. Small group spirituality has come to mean no more than reorganizing the congregation

into "cell groups" to make them serve the needs of individual members better.

Most evangelical thinking, particularly in the area of church growth, has been along this line. Something more promising has come along in the form of small groups organized as effective agents for change in the church and in society at large. They deepen spirituality, since they require from their members a high degree of commitment to an objective ideal.

Chan, 1998, p. 104

The task of Christian community is not a democratic process, not a meet-your-neighbor club, not a platform for diversity or an assembly line for accomplishment, it is movement toward Christ. And groups, with their interactive connections between Christians, can become significant structures toward this end.

The fellowship of the church is that most remarkable phenomenon where all of our talk about the importance of the Christian community becomes a practical reality for transformation. . . . Fellowship is one of the great mysteries of God's work. It only happens, though, if there is a real coming together/Community. When that happens, we are shaped by each other, and as such, fellowship is a basic tool in the task of spiritual formation.

Lawrenz, 2000, pp. 96, 98

To experience this unity with the people of God necessitates—and fosters—connection with God. To maintain relatedness with God requires relational connection with those who house the Spirit of God. "For anyone who does not love his brother, whom he has seen, cannot love God, whom he has not seen" (1 John 4:20). This commitment to the objective standards of God within the life of an intentionally grouped community of people in whom the Spirit dwells becomes major motivation, means, and environment for spiritual formation.

The Nature of Change

Change is seldom neutral. We talk of "change for the better" or "change for the worse." We are exhilarated by the prospect of change or threatened by its demands. A significant factor today that propels us toward personal relationships is living with rapid change. We need someone to hang on to in a changing world. For the most part people initially resist change because it means leaving what is comfortable and moving to the unknown. But there is no forward motion without change. The Christian life is expected to be one of transition and transformation as believers are continually formed more wholly in the likeness of Christ. At the heart of all life is growth and development, positive or negative. Scripture identifies this change. Paul the apostle wrote to the Galatians, "My dear children . . . I am again in the pains of childbirth *until Christ is formed in you*" (Gal. 4:19, italics added). And to the Corinthians, "We, who with unveiled faces all reflect the Lord's glory, are *being transformed* into his likeness with ever-increasing glory" (2 Cor. 3:18, italics added). To the Romans he sent this word, "*Be transformed* by the renewing of your mind" (Rom. 12:2, italics added). Such texts suggest a process involving both Spirit power and prompting in spiritual formation. This formation is enabled by focusing on and then reflecting back the image of Jesus. Evidence points to the will and the attitude as being major participants in this formation process.

Formation also involves our actions; it requires "walking in the truth." Scripture indicates that the intentional practice of putting God's truth into action is necessary for the production of Christlike qualities in us. "Solid food is for the mature, who *by constant use* have trained themselves to distinguish good from evil" (Heb. 5:14, italics added). "Constant use" leads to a maturing discernment of what right living is. Jesus himself extolled the coupling of both hearing and putting into practice his words. The parable of the wise builder is an illustration of acting on known truth. "Everyone who hears these words of mine and puts them into practice is like a wise man who built his house on the rock" (Matt. 7:24). The rich young ruler was told, "If you want to be perfect [complete, mature], go, sell . . . and give to the poor" (Matt. 19:21). In other words, "Practice the truths you claim to know." Be changed!

Purpose

The purpose of a small group is not meetings but maturity. Not making connections as much as knowing God. True spiritual community leads to growth. Stuck groups are usually those that have closed their minds to change. They have chosen to remain within their comfort zones. Group vitality is energized by movement and growth, both in the individual and in the group as a whole. The presence of the Spirit, the gathering of believers in the name of Jesus, and the living, active Word of God combine to produce an amazing climate for growth. When every occasion of Christian community is viewed as an opportunity for Christian formation, groups take on new importance and the structuring of the time together becomes one of purposeful interaction. Group times then become more than just finishing a project, spending time together, or even getting to know each other.

Spiritual formation comes in many forms. In their journey toward Christlikeness, group members may grow in character, may discover new understandings, may develop skills that enhance their relationship with God and others, and may accomplish ministry to the body or to the world. A God-centered focus redefines whatever is done. People don't treat others with esteem and care just so they will feel at home in the group. Their at-homeness and experience of genuine love enhance openness to the formation of Christ within them and within relationships in the group. Members don't share openly just because they want people to know them and like them. Honest communication can be a means of personal formation. One person's disclosure may be used by the Spirit of God to help someone else gain perspective and encouragement. Refreshment times are more than icebreakers or small-talk time. They become occasions for informal formation and enjoyment of God's unique work in people made in his image. The intent of every facet of a gathering of spiritual community is to be formational.

The Latin phrase *coram Deo* sheds light on this perspective of formation. *Coram Deo* means "in the presence or before the face of God." Everything is done as it were with God being present to enhance and make use of acts and conversations to achieve his purpose. Words, activities, even rituals of a community become filled with his presence and are made more than mere human expressions—they are carried out to the glory of God. Even the most mundane act becomes an investment in the process of formation. With this kind of focus, words are chosen, actions are carried out, and group events become occasions for seeing God at work in who we are and what we do. Reports become offerings, expressing worship.

We must look at all of life from the central core of being "in Christ." How does being in him, knowing him, reshape our view of life things? We find God in the ordinary and discover that the former "ordinary" becomes significant and purposeful. When God is in our midst, formation is possible. It happened to Peter in a work group (his fishing team), to Cleopas and companion at table, having dinner together (in their Emmaus home), to Martha in the midst of grief (at Lazarus's wake), to a Samaritan lady during a routine household duty (getting water from the well). Every group occasion, whether support group, study group, or committee meeting, is an opportunity for our formation when seen as *coram Deo.*

Agents of Change

The Spirit of God is the agent of formation. Only the Spirit can form us in his likeness, and that can occur in the midst of any spontaneous happening. Our role is to prepare for his coming. John the Baptist was given the mission of making crooked places straight, so those moving toward the Messiah would not stumble over unnecessary hurdles. All focus is on the Coming One and enabling people to get to him. Knowing God in our midst does not evolve from group dynamics. We do not convict or transform or reform people. Groups are not one more self-help mode. Spiritual formation is the work of the Spirit. "If you want to prepare for involvement in spiritual community, acknowledge that no amount of knowledge and skill and effort will make it happen" (Crabb, 1999, p. 128). We, as human enablers, work with the Spirit to do whatever is necessary to prepare the way for his arrival. This is our ministry—creating conditions receptive to his working among us. These conditions do not cause the actual transformation in themselves but rather create an environment that helps put us in a place where God can move among us and shape us to reflect more fully his image.

Climate for Transformation

Expect It!

The leader who plans with transformation in mind will lead differently. The member who comes expecting to be changed by this group encounter will respond differently, to both information and interpersonal relationships. This openness to God's action in transforming attitudes, changing behavioral patterns, and moving us into deeper insight is in essence faith. Such belief in the power and person of a God who works in community to grow us up is essential to the Spirit's working God's will in our midst. Nazareth was left barren when it came to experiencing miracles that its native Son performed elsewhere. The inhabitants chose not to esteem him as more than a carpenter's son and thus their expectations were limited.

Regrettably, many groups become humdrum and lose vision as time sets in. People who have become old hands at group meetings fail to expect more than what has already been experienced. It takes intentionality to maintain the expectation that because God is at work here, every encounter, every happening is an opportunity for life change to occur. It is easier to settle for the status quo of our present situation. Groups where people are new to each other often see more formation and increased insight because of their openness to change.

Leaders who expect transformation lead with a different end in mind. Teachers who believe individuals and groups will be reshaped as a result of insights and processes will teach content in a more focused, life-related way. Members who come expecting to be changed experience significant growth. Perhaps this is why we so often grow through crisis events—we are forced to change and we open ourselves up to God to work newness in our lives. Expect transformation when the people of God gather around the Word of God with the Spirit of God present. Our expectations are never too high when these conditions are present.

Cultivate Safety

Developing a climate of security and belonging is essential to people opening themselves up to make changes. Threat, being unsure of how one is accepted, and feeling one can't be honest about who he or she really is, keep a person protective and promote a desire to maintain the status quo. Willingness to let go and to trust are conditions that grow out of knowing and feeling at home with others. Leaders should encourage members to share facts and feelings, to let the leaders get to know them. Those who are leading should communicate expectations and boundaries that provide a sense of security. They need to emphasize the group's areas of commonality and express value for differences. It's the leaders' responsibility to exhibit appropriate behavior themselves before calling others to do it. The group as a whole needs to affirm a desire to grow, to accept its present stage, and to acknowledge the power of the Spirit among it to transform individuals. It's important for leaders to express the value of each person as a unique expression of God and as someone in whom he is at work.

Foster Cohesion

Chances for retooling attitudes and revising concepts and habits are increased whenever a strong "we-feeling" is developed within a group. A sense of togetherness creates openness whereas individualized competition nurtures a closed attitude toward change. Studies show that a person is more likely to want to change if he or she has the support of and solidarity with those around him or her. A desire for change may begin with one, but that hunger must spread or the individual will simply be written off as a deviant from the group's norm.

Support and recovery groups are often significant in helping people develop new patterns of coping because members realize others accept them. Cohesion is built on identifying common connections, recognizing each needs the other, and developing shared memories, stories, and acts unique to the group. God built this into Israel in their shared events (Exodus), mutual celebrations, common history, and forebearers. Mutual growth builds connection. Crabb declares, "All substantial change depends on people experiencing a certain kind of relationship" (Crabb, 1999, p. 45). Spiritual community with its allegiance to the one Lord, one faith, one baptism promotes "we-ness" in relationship.

Actively Involve

After surveying small group Bible study, Wuthnow's landmark study observes,

> The key point that our research suggests . . . is that the group process counts, not simply the raw content of the lesson being studied. If spiritual development were only a matter of exposing people to a certain body of ideas, getting them to read the Bible on their own, or inviting them to listen to sermons, these activities might function just as effectively as small groups. But the reinforcement that comes from considering ideas as a group gives them added significance.
>
> Wuthnow, 1994, p. 280

A major element in transformation of ideas, of attitudes, of behavior patterns is the personal interactive involvement of the one being transformed. Planning in opportunities for talking about meanings and experiencing of truth, voicing fears, and sharing questions with one another prepares the ground for new formation to occur. As people process aloud, they become instruments of change in one another's lives. Active involvement frees a person to present and confront misconceptions as well as insights being prompted by the Spirit of Christ in individual members and in the group as a whole.

Perspective on Scripture

The place of and perspective on Scripture in a group is a determining factor in the formation of individuals in a group. This is more than simply the inclusion of Scripture or the study of Scripture. It is an attitude of commitment to the Word of God as being the primary source of reality for a believer. And that reality—if it is to be recognized as a reality, not just an alternative among others—is a reality that must be lived. Many base their responses on common sense or experience. Neither of these can be trusted to be true. Spiritual formation in a believer's life occurs when the Word of God is viewed as the only way of operating, the only way to live if fullness of life is desired. God does not say things just to sound pious. When he speaks, he utters essential truth for right living. The way of the Spirit is prepared by asking,

"How can we live out the meaning of this truth in the issue we discussed? If we were to operate on the basis of what God declares in this passage, how would we operate differently in this circumstance? In what way does this perspective of God's change our perspective on the situation?"

This preparation for formation by the Spirit feeds on the assumption that, of course, the Word of God is true. It is the authority to be obeyed. It is to be lived out in our present situation, and that living out will change us and our view of present reality. With this being our mind-set, the Spirit can call forth newness of person and perspective out of responsiveness to God's Word. Hence, the Word becomes a "Living Word" in our midst, and we become a people transformed by the truth.

Know People

A factor to be considered in this process of change is the person in the process. "You can't sell refrigerators to Eskimos" or "combs to bald men." In other words, you have to know the people you're working with. They're going through a process of change. This development of the person in sequential stages is called developmentalism. This theory says we never just teach content or just run a group. We always factor in who the people are in terms of characteristics and abilities, what they have experienced, and what they are currently experiencing. Knowing this can enable us to relate group content to current circumstances. Again, we realize we cannot, nor do we want to, manipulate or maneuver a person into change. That is the Spirit's work. He will use the content to prompt inwardly in the direction of God's will. But in our illustrations, our questions, and our process, we can present truth as it relates to particular issues pertinent to the group members. For example, in a Bible study focus on trusting in place of fearing, a group of elderly people would identify with the emphasis differently than a group of young adults. By taking this age level factor into consideration, we prepare the way for the Spirit by referring to pertinent life circumstances. Jesus did this in relating to a Samaritan woman by referring to her husband, but he called Nicodemus to face up to his need for rebirth. This sensitivity to individuals and their situations is an asset in preparation for formation.

In the same way, groups as a whole go through different phases of development and thus should be led differently, structured differently, and refocused to meet the kind of insights and experiences needed by members going through that transition. The Scripture is always relevant. But how we package it and draw relationships to life changes so that people are met with the truth at every point of life. Maturing developmentally can enhance growth in Christlikeness but does not automatically produce it. Each stage of life presents a unique opportunity to challenge people with the lordship of Christ over strengths and challenges of that stage.

Change Agent in History

What has been the impact of spiritual community on society in history? How have groups been transformational in our culture? A noted historian asserts,

> The strongest organizational unit in the world's history would appear to be that which we call a cell; for it is a remorseless self-multiplier; it is exceptionally difficult to destroy; it can preserve its intensity of local life while vast organizations quickly wither when they are weakened at the center; it can defy the power of governments; and it is the appropriate lever for prying open any status quo. Whether we take early Christianity or sixteenth-century Calvinism or modern communism, this seems the appointed way by which a mere handful of people may open up a new chapter in the history of civilization.
>
> Butterfield, 1979, p. 24

The small group format exists as far back as the creation of the family. And the group experience appears within every time period of human existence in varied expressions of human attempts at collaboration and community development.

Israel

A small community experience was part of God's plan. Ancient Israel's traditions were clearly expressed in family and tribal units with life and faith enriched and framed by these corporate boundaries. Days of remembering God, such as Passover and Sabbath, were celebrated with the family. Rites such as circumcising male children took place within these units. And the vital role of instructing the young in their faith and insuring that God was honored were intentionally positioned in the intimacy and accountability of the household unit. Israel's identity was reinforced and influenced aliens through these strong units of relatedness.

New Testament

Jesus perpetuates this practice of instructing and celebrating within the intimacy of a small group, now with those who have become family to him. In Acts the new covenant community continues gathering together in houses and upper rooms for praying, mutually sharing the faith, and expressing devotion to the same Lord and support for his cause. Robert Banks, a champion of the house church movement, suggests that the New Testament church existed primarily in people's homes (Acts 2:43; 16:40; 20:8; Rom. 16:5; 1 Cor. 16:19; Col. 4:15; Philem. 2). He further observes that Paul and other apostles primarily chose converted household units as nuclei for founding churches (Acts 11:14; 16:15, 25–34; 18:18) (Banks & Banks, 1998, p. 31). The small home group was central to the development of the church.

Second Century through the American Revolution

Groups often arose in reaction to the institutionalized practices of the church hierarchy. As far back as the second century small closely knit bands (Montanists) were formed, patterned after the model of the Jerusalem community for the purpose of encouraging participative contributions and supportive accountability (Banks & Banks, 1998, p. 50).

In the following centuries this was replaced by various monastic movements famous for their emphasis on communal living. One of these groups, Brethren of the Common Life, influenced Martin Luther. In the sixteenth century the fires of the Reformation were fanned in home gatherings. Across the German border persecuted Waldensians grouped in French homes. Across the Channel in England Lollards met for mutual encouragement through prayer and study of the Bible. Anabaptists committed themselves to one another in small group gatherings. This commitment included living out their faith in everyday life, exercising special care for one another, seeking as laity bonded together to influence the world around them by their love, unity, and practice of the faith. Group gatherings consisted of instructing in the Word and motivating the faithful living out of faith in society.

Succeeding centuries experienced the Pietist movement in Germany. This brand of Lutheranism spawned small spiritual gatherings for the expression of mutual support of believers in realms of Word and prayer and mission. Many of these movements shared common characteristics and priorities. Among these were the emphasis on the priesthood of the believer and the active involvement of the laity. In typical group fashion they exhibited an openness to active participation by all, stressed the disciplined study of the Scriptures, and required strong accountability of one another. They demanded an intentional practice of God's Word in everyday life, attention to caring for their own, passion to influence the world outside, and a response to the organized church's need for relevance.

Many of these small groups (Pietists, Quakers in England, and Moravians in Germany, among others) pursued renewal in the church through their actions. One outstanding result of these groups was the creation of a new high in the credibility of the layperson as priest serving both God and humankind. As such this small group influence was profound (Banks & Banks, 1998, pp. 52–58).

> When the first settlers came to America, they . . . modeled their interaction on the close-knit cells of religious dissenters from which they had come in England and Scotland. Subsequent waves of immigrants often came as small groups as well . . . and in many cases they settled in neighborhoods and in farming communities where they could share a common faith.
>
> Wuthnow, 1994, p. 41

Wesley

Outstanding in the history of small group influence is the name of John Wesley. His famous "heart strangely warmed" Aldersgate experience resulted from the ministry of a Moravian. For Wesley the small cell was central to the church. In *The Radical Wesley*, Howard Snyder declares, "The class meeting was the cornerstone of the whole edifice" (Snyder, 1980, pp. 53–54). These small groups promoted unity, quality control, and fellowship and became sites for progress reports, praying, admonishing, and enabling members to grow. Methodism brought this small group network across the ocean to the New World.

Nineteenth Century

While the Methodists operated through class meetings, Baptists brought unity to their constituents through midweek prayer meetings. As immigrants continued to flood into America new organizations, like the Young Men's Christian Association and the Salvation Army, discovered that small groups were effective in incorporating immigrants and in reaching new populations in the growing urban areas (Wuthnow, 1994).

Twentieth Century

Increasing size forced churches to redesign to continue effectiveness. The Sunday school became the major way to separate people into small units for greater benefit. Weekday groups for women (Women's Missionary Society), youth (Christian Endeavor), and various denominational specialized groups became popular to meet the increasing demands of diversity and to respond to the need for discussion after didactic instruction.

1940s–1960s

The scientific study of what occurred in groups was undertaken by Kurt Lewin, now labeled the father of "group dynamics." By creating a Research Center for Group Dynamics at Massachusetts Institute of Technology in the 1940s, he set the stage for research into this process that would provide significant insights and seek to establish theories and guidelines. In the years following the war, Americans moved toward a more privatized view of faith. The role of churches was seen as that of servicing individuals. Parachurch organizations such as InterVarsity, Campus Crusade, Navigators, Faith at Work, Yokefellows, and others enthusiastically engaged the small group methodology. In so doing they opened the door for the small group invasion of the institutional church.

The 1960s reflected primary emphasis in the realm of social issues. The small group movement responded to this concern and its call for changes in the person and in society. This decade saw the rise of many influential pioneers in small group ministry. They enthusiastically took up the challenges of facing realities present at this time in history. The movement was shaped by such gurus as Keith Miller, Bruce Larson of Faith at Work, Gordon Cosby, Elizabeth O'Connor who developed the model at Church of the Savior, Washington, D.C., and Samuel M. Shoemaker who recorded the Pittsburgh Experiment, an attempt by laity to integrate work and faith (Gorman in Clark et al., 1991). Outside the walls of the church such responses as T-groups (training groups in business), encounter groups, and retreat centers helped develop small groups into a movement of national proportions (Wuthnow, 1994).

1970s–1980s

In the decade of the 1970s the focus changed to healing, self-awareness, and self-expression. "Furthering the cause" was exchanged for an inner focus on "me." The 1980s reinforced this self-centered inner focus and groups experienced a decade of rapid growth. Groups moved to balance inclusion of Bible study, social action, and personal growth (Gorman in Clark, et al., 1991). Religious leaders viewed the movement as the magical formula that would revitalize dying congregations and stimulate growth in fledgling congregations. Other organizations turned to small groups as acceptable sanctuaries for group therapy, particularly highlighting self-help in recovery from addictions. Churches hosted Serendipity Conferences. The Church Growth Institute of Fuller Seminary and the American Institute of Church Growth identified small groups as a rich resource for increasing vitality and numbers in congregations. Out of Korea came awesome reports of the spectacular growth issuing out of Paul Yonggi Cho's implementation of the home church group. Stephen Ministries fostered emphasis on developing caring centers for Christians. Many would label this the golden age of groups in the church.

1990s

The small group momentum continued into the 1990s embracing Catholic dioceses, Jewish communities, Protestant parishes, Twelve-Step programs, and countless self-help, support, and recovery groups along with targeted congregational groupings such as antique car buffs, surfers, skateboarders, and the like. One reviewer announced, "From job-seekers groups, to weight-control groups, to support groups for the dying and the bereaved, the small-group movement shows signs of enormous and continuing vitality" (Wuthnow, 1994, p. 45). And there is no indication that this trend will diminish as we move into the next hundred years. The movement will continue in new forms as it adapts to the changing culture, proving an attractive essential for life in the twenty-first century.

Outside the United States

The small group endorsement is worldwide in scope. In addition to the above-mentioned Korean experience of spectacular growth, in South America the Catholic church incorporated the assets of this cell format in its base communities. Reflecting the pattern of liberation theology, these small groups burst forth among the laity to express concerns for the poor and to foster promotion of justice. They found an eloquent spokesperson in Leonardo Boff (*Ecclesiogenesis of the Church*).

In Russia and mainland China, Christians facing persecution and the impossibility of institutional church gatherings, formed clandestine, underground house groups that essentially kept the church alive during the dark days of communism and the cultural revolution. "Although estimates vary, there are probably more than fifty million believers in China today. The number attending official churches is at most only several million, which means that house churches are far and away the 'mainstream' form of church life in mainland China" (Banks & Banks, 1998, p. 61).

Reports indicate that cell groups and house churches are on the increase in India, Philippines, other parts of Asia, and Africa, where group communities are well integrated into the mainstream church. The influence of David Prior, Michael Green, and the Alpha course have kept alive small cell and house groups in England and Scotland. In Hungary one source reported six thousand groups in existence in 1987. Even in East Germany before the Wall came down, small Christian communities were keeping the faith (O'Halloran, 1996).

Summary

Small groups appear integral to the ministry of the church. The creation of intimate, participative, laity-run units allowing people to talk about their faith becomes a site for spiritual formation. Under the direction of the Spirit such cells can purify and revitalize the church, energize its mission, and transform adherents into active, knowledgeable participants. In the words of Butterfield, spiritual communities may "well become an appointed way by which a mere handful of people may open up a new chapter in the history of civilisation" (Butterfield, 1979, p. 24).

Firestarters

On a long sheet of paper, chart a "Journey of Transformation," examining the years in your life. Where did a person or persons play a major part in your formation? How did this occur? What else did the Spirit of God use to help you be formed in Christ?

Who are the people in whom you are deliberately investing your life at this time? What evidence of transformation in you or in them has been revealed?

Why do you think relationships play such a key part in the formation of a person's life?

PART III

GROUP
DEVELOPMENT

6

The Genesis of a Group

When is a group a group?
> Julie Gorman

Which of the following would you place under the label of group?

- A crowd of people gawking at an accident
- Contributors to an on-line chat room
- A police battalion
- Several fans in line discussing their hopes of getting a ticket to a crowded sports event
- A traffic school class

While each of these collections may be casually referred to as "a group," in the use of the word in this book, none of them qualifies as a group. Below are several definitions of a group. Compare the qualifications that are similar in each of the examples.

> A group consists of a small collection of people who interact with each other, usually face to face, over time in order to reach goals.
>
> Adler & Rodman, 1991, p. 224

A small group is a collection of individuals, from three to fifteen in number, who meet in face-to-face interaction over a period of time, generally with an assigned or assumed leader, who possess at least one common characteristic, and who meet with a purpose in mind.

L. Barker, Wahlers, Watson, & Kibbler, 1991, p. 9

A Christian small group is an intentional face-to-face encounter of no more than twelve people who meet on a regular basis with the purpose of growing in the knowledge and likeness of Jesus Christ.

Hestenes & Gorman, class syllabus

A group isn't a group without interaction. Students in a lecture or believers in a congregation can feel very much alone even though surrounded by other people if they are expected to passively listen. Simply occupying the same area at the same time does not turn people into groups. For face-to-face encounters, groups are limited in size, usually no more than twelve, with seven or eight as the optimum number. The common characteristic that unites people may be assigned, self-realized, or assumed, but it must always be there. It may range from having a common cause or goal to having gone through similar experiences. Groups tend to be intentional, not just spontaneous gatherings, and they must occur regularly. To be one, a group must meet at least once a month.

think about this:

- Think of some groups you've encountered. Which of them fulfilled these criteria for small groups? If you have experienced a "group" that never seemed to become a group, were any of the above factors missing?

The shared purpose that group members have usually determines the kind of group being formed. Notice how these broad categories suggest definite purposes: contact/friendship groups, evangelism groups, nurture/discipleship groups, study groups, support groups, recovery groups, equipping groups, prayer groups, mission/project groups, worship groups, committees. Some groups are categorized by the people targeted: singles groups, seniors groups, intergenerational groups, grief groups.

Every group is confronted with three necessary goals and a fourth that is distinctively Christian: accomplishment of purpose; caring for personal needs of individuals in the group; maintaining healthy relationships; and—overarching all three—becoming the people of God in process.

Group Needs

Achievement Goal

Groups need a reason for being. Purpose is a key element in the survival of a group. Without a purpose, groups flounder and eventually die. Every group needs a task growing out of that purpose for its existence. The task may range from completion of a project to the development of friendly relationships with others in the group. Tasks may be multiple in number such as developing a sense of togetherness while learning how to minister to a group of refugees who recently arrived in your city.

Personal Goals

Each member has results in mind (consciously or unconsciously) when joining a group. While not all of these results can be achieved, good groups are aware of what can happen in a group to help people balance their personal needs with those of the group. A person's individual goal may be in sync with the group purpose or, at times, in competition with it. For example, the need to be safe and secure might cause a member to hold back what he or she has to offer when the group climate seems risky. Because a person so strongly wants to belong, that individual might refuse to critique the group's actions with questions that could prevent problems later. An example of this would be a woman knowing that the presentation planned by the males in her group would come across as authoritative and controlling, but she refuses to interject her insight for fear she would be labeled as too sensitive.

All of us come to group encounters with histories, wounds, and sensitive areas where we doubt and fear. Each of us consciously or unconsciously operates out of needs for feeling valued and understood, for feeling loved and accepted, for feeling we can achieve something worthwhile. Until trust is built, people in groups can be expected to operate primarily on the basis of these individual motivators to feel whole and significant.

Unusual behavior or intense emotions expressed by individuals usually means they are working from some subconscious agenda that is inherent in who they are as individuals. For example, always having to be right may indicate that a person is unsure and needs to validate his or her identity by being in control. Initially a group goal is made up of a composite of personal or individual goals owned by members of the same group (L. Barker et al., 1991). That makes it imperative that every member place his or her desires for the group on the table so those expectations have a part in shaping the group goal.

think about this:

• What is an individual need of yours that you bring to a group you are currently in?

Healthy Relationships

Finally, besides task and individual needs, every group is concerned with the need to enhance the group climate and be built together as individuals. This need is called group maintenance. It involves strengthening the group through such behaviors as affirming and listening and caring or establishing safe boundaries and building cohesion among members. It may seem difficult to balance these two goals of task accomplishment and group maintenance. Often a project is pushed through by a leader or strong subgroup only to find that the group is left with anger, apathy, and little enthusiasm for the results. Committees are notorious for concentrating on business and covering the agenda while ignoring interpersonal relationships, misunderstandings, and members' self-esteem. On the other hand, some groups focus so strongly on positive interpersonal relationships that they neglect to achieve a goal that could introduce conflict and strong feelings within the group.

Group relationship and group efficiency appear to feed each other. Both are needed (Wheeless, Wheeless, & Markman, 1982). Wheeless and Markman (1982) found a positive correlation between group solidarity, satisfaction, quality of interaction, and goal attainment. Working together, members become aware of one another's competency and thus are drawn closer together, which in itself increases the possibility of their successful performance (L. Barker et al., 1991). When groups seem to have a hard time achieving their goals, examine the amount of time spent on the task compared to time building interpersonal relationships. Adjust the focus appropriately to spend more time on relating. This will be difficult to do because when a project gets bogged down, we tend to push harder, not pull off and build nurture and concern among people.

Groups constantly face the dilemma of sacrificing productivity for member relations or vice versa. Berkowitz (1954) and Thelen (1954) both found that groups had greater long-term efficiency if they spent more time initially in building interpersonal relationships (L. Barker et al., 1991). In getting to know each other and each other's agendas, people build foundations for problem-solving and goal-reaching.

Live as Community

As Christians we are not together to get tasks done or to see that everyone achieves self-determination or to produce a model group. Our focus is on giving pleasure to the One who called us together and on increasingly responding to him. The motivation for any achievement or relating is to experience him more completely. This conditions our responses to one another and can cause us to live above our natural inclinations. What makes for good group dynamics is the presence of the Spirit in attitudes and actions so that love triumphs over self-fulfillment. Spiritual formation takes precedence over using people and having one's own way. What drives this kind of group is a passion to honor God as God in our lives, a passion to trust, a passion to grow, and a passion to obey (Crabb, 1999). When these four drives are present, the aforementioned three goals will be realized though perhaps transformed from their originals. Tragically, many Christians group together to achieve one or more of the first three goals without prioritizing the critical nature of the fourth. Thus Christian groups can become as divisive and painfully self-centered (if not more so) than their non-Christian counterparts.

Personal Needs Affect Group Structures

Personality often serves as a factor in group emphasis as some people want to get the job done, being task-centered, while others gravitate toward cultivating warm interpersonal relationships. Interestingly Blanchard and Hershey recommend knowing and using various leadership styles to help balance these complementary foci. Paul the apostle would probably agree—each strength of a member, while different, reflects the wisdom of God in placing all in the body of Christ just as he wanted so that the body would reflect the fullness of Christ and thus be built up as each part supplies the strength it has for the good of the group (Eph. 4:16). Those strong in task achievement cannot say to the others, we have no need of you. And those who have the ability to discern and respond to personal needs cannot disparage the emphasis on cultivating group strengths that may go beyond the individual's need.

Personal needs of members also have an effect on how groups are structured. Luft observes such a preference:

> Individuals searching for safety or security are likely to feel better in a more authoritarian group, and their performance seems to improve. The person for whom self-esteem is important, however, seems to prefer groups in which the structure and leadership are more egalitarian.
>
> Luft, 1984, p. 17

Because these personal needs come with members into group structures, they have an effect on achievement of the task and satisfaction over group relations, both of which determine effectiveness of a group.

Safety

Every person feels a need to gain a measure of safety in a strange and uncomfortable situation. When people join a group there is a natural anxiety that comes from concern about how others perceive them and about their own perceptions of others in the group. "Anxiety, to one degree or another, is the prevailing and dominating emotion at the start of any group setting" (Napier & Gershenfeld, 1989, p. 7). There is also present a vacillation between belonging and withdrawing, a paradoxical tension that is born out of being an individual and a group member at the same time. This creates insecurity as members are torn between interacting and protecting. We feel the need to share "this is me," and then pull back wondering what others think about us. In reality, others are primarily preoccupied with their own needs and figuring out ways of coping with tensions they feel.

One way we gain a sense of security is by ordering, looking for ways of comparing, and finding similarities in the great amount of new data that confronts us when forming a group. By this means we keep from being overwhelmed. For example, we will begin to align ourselves with people in a group who fit our idea of what a good group member is like— those who are most like us and thus least threatening because they don't cause conflict with our own values and desires. We identify with these individuals and therefore feel safer in a tense situation. Later we may realize how inaccurate and incomplete our assessments were. But at this point such "ordering" gives us a sense of mooring and control in an uncharted territory. It becomes evident that needs constantly arise in the act of group formation. While group members may be talking objectively and calmly, in actuality they are actively working to bring a sense of well-being and harmony to an unsettling scene (Napier & Gershenfeld, 1989). This is bound to affect behavior and is one reason individuals may appear to be entirely different persons inside a group than when outside it.

A Systems Perspective

The previous multiple motivations suggest the importance of viewing group behavior in a systems perspective. Complex behaviors do not result from a single cause. Rather, an individual's behavior grows out of a blending of interdependent forces relating to one another and multiple causes joining together. For example, a member's personality combined with a certain group size and group leadership style when set in the midst of a group's interpersonal relationship conditions may cause a person to act in a way never before observed. A complex network of needs and esteem requirements may influence group participants to interact in unusual ways. Changing the leader may not eliminate negative reaction because that is only one factor in a system of causations.

Factors in the System

Other People

The very presence of other people has an impact on individuals that is not present when one works alone. The presence of others can provide a source of support and comfort when one faces an anxious situation. On the other hand, it may create defensiveness and protectiveness within us when we realize that others are watching. Knowing that others are there and will observe with resulting reward or condemnation influences our behavior in groups. The presence of others can provide guidelines about what is acceptable and what is unacceptable behavior as they model what is appropriate. The presence of others may inspire us to new heights of productivity or may distract us from our task achievement. Groups by their very social structure trigger reactions within us (L. Barker et al., 2001).

The presence of people, however, is not the only factor affecting how groups form. Natural environment plays a largely unconscious part. Three major factors are space, seating arrangement, and size.

Space

Space communicates silently. One has only to observe people crowded into an elevator or seated closely on public transportation to become aware of how people react when the relationship does not fit the distance dimensions. Anthropologist Edward Hall identified four distance zones in human interaction. Intimate distance moves from zero to eighteen inches while personal distance ranges from eighteen inches to four feet. Social distance varies from four to twelve feet. Public distance extends from twelve to twenty-five feet (E. Hall, 1959). Women have been observed to use shorter conversational distances than men (Heshka & Nelson, 1972; Willis, 1966). Children interact in shorter distances than adults (Meisels & Guardo, 1969). Cultures have varied rules about space. Too close proximity is more tolerable at our sides than when directly in front of us (Blumberg et al., 1983). Observe this variable at work in your day. What makes you feel uncomfortable? How do you find yourself automatically reacting?

Seating Arrangement

Seating has an effect on interaction and appears to be affected by a person's attitude toward leadership. People who are in or desire leadership positions gravitate toward the ends of rectangular seating arrangements. Members of a group generally viewed those sitting in these positions as leadership whether in actuality or as viable candidates (Blumberg, Hare, Kent, & Davies, 1983). Leadership is usually affected by the ability to have eye contact with each person in the group.

The task to be performed will often dictate where people naturally sit. Casual conversations select corner-to-corner or face-to-face arrangements. Competing individuals often sit opposite and often at a distance from opponents (Tubbs, 2001). The arrangement most advantageous to interaction is the circle. Motivation to speak is higher when one faces others and can see them clearly. Because of that factor more interaction takes place across a circle than side by side. One of the more difficult interaction positions is three on a couch. Being out of the circle or seated at a corner in a rectangle usually means the person in that position will remain outside the interaction. In a small room people feel comfortable sitting farther apart than in a large room, which will cause them to sit closer together. High background noise whether loud music or multiple conversations drives people to decrease the amount of distance between them. This principle explains the presence of loud music in bars and discos and how certain high-pressure sales situations occur amid music and multiple conversations in one large room (Blumberg et al., 1983).

These are a few factors to consider when structuring for interaction among people in groups. Such factors are usually in our awareness at the forming of a group but lapse into unconsciousness as time goes on. Nevertheless, seating factors play a part in the roles and interaction group members exhibit. It also affects where the leadership sits and the way that leadership comes across. A leader who sits along the side of a rectangular table silently expresses a desire for a more democratic style than the leader who leads from the more authoritative end of the rectangle position. Most people in a group feel uncomfortable if the leader is not seated in a leadership position. Try sitting in a corner position and watch the uncomfortableness of the group. The corner seat is usually a silent member. Likewise in a circle arrangement the leader set apart from the group creates a leader-oriented discussion pattern of interaction where most, if not all, conversation is directed to and from the leader. Seating of participants becomes the quiet controller of the interaction that takes place in the group.

Crowding has a physical and a psychological side. Generally speaking females tend to feel more comfortable in smaller rooms that promote intimate conversation among them while males prefer larger rooms. Moving people closer together for conversing or turning up the heat in a room both create the sense of crowding and cause people to respond negatively to one another (Napier & Gershenfeld, 1989).

Size

Size has been shown to be a factor affecting leadership, the participation and reaction of members, effectiveness of the group, satisfaction of members, and ability to reach group consensus (Wilson & Hanna, 1986). Size is best determined by the objective of the group. Those desiring to stimulate individual thinking and questioning require a small group while objectives that incorporate broad exposure with many points of view will be best achieved in a larger group (Brilhart & Galanes, 1989). Most researchers agree that for optimum discussion and involvement five to seven is an ideal number (Brilhart, Galanes, & Adams, 2001; Tubbs, 2001). The upper limit varies between twelve and twenty (Rothwell, 1992); from twelve to fifteen (Cathcart, Samovar, & Henman, 1996); and eleven, twelve, fourteen, or twenty-five (Brilhart & Galanes, 1995).

Time, task, amount of interaction, and member mix can influence the limit. An example of such a group would be an intergenerational group where the group is broken into subgroups of families. Brilhart,

Galanes, and Adams suggest the group should be as small as possible, but including all the diversity and expertise necessary to accomplish the task. On the downside, increasing size tends to produce lower satisfaction, less cohesiveness, increased aggression, competition, and withdrawal (Brilhart et al., 2001). This, of course, affects other dynamics of the group.

Larger groups provide anonymity for individuals who don't want high involvement. They also provide a broader pool to draw from in accomplishing group tasks with a greater variety of skills and abilities available along with greater knowledge and experience. On the other hand, member participation decreases with increasing size, the conversation centering on the talkative few who tend to speak to each other instead of to the whole group. The central person tends to do more and more of the speaking. "Speeches" made by participants usually increase in length. Some evidence suggests that the total amount of talking lessens as size grows. All of this contributes to lower satisfaction with a group (Brilhart et al., 2001).

Larger groups—of ten or more—require an inordinate amount of time to handle organizational procedures just to keep the group functioning. This means less time spent on the task (Tubbs, 2001). People who want to join a closed group will often plead, "It's just one more." But the number of potential relationships multiplies astronomically with each member added. In a four-person group the possible initiating interactions total twenty-eight while in an eight-person group the number jumps to 1,056 (Tubbs, 2001).

Relationships

"Each group member is under increasing pressure to maintain appropriate relationships with an increasing number of group members. There are more relationships to maintain and increasingly less time in which to do so" (Palazzolo, 1981, p. 167). Such pressures cause increased evidence of tension release while the actual showing of tension decreases dramatically, going underground. Suggestion making and information sharing grows while opinion seeking and opinion giving fades. With increase of size comes a more formal, mechanical style of offering information such as the typical round-robin method. Members seem less sensitive to exploring another's point of view and give evidence of trying to control others, pushing them to conclusions and reaching decisions regardless of whether all are in agreement. Because there is less "check-in," there is likely to be more resentment and less feeling of ownership. People are more likely to withdraw.

Subgroups

As groups grow larger, they tend to subdivide into smaller unit groups. It is possible to have several subgroups functioning, sometimes at cross-purposes, at the same time. The forming of these blocks can slow down progress and drain energy from the group. Their side conversations may annoy the others in the group. When subdividing, *even sized* groups tend to divide into equal parts that can increase conflict, disagreement, and a struggle for power while *odd sized* groups are more likely to reach decisions sooner aided by their unequal division (Palazzolo, 1981).

Participation

The larger a group becomes, the greater the amount of inequality of member participation. A few will participate heavily while others may not be involved at all. In any group over eight there is great likelihood of silent members who don't contribute at all. The talkative few usually address each other rather than the other members. Talkers are usually considered to have a lot of influence whether saying something significant or not.

think about this:

- From your experience how many people do you think will dominate the conversation when the group numbers twenty? How many would dominate a group of ten? When eight people comprise the group? In a group of five? A group of three?

When the group size is twenty, five or less will dominate. With eight or ten people, three. With five the number is likely two, and with three, probably no one (Napier & Gershenfeld, 1989). With increasing size comes less time for each member. This is complicated by the need to hear from every member so as to feel that all are involved and contributing. The larger the group, the more requirements are placed on the leader.

Leadership

The larger groups become, the more the leadership tends to take over and the more members in the group desire and accept that takeover of the important group functions (Wilson & Hanna, 1986). At the same time, the influence of a leader seems to be lessened as the size of the group grows. Paul Hare discovered that leaders tend to be more influential in smaller sized groups while John Hemphill found members from increasing sized groups require leaders to exercise more effective control (Hemphill, 1950).

Another major factor that sets the scene for a positive group experience is the presence of a shared agreement variously known as a covenant, contract, or group agreement.

Shared Agreement

The old saying, "What you don't know can't hurt you," proves untrue in life and in small groups. Hidden agendas undermine a group and keep it from functioning effectively. Some expectations are unconscious and remain so unless group members are encouraged to explore them. A "contract discussion" allows for that exploration.

A group's contract is basically a shared agreement of the purposes this group is set on accomplishing and the responsibilities required of each member if that purpose is to be achieved. Such a statement of expectations lets everyone know what he or she is getting into. Many prefer the term *covenant* because this word expresses our commitment to one another as those under God's love.

A group's covenant can be determined by the leaders and then shared in such a way that allows others to buy into that depiction of purpose and responsibility. For example,

> This group is for those who want to actively share in the study of Scripture together always culminating in the specific practical application of truth to their everyday lives. Members will study a chapter ahead of time and be present to contribute their ideas and personal implications to the group time. We will meet every week for twelve weeks with members contributing refreshments on a rotational basis.

In describing what is expected, the leaders realize that this group isn't for everyone but only for those who want these ingredients in this purpose. Before committing to such a group, each potential group member needs to be made aware of what that commitment means. Too many times people join a group thinking it will be one thing when there was no intention of going that direction. Or they get involved in a group that will ask from them something they are unwilling or unable to give.

Another method of covenanting is to ask interested persons what a group needs to be if it is to be fulfilling to them. Sometimes the reverse is helpful: What is something you don't want in this group?

As each shares hopes and plans, the group begins to take shape and people begin to determine whether or not that shape fits them. Talking about expectations and commitments at the beginning helps to prevent frustration later when the group doesn't fulfill the plans of the joiner. Most people investigate a car make and model prior to their purchase and check out loan commitments before signing up. Premarital counseling at its best seeks to enable couples to talk through their values and dreams before making commitments, to realistically talk about where they are headed and what each expects of the other. A small group covenant is similar to each of these practices.

Some groups even place their agreements in writing so there is no confusion and so the agreed-upon items can be referred to later as group-owned. When the group agrees to responsibilities ahead of time, the leader is not seen as foisting upon the group the leader's hidden plans. Almost anything can be discussed in a group covenant discussion, but it is better not to overburden members with too many details. Allow them, however, to make decisions wherever possible about what the group will do, how it will develop, and what priorities are in place. Some personalities can live with greater fuzziness than others. Some items you may want to include in your covenant discussion are

- what you hope to achieve—your purpose
- what you will do as a group—your task(s)
- what the leader can be expected to do
- what members are required to do
- time commitment
- place shared
- refreshments
- baby-sitting
- special requirements (abilities, events outside meeting times, age, sex, marital status)

Em Griffin (1982) suggests these commitments:

1. *Attendance:* I need everyone in the group in order to grow. One person's absence will affect the whole group. . . . For the time I am here I will concentrate on what I am feeling at the moment

and on my response to others in the group. . . . I will stay in the here and now.

2. *Affirmation:* There is nothing you have done or will do that will make me stop loving you. I may not agree with your actions, but I will love you unconditionally. It is more blessed to care than to cure. This is not a therapy group. I will avoid the tendency to fix people.

3. *Confidentiality:* What's said here stays here! A permissive atmosphere flourishes when others are trustworthy. I will never repeat what another has said unless given specific permission.

4. *Openness:* I will strive to reveal who I am—my hopes, hurts, backgrounds, joys, and struggles—as well as I am able.

5. *Honesty:* I will try to mirror back what I see others saying and doing. This way I will help you understand something you may want to change but were unaware of. You can help me in the same way. This may strain our relationship, but I will have confidence in your ability to hear the truth in love.

6. *Sensitivity:* I will try to put myself in your shoes and understand what it is like to be you. I will try to hear you, see you, and feel where you are, to draw you out of the pit of discouragement or withdrawal. But I recognize that you have the individual right to remain silent.

7. *Accountability:* I am responsible for my own growth. I won't blame others for my feelings. None of us is trapped into behaviors that are unchangeable. I am accountable to myself, others, and God to become what God has designed me to be in his loving creation. I will help you become what you can be.

8. *Prayer:* During the course of this group, I will pray for the other members and bask in the confidence that they are praying for me.

Joining together in committing oneself to these kinds of goals not only brings a sense of security and direction but also sets before the group the possibility of transformation. Groups will never reach their highest potential until people are willing to sublimate personal needs not in harmony with the group's objectives. Shared values that reinforce the group's purpose and shared commitment to responsibilities that will build the group's health are a powerful dual contribution to member satisfaction and growth. Spelling it out at the beginning is imperative for the survival and progress of a group.

Covenants, because they are ventures, require the support of all parties. They ensure that one party doesn't have greater responsibility than the other so the group doesn't become the leader's group with the leader responsible for enforcing, doing the caring, and getting the task done.

It helps to develop a member-owned group with leader and members aware of their mutual responsibilities.

Covenants may be discussed and revised at any time. In fact, it's important to keep current on commitments. If people renege on what was agreed upon, the group can rethink its decisions. For example, "It seems to be hard for all of us to be here at the time we decided to begin our group. What would you like to do: adjust the time, recommit ourselves to what we decided, discuss issues that prevent our being present on time, or what?" Such open, responsible discussion helps to eliminate frustration, anger, and gunnysacking that comes out later over some other issue. It prevents blame and judgmentalism and promotes sensitivity and harmony.

Beginnings are *prime*. They establish foundations for what is to come. Being aware of and consciously designing with the above issues in mind can mean the difference between a healthy, fulfilling group and a frustrating experience of involvement with others in a group setting.

In a Different Voice

Gender can affect placement. Sommer discovered that North American women are inclined to sit closer to others (regardless whether male or female) than men do. Males prefer greater personal space when seated next to other men (Sommer, 1959). Men generally feel more comfortable in a larger room while women prefer a more intimate space. Some have connected this factor with women's direct eye contact issuing in greater awareness of nonverbals displayed in the group. Crowded conditions therefore cause men to respond less (Pearson, Turner, & Todd-Mancillas, 1985, p. 172). Men will disclose more about themselves in a dyad than in a small group made up of three or more. Females share more in a small group than in a dyad (Pearson et al., 1985).

Through Others' Eyes

Personal space for the dominant culture in the United States is about eighteen inches. To Anglo Americans a fundamental right is to be left alone if they so choose. Approaching or touching another is off-limits. Other cultures such as Middle Eastern find men moving much closer to other men as they are talking (Samovar, Porter, & Stefani, 1998). A forty-page booklet on gestures and body language among the Arabs was distributed to military forces sent to Saudi Arabia during Operation Desert Storm and included the following. Do not cross the legs so that the sole of the shoe is pointed at someone, "don't be upset if Arabs stand very close, even touch you, when conversing . . . [and] the 'O.K.' gesture (thumb and forefinger forming a circle) may be interpreted there as giving a curse" (Axtell, 1991, pp. 12–13).

A Latin American is comfortable with culturally conditioned closeness and ease in touching another. African Americans also exhibit a more demonstrative and expressive way of sharing themselves and their thoughts. They tend to maintain closer distance to Caucasians than Caucasians do to them (Booth-Butterfield & Jordan, 1989). Chinese prefer sitting side by side rather than directly across from each other (Dodd, 1997). Imagine a group in initial stages of formation composed of an Arab, several Anglos, two Latin Americans, and two African Americans.

think about this:

●   How would you lead such a group through its get acquainted sessions? Place yourself in each member's shoes and become aware of misunderstandings that might take root that first session.

Another area in which misunderstandings can occur is in the viewing of time. For some it is to be harnessed and used by scheduling, and by beginning and ending at definite points. For others, time is to be expended according to the needs of the moment and the needs of the person take precedence over the domination of a set time frame. Jim and Carol Plueddemann have summarized this aspect of time according to perspectives of high- and low-context groups. In high-context small groups many things can happen at the same time. It may be difficult to begin and end on time, or isolate one activity at a time. In low-context small groups the group will begin and end on time. Events can be scheduled in an orderly sequence. People will want to stick to the passage (Plueddemann & Plueddemann, 1990).

Time may also be focused on the past, the present, or the future in certain cultures. Past-orientation cultures value tradition and roots. Present cultures see only the "now" as important and real while future-oriented cultures usually value change highly and see the future as enabling that. Bible history and savoring the stories of Israel and our Judeo-Christian heritage will be favored by groups with a bent for the past, while the didactic passages that lead to present or future active involvement in living out the teachings of Christ in a changing world will appeal to the future-orientation group.

Firestarters

"Off to a Rocky Start"—The Birth of a Group?

Ralph: (fearless leader) Okay, people, let's get started.

I realize it's kinda crowded in here. It's hard to fit twenty people in. Can you squeeze a fourth person on the couch there? That's good.

I can't see you folks in the dining room. Don't want you to get into trouble out there. Here, put your chairs in front of those four people. You'll be on the front row. Can you folks see around them?

Okay, everybody got a place? Are we ready for liftoff?

To get acquainted I want us to do something fun tonight. Last summer my family went rockhounding in Colorado, and we brought back some gems. All you have to do is look out in my backyard and you will know that we found rocks. When I was picking up those stones I got to thinking that people are a lot like rocks. Sometimes you don't even notice them till the sun comes out. You have to turn some over to see their beauty. Sometimes you walk right over them. Most rocks are hard. You notice that when you have to sleep on them. Remember Jesus said we ought to build our house on a hard rock so when the rains come it won't collapse.

Let's start out by sharing "what kind of rock are you like?" Or maybe you're not a rock lover—"how do you feel about rocks?" Or if none of that grabs you, then talk about a time when things got rocky for you. Now that ought to give something for everybody. Okay?

Oh, and I only have twenty minutes down for this 'cause we need to get to the important stuff like Bible study. Now you math wizards have already figured it out—that means about one minute apiece. Okay. Who's first? Let's get acquainted.

. . . . Oh, come on—our twenty minutes are going by. Tom, you start us out.

Tom: Uh, can you tell me the questions again?

(Ralph repeats questions)

Tom: Well, to tell you the truth, I hadn't thought much about rocks till you mentioned it. But I guess they are pretty important. I just had a rocky experience last week. I was driving down the 605 freeway— you know, out there by the quarry. And suddenly a rock bounced off a truck and hit my car windshield smack in front of the driver. It chipped a little piece right out. Now I have to take it in and replace the windshield 'cause I know it will spread. And this is the second time in two years. So I guess I don't feel real good when I think of rocks.

Phil: You can get those people to come to your house and fill in the chip with something. It keeps it from spreading and saves the cost of replacing the windshield. I talked to a guy in my office who had it done.

Ralph: Alright—we need to keep it moving. And try to keep it to one minute. Who's next?

Carolyn: I had that happen to me too—three times! I wanted to report the truck to the Highway Patrol. I think they should be required to have covers put on those stone trucks. (Catches sight of Ralph's face) Oh, have I used up my minute? . . .

Ralph: That was good, Carolyn. Marsha, you're beside Carolyn. Why don't you go next.

Marsha: Can I just pass and you can come back to me at the end?

Ralph: Are you sure you can't think of anything? Maybe a rocky time in your life?

Marsha: (squirms) I suppose most of you know about my divorce. That was one of the toughest times for me. . . .

Ralph: Good! See, you did have something to share. And I think you helped us pick up a few seconds. Heh, heh. Let's go on around the circle.

Beth: I remember picking up rocks when I was a kid. Dad hated it. We always carried them home in the trunk. And he always complained about the mess it made. Lots of times he made me wash them off before he would put them in the trunk. I guess my mom eventually threw them out 'cause I can't remember what happened to them. I always had a suspicion that my brother was leaving them alongside the road whenever we would stop. But I never did catch him at it.

Ralph: Next?

Tina: When I hear the word "rock" I always think of "The Lord is my Rock and my Salvation." I love it when the choir sings that song about him being that. It gives me such a safe feeling . . .

Brent: I thought that song was about him being *light* and salvation.

Tina: Well, one of their songs is about him being a rock. I may not quote it right, but it always says something to my soul. Sometimes it's hard to remember the words exactly. I know it talks about God as a rock. And then there's "A Mighty Fortress Is Our God"—that's one of my favorites too.

Ralph: Okay, Brent, let's make you next.

Brent: Well, one of my all-time favorite movies is *Rocky!* Heh, heh. I think I like *Rocky II* better than *Rocky I*, though. How's that answer, Mr. Rock man?

Ralph: I think that's all we have time for tonight. We'll get you others next time because I do want to get to the Bible study since I know you came for that. I guess we got off to a rocky start. Joke. Joke. Well, anyway, did you all bring Bibles?

Phil: What will we be studying in this group?

Ralph: I haven't decided yet. I'll tell you next time. This time I want to talk about doubt. Everybody struggles with doubt. And the Bible passage we are going to study talks about doubt and rocks! You all know it—David and Goliath. Course David didn't doubt, but the army did. Find 1 Samuel 17. Let's read around—verses 1 to 50. We may have to skip some verses because of time. Sara, you start . . . You don't have the Old Testament? Well, just listen then. Mike—you have the Old Testament? Okay. You start.

(Group reads 1–50)

Ralph: Well, it took us so long to read that we can't spend too much time talking about it. You all know it anyway? Who was Goliath? . . . How tall was he? . . . And who were the Philistines? . . . Who were David's brothers? How did they react? . . . And what did David do first? . . . What did Saul do? . . . We're a lot like that army. We doubt God and then can't kill those giants in our lives. We don't even pick up the rocks. Now I want all of you to complete this statement: "An area where I struggle with feelings of doubt is . . ." Think about it. We all doubt God sometime. Where do you do it? Let's have those people who didn't share give us their answers. Who wants to be first?

(Silence)

Ralph: Carrie Sue?

Carrie Sue: I don't like to talk in front of groups. So just pretend I'm not here.

Ralph: We'll get you next time, Carrie Sue. Richard?

Richard: I don't know about now. I remember questioning if God was real when I was a teenager. I was having a hard time finding myself and I guess I kinda took it out on God. I didn't want to pray or go to church. I'm not even sure that I was a Christian at that time. Do you have to be a Christian to doubt God? or do non-Christians doubt him too?

Ralph: Well, we're just talking about Christians here and I'm afraid we have to quit now. Time sure flew. We've got the beginnings of a good group here. Next time I'll have some surprises for you. So see you all next week.

Wanna bet?

Warming Up

1. What feelings were generated in you as you vicariously partici-
   pated in this group?
2. What did you learn about the leader? about others? about the
   group sessions? How did you pick this up?
3. Put yourself into the shoes of the members as they arrive at this
   first group session. What are their feelings as they come? What
   are the questions they arrive with? What would be most important to you as an arriving newcomer?
4. From a member's vantage point what would be the most important first acts of the leader?
5. What do members need to know? How can they learn that?
6. What do members need to do? How can they experience that?
7. What did you learn about questions?
8. What three or four outcomes are the most important ones for
   the first time a group gets together? What three or four major
   things need to be accomplished? What do you want members
   to walk away knowing and saying and feeling?
9. What structures would help to accomplish those three or four
   things? What could the leader do to help accomplish those
   things?
10. What feelings about your own experience did this scene raise?
11. Why is it difficult to break old habits of group leadership and
    response?
12. What is a habit pattern of which you are conscious?
13. What is one specific response you could choose to make in the
    initial get-togethers of your group?
14. What will you commit to doing as a result of having been
    exposed to this "Firestarter"? What will "cue" you to remember
    to do this?

7

GETTING TO KNOW YOU
Self-Disclosure

In order to see I have to be willing to be seen. If a man takes off his sunglasses I can hear him better.

Hugh Prather

While he was still a long way off, his father saw him and was filled with compassion for him . . . he ran to his son, threw his arms around him and kissed him . . . the father said to his servants, 'Quick! Bring out the best robe and put it on him; . . . Bring the fattened calf and kill it. . . .' So they began to celebrate.

Luke 15:20–24

No parable is more moving than this reunion between father and son. It mirrors the Old Testament story of Joseph and his brothers. It speaks of embrace as the beginning of renewed relationship. It is expression of acceptance and trust. The embrace is the precursor to lavish giving. It is the threshold for letting people into our hearts and homes. It is the symbol of reconciliation and the enjoyment of community.

Miroslav Volf selects this metaphor of embrace to express a Christian's personal and communal identity in the interplay between self and others. To those whose cultures would see this choice as too intimate, he suggests a wide range of embraces—interlocking fingers, palm meeting palm, arm over shoulder. Explaining his choice he notes four elements in the transaction of embrace: "opening the arms, waiting, closing the arms, and opening them again. For embrace to happen, all four must be there and they must follow one another on an unbroken timeline." All are necessary as four steps essential to the embrace. Notice how they describe the essentials in community:

1. The open arms speak desire to allow the other to be a part of self and a desire to have self become a part of another. "Open arms are a sign that I have created space in myself for the other to come in and that I have made a movement out of myself so as to enter the space created by the other." There is an opening made in the boundary of the self that allows the other to come in.
2. The waiting arms demonstrate respect for the other, a refusal to demand the other respond. "Waiting is a sign that, although embrace may have a one-sidedness in its origin, . . . it can never reach its goal without reciprocity." I respect you as a separate individual with your own uniqueness. Therefore, I invite, not compel.
3. Closing the arms completes this reciprocity as each person both holds and is held by the other. Each knows the presence of the other, each moves into the space of the other. Each is fully individual but enhanced and transformed by the gift of the other.
4. Opening the arms allows the other to retain its own separate identity, now enriched by the marks that the other has imprinted on it in the embrace.

Volf, 1996, pp. 141–45

As God embraces us, so he longs for us to embrace him and each other. His desire is that we relate to one another in open self-disclosure and trust. It reflects the way he has designed us to desire and contribute to each other as community. Jesus called his disciples to embrace the needs of each other, washing each other's feet. Such posturing seems risky from a human standpoint. To trust another is not natural. On this note, Crabb writes, "All of us enter life with a severe handicap: We trust no one, and our deepest inclination is to seize from life what we need while protecting ourselves from its disappointments and threats. That strikes me as a rather substantial handicap if we are designed to be in true community" (Crabb, 1999, p. 50). This means that the presence of mistrust, masquerade, and cover-up will undermine the formation of spiritual community. They must be faced for what they are—an expression of our sinful state. Crabb goes on to picture the difference this makes:

> When Jean Vanier [founder of L'Arche communities for the mentally challenged] states that community is the place where ego dies, I understand him to mean that our determination to fully trust no one must die and an eager willingness to receive what is best from others and to give what is best from within ourselves must take its place. That only happens when people feel loved, safe enough to face their dependency, trusting enough to enjoy what someone else gives, and courageous enough to offer who they truly are to another. It is a risk.
>
> Crabb, 1999, p. 47

Whenever God wanted to move in a significant way in the life of his people, he built trust. Trust grows out of knowing. When God called his people to trust him or one of his own, he disclosed himself. In response to Moses' stuttering refusal, he proclaimed himself the "One who made your mouth." The exodus caravan observed the plagues and desert signs that shouted, "I am the Lord!" They could see the cloud by day and the fire by night that let them know he was their ever-present protector. Self-disclosure is important to trust. The willingness to reveal who we are grows out of knowing the embrace of Christ in our own broken lives. The prodigal became the best candidate for becoming an embracing father.

To Disclose or Not to Disclose

Smith and Berg in their excellent work *Paradoxes of Group Life* pinpoint the contradictory issues from a human standpoint. Before disclosing who we are, we often feel the need to know another so we can disclose in a climate of safety. But how can we know about others unless someone is willing to reveal himself first (Smith & Berg, 1987)? And so we proceed cautiously, offering each item of personal information as a test to determine the safety of revealing ourselves further. As each bit of information is safely received, more is revealed. And so it often happens in a newly begun group that the self-disclosure becomes greater with each person's sharing so that those who took the plunge at first may end up feeling that they didn't share deeply enough.

Of course, to be acceptable, we only show our good side with great reserve. This results in politeness and an air of unreality or boredom with stilted and often open spaces between conversations. This game of showing only the "acceptable me" usually results in ambivalent feelings—positive feelings over being accepted and having navigated successfully through the cultural mores of the group—but also a disturbing realization that the *me* that has been accepted is a sham. Because I know there are parts of me that others would find difficult to accept, I find unacceptable the acceptance I have gained. As John Powell writes, "I am afraid to tell you who I really am, for if I tell you who I really am you may not accept me and that is the only me I have" (Powell, 1969, p. 12). The dilemma we face is not only in what do we share with others about who we are but also in the fact that we will never know if others will accept us as we are until we attempt to disclose the real us (Smith & Berg, 1987).

In the formation of a group no one overtly refers to this stress of paradoxical needs, but it is there. People will seek to relieve some of the tension with humorous comments such as "Well, I suppose I should tell you the good things so you'll want me in this group." Or to balance the guilt we feel about such a biased picture, "Now don't ask my wife (husband) about me because she'll probably tell you the opposite." Or, "Of course I do have one or two faults, but you'll find that out soon enough."

Leader or group assurance that I will be accepted is never enough—I can only find such acceptance as I trust the One I have come to know as always trustworthy. Knowing I am embraced by God in Christ frees me to be an "embracer" in relating to others. Knowing the One who is Truth sets me free to open myself to another and to be open to his longing to be loved as he is.

> The passion to protect ourselves, to keep our wounds out of sight where no one can make them worse, is the strongest passion in our hearts. And it will remain so until we experience a certain kind of relationship, until we meet the crucified and resurrected Christ, and experience a person like Christ, someone broken yet beautiful.
>
> Crabb, 1999, p. 35

Cultural and gender differences affect disclosure. And that's another reason "kingdom perspective" must transcend cultural patterns if spiritual community is to take place. We share what God has given us (giftedness, experience, insight) not because it is culturally acceptable but because it is the way of love (1 Cor. 13). And the way of love causes us to be sensitive to the other who may be conditioned to respond differently. Expressing feelings, caring for people becomes an act of love when it is done in a way that others can receive and be built up by it. This is the way of Christ in the body. We may choose to restrain ourselves from blurting out frank comments, which is our natural way or cultural upbringing, and adapt our response to what can be heard by others.

To Trust or Not to Trust

"To know" may lead to trust, but this area is also marked by paradoxical feelings. Groups depend on the development of trust for their being, but before we can trust we want to know how others will respond to us. To discover their trust we must be willing to expose and trust. Cultivating such a climate when others are fearful of trust is a challenge to an inexperienced group leader.

In beginning groups it is hard to get an honest reading on the group because no one wants to risk being branded negatively. People often hide their true feelings and seek to blend into a "we all feel the same way about everything" climate, a pseudocommunity. They may exhibit a politeness and patience they don't feel because they don't feel safe voicing their actual feelings. Feedback (positive and negative) must be presented if a person is to experience a climate of trust, because reality tells us that no one is received favorably all the time. Yet we fear the negative because it may imply rejection. Trust says it is safe to share both negatively and positively, and the person is accepted with the realization that both negative and positive traits comprise that individual (Smith & Berg, 1987).

Again the hunger for spiritual community, brought about by focusing on the central relationship with Jesus, can remarkably change attitude toward trust.

> Everything in spiritual community is reversed from the world's order. It is our weakness, not our competence, that moves others; our sorrows, not our blessings, that break down the barriers of fear and shame that keep us apart; our admitted failures, not our paraded successes, that bind us together in hope. A spiritual community . . . is full of broken people who turn their chairs toward each other because they know they cannot make it alone.
>
> Crabb, 1999, p. 32

To Risk or Not to Risk

Another aspect of paradox is that of intimacy. We feel freer to share risky thoughts and feelings once we have discovered a commonality with others. This discovery promotes intimacy. But the only way we can find the acceptance of commonality is to risk sharing what we truly think and feel, and then discover that others connect with us. We accept ourselves as we are accepted by others, but we can accept others only as we discover that we ourselves are accepted. John writes, "We love because he first loved us" (1 John 4:19). "That's what I was thinking" is an affirmation of our disclosure by another. But to receive that affirmation of acceptance we must accept our own value enough to venture forth with a statement of risk. That comes from knowing that we are securely sons and daughters of the Almighty One. Confidence that gives us the courage to risk (vulnerability, future, even our lives) always grows out of knowing God and resting in the assurance that God knows us and loves us.

Often in a group forming trust, you will hear qualifying statements prefacing remarks. These qualifiers include: "I may be off base, but I think . . ." "I may not totally understand the issue but it seems to me . . ." "I'm probably biased, but I. . . ." Such hesitations are not so much indicative of humility or tactful understanding as they are of self-doubt and fear of rejection. Later in the saga of the group these conditional statements will disappear as people realize they are accepted and can state things as they see and experience them without fear of rejection.

All of this underscores the absolute necessity of building a base of connectedness to the God whom we are increasingly coming to know and trust and to each person who is an expression of his presence. The absence of this may help to explain why committees take so long and often fail to become one. We do not allow for the time needed to connect with one another and for the God-focused time that positions us to receive each other.

In developing a sense of intimacy and trust through self-disclosure, there are numerous factors that will impact what a leader does. One of these is how members feel about the level of risk involved.

Why is it some things seem of higher risk than others? Each person has his or her own personal ranking. Read the list below and indicate how appropriate you feel each item is for disclosure. Use the following scale:

L = low risk, appropriate to disclose this item to almost anyone
M = moderate risk, appropriate for persons in established friendships or fairly well known
H = high risk, disclosed to only a few most intimate friends
X = disclose to no one

____1. Style of music you prefer or dislike
____2. Things you feel angry about
____3. Your personal political views
____4. What you and your spouse (closest friend) fight about
____5. Your personal view of God
____6. The nature of your present relationship with God
____7. Area where you question God's ways or Word
____8. Your educational background and feelings about it

____9. Weaknesses of yours that disturb you
___10. Personal achievements and characteristics that bring you pride
___11. Details of your secret ambition
___12. An area of self-doubt
___13. Unfulfilled dreams and desires of your life
___14. What you do to relax
___15. Parts of your body you are most pleased with
___16. Features in your looks you would most like to change
___17. Parts of your personality you would like to change
___18. A person you resent highly and why
___19. What you enjoy most about the opposite sex
___20. What you would most like to cover up if your life were revealed

If you qualified any response, why did you choose the qualifier you used? In addition to the personal assignments of risk we make to certain topics, there are generally agreed-upon items which project more risk than others.

Risk Factor: Time

Time is a variable when it comes to disclosing. Typically the past is the safest time frame to disclose. Our histories contain events that seem less risky to share because there is nothing we can do about them. Sharing of future plans, however, contains more risk because we lock ourselves into having to follow through on what we said we will do. The greatest risk of all is contained in disclosure of present acts because they are open to evaluation, to affecting relationships, and to being changed by others right now. Note how the risk factor goes up in the following: "I tried to impress people in high school by covering up my feelings and coming across as confident" *(past)*. "I'm going to set up a neighborhood barbecue to introduce my neighbors to the gospel" *(future)*. "I'm trying to impress you right now with a recital of my abilities because I know you are impressed with confident, capable people" *(present)*. The time frame of the disclosure affects the risk.

Risk Factor: Feelings

In general, disclosing feelings is more risky than sharing facts. "Most people list speaking to a group as more stress producing than any other activity" *(fact)*. "I feel very nervous and fearful right now in telling you how I feel because I am afraid you won't think I'm a good Christian" *(feelings plus fact)*. Feelings are seen to be more personally owned than facts. Feelings often reveal the real us while facts are nonjudgmental. For example: "I came from a single parent home *(fact),* and I hated it for what I felt I missed" *(feeling).*

Risk Factor: Evaluation

Being asked to disclose an evaluation of yourself or others takes on a higher risk than nonevaluative statements. "Let's share with Bill how he could be a better leader," or "In groups of threes, discuss your evaluation of our group." Another high-risk factor in the previous statements is disclosure given about someone present as opposed to giving information about someone not present.

Risk Factor: Group Size

The larger the group, the safer must be the topic chosen. What the person is asked to share can be balanced by the audience addressed. *High-threat content* ("Share how you were hurt by someone you cared about") can be offset by *low-threat structure* (one to one), or a *high-threat structure* (in front of the whole group) can be tempered by *low-threat content* ("Where do you enjoy going on vacation?"). When several of the above factors of risk are mixed so some are safe and some are threatening to disclose, the participant has to weigh the pluses and minuses and decide on the level of risk. For example, a secure person who is new to the group is asked to share with the whole group what gifts and abilities he or she brings to the group from past experience.

Johari Window

The Johari Window is a model that provokes self-disclosure awareness in interpersonal relationships. It's named for its two creators, Joseph Luft and Harrington V. Ingham, a combination of *Joe* and *Harry.* The model consists of four quadrants called *Open, Blind, Hidden,* and *Unknown.*

The *Open* area, Quadrant 1, consists of behaviors, feelings, and motivations that are known to you and known to others. This area includes common knowledge of which both you and others are aware.

Quadrant 2, the *Blind* area, includes behaviors, feelings, and motivations that others know about you but of which you are unaware. We commonly refer to such lack of self-awareness on the part of a person as a "blind spot." What may be very evident to those around us is closed to us. Feedback may help us move this information into Quadrant 1.

There will doubtless always be a blind area that we reveal to others but are not aware of ourselves.

The *Hidden/Secret*, Quadrant 3, symbolizes the behaviors, feelings, and motivations that are known to you but that are hidden from others. Each individual's responses are colored by an awareness of thoughts, motives, agendas, and experiences known to the sender but unknown to others in the relationship. Relationship-building consists of disclosing the hidden area and bringing it into the *Open* quadrant. Such action usually results in a reciprocal action being taken by others, thus developing a basis for trust and growth in relationship.

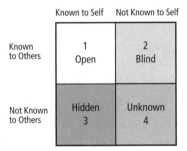

Quadrant 4 houses the behaviors, feelings, and motivations that are known neither to self nor to others. These four quadrants represent the whole person in relationship to other people. The size of the quadrants increases and decreases accordingly as the relationship changes. For instance, as disclosure takes place, the *Hidden* quadrant decreases while the *Open* quadrant increases. As Quadrant 2 becomes known to an individual because of feedback from others, the *Open* quadrant grows and the *Blind* quadrant decreases. Each encounter with others moves quadrant lines within the window, but the window continues to contain all four quadrants. The following diagram illustrates the shifting of boundaries as a relationship is developed.

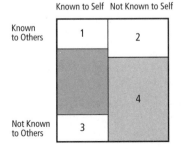

Note that a change in one of the quadrants will affect the other quadrants. The larger the first quadrant, the better the communication. When Quadrant 1 is small, threat is high and communication is usually poor. As trust develops among members, awareness of *Hidden, Open,* and *Blind* facets of the relationship increases along with a desire to move into the *Open* quadrant items from *Hidden* and *Blind* quadrants (Luft, 1984).

Beebe and Masterson in their third edition of *Communicating in Small Groups* present a helpful exercise that illustrates the Johari awarenesses.

- Form groups of three to five known people.
- Check five or six adjectives from the list below that best describe your personality as you see it.
- Select three or four adjectives that describe the personality of each person in your group and write them on separate sheets of paper. Distribute these lists to the appropriate group members.
- Fill in square number one ("known to self and known to others") with adjectives from the list that both you and at least one other member of your group have selected to describe your personality.
- Fill in square number two ("not known to self but known to others") with those adjectives others in your group used to describe you but you did not use to describe yourself.
- Fill in square number three ("known to self but not to others") with adjectives you have used to describe your self but no one else used to describe you.

able	dependable	intelligent	patient	sensible
accepting	dignified	introverted	powerful	sentimental
adaptable	energetic	kind	proud	shy
bold	extroverted	knowledgeable	quiet	silly
brave	friendly	logical	reflective	spontaneous
calm	giving	loving	relaxed	sympathetic
caring	happy	mature	religious	tense
cheerful	helpful	modest	responsive	trustworthy
clever	idealistic	nervous	searching	warm
complex	independent	observant	self-assertive	wise
confident	ingenious	organized	self-conscious	witty

Feedback is vital to any formation. Verbal and nonverbal responses to people and/or the messages they are sending helps the originator know what and how he or she has been received. A nodding head, wrinkled brow, or "I could hear better if you let me ask questions"—all convey meaning and can help the sender grow in ability and sensitivity. Asking for feedback, "I need to know what you heard me say," or "How could I have been more clear?" brings not only understanding but builds relationship and trust.

Sharing Questions

Besides factors already mentioned, seating so as to be able to read nonverbal responses in others is a must for enabling sharing. An important means of cultivating knowing and trusting one another is to create opportunities for group members to disclose and give feedback. Begin a group with a question designed to help people reveal safe information and find those who are like and unlike them. Sharing questions should be used for at least ten weeks in a beginning group and reintroduced whenever members sense a distancing from one another or seem to remain at a shallow level of interaction. Simply being together in a group does not guarantee that members will be building personal relationships. Sharing questions and relational games can free people to bond.

Developing appropriate sharing questions requires a knowledge of your group and an awareness of group principles. In light of the risk factors shared above, determine where your group is in its life cycle. If just beginning, center your questions on history giving, the safe past. When you assess that trust has been growing, you may move into the future and present tense. Even further trust is required for a question of affirmation or one that requires personal accountability. "How have you seen yourself or another grow in the time we've been together?" In the course of a group's life, people appear ready and desirous of moving into these areas of greater openness and commitment.

Questions asking for factual information are low threat as long as they do not involve expertise. "What was your placement in the family? Firstborn? Baby? Only?" Good sharing questions usually evoke some kind of emotional response. Combine the informational question with a request for personal self-disclosure and a feeling response. "What was your placement in the family, and what did you like about it?"

Keep questions simple so they don't require explanations and can be answered in a brief amount of time. There is a major difference between asking, "What kinds of things would you like to change about your job?" and "What one aspect of your work last week made it enjoyable?"

Beware of asking questions that could be very psychologically revealing or painful. This could include asking people to confess sins or to admit negative things about themselves before trust is built. Groups that have been together for a long time may be open to this kind of trust, but not beginning groups. It can be helpful to identify the primary feeling that your question will likely arouse. Feelings of regret over the past where nothing can be done, or anger and depression over unfair treatment can color what goes on in the group for the rest of its life together.

Good questions reveal something about the individual that is helpful in understanding and caring for him or her. Don't take up time sharing trivialities that give little insight into the person, such as "What is your favorite fruit?"

Avoid superlatives like the *best,* the *most,* and the *worst* because they force people into evaluation and hairsplitting. "What was the best birthday present you ever received?" *Best* can be interpreted many ways: Best for that age? Best in terms of desire? Best in terms of size or expense? Also people fear inadequacy in remembering the top selection and will change the question to provide credibility. "Well, I don't know if this is the *most* important, but. . . ." Change superlatives to *a very memorable,* or *a difficult,* or *highly appreciated.*

Check your questions' inclusiveness: Can they be answered by all, not just a few? Experience and expertise can exclude people from responding to a sharing question. "What are your childhood memories of Sunday school?" can eliminate those who did not attend Sunday school while growing up.

Where possible connect your request with the purpose or topic of the group. "In two or three sentences, describe an experience of worship where you came face-to-face with God."

Sharing questions are not intended as occasions for discussion, comment, or critique. Members should have permission to reshape a question into one they feel comfortable answering, or to pass and be given another chance to share after others.

The leader can begin the sharing and set the pace, or can call on an individual known to be comfortable with disclosure. The group depends on the leader to keep the sharing from bogging down, and from becoming controversial, judgmental, or painful for anyone in the group.

Examine the following sharing questions. Which need to be revised because they don't meet the criteria listed above?

1. What's an area where you feel like a failure?
2. What is a prayer you are glad God didn't answer and why?
3. Share your most significant learning experience.
4. What is your opinion of capital punishment?
5. How do you feel about foggy days?
6. What's one thing you like about our church and one thing you'd like to improve?
7. What did God do to get you into this group?
8. What one thing have you worried about the most this week?

Answers: 1. Negative, arousing guilt. 2. Confusing, interpreted differently. 3. Superlative, hard to select. 4. Controversial and divisive. 5. Not significantly helpful in getting to know person. 6. Good—balanced and realistic—not everybody likes everything. 7. Good as long as it involves how you felt about it in the answer. 8. Psychological striptease, superlative.

Relational activities also provide opportunity for self-disclosure, using materials or activities as expressions of inner feelings. An example of such is the drawing of your dining room or kitchen table as you remember it at age ten. Colors identify relational feelings as each person draws where family members sat around the table. This picture becomes the gist for discussion questions about the family of origin. Other relational activities use sculpting an individual's perspective in clay or paper, sharing from card or board questions in Ungame fashion, or creating want ads that describe one's person. Assigning people on teams with limitations ("You can't speak," or "You have only one leg") and then sending them on an obstacle course as a unit can produce some interesting insights. Using media frees some people to express inner thoughts and feelings. It can frustrate others who are not used to such creative expression. Because of their nature, relational games tend to take longer to process and may be remembered for a greater period of time because of the involvement required.

The best self-disclosure grows out of the purpose or content of the group so there is a relationship between what is shared and what goes on in the group.

Listen

Listening helps to build trust and enables self-disclosure. Jesus frequently finalized his teaching of truth with "Let the one who has ears to hear, hear." In this manner, he suggested that the listener must become involved if hearing is to truly take place. In the Old Testament, when given opportunity to request anything of God, Solomon asked for a listening heart. He wanted to hear with the inner ear. Though this word is usually translated "understanding or discerning," the Hebrew literally means "hearing." God granted Solomon a wise and listening heart, made competent to hear with the inner ear and discern wisdom in ruling his people (Wakefield, 1981).

Speech is difficult, but silence is impossible.

Chinese proverb

Hearing is one of the body's five senses. But listening is an art.

Frank Tyger

Hear twice before you speak once.

Scottish saying

Sperry Corporation's senior news specialist Cynthia Swain documented that 80% of a person's waking hours are spent in some type of communication. Writing occupies 9% of that time, reading 16%, speaking 30%, and listening a whopping 45% (Bittner, 1983). We spend at least six elementary school years learning to read and write, and both high school and college offer specialized courses in speaking. Yet little, if any, formalized training in listening skills is given. The student graduates into a society in which he or she will spend three times as much time *listening* as reading and five times as much time as writing. Though we pick up our speech habits from our environment, we spend time correcting and perfecting these habits so as to be successful. Yet we do not deliberately work at improving listening skills. In job interviews we rarely test for listening competence. In his autobiography, Lee Iacocca stresses the importance of listening.

> I only wish I could find an institute that teaches people how to listen. After all, a good manager needs to listen at least as much as he (she) needs to talk. . . . You have to be able to listen well if you're going to motivate the people who work for you. Right there, that's the difference between a mediocre company and a great company.
>
> Iacocca, 1984, pp. 54–55

One of the reasons that listening is difficult is rooted in the fact that an average person speaks at approximately 125 to 150 words per minute while listeners can easily process some 500 words per minute (Wolvin, 1982).

Hindrances and Helps

The most common hazard for people newly formed into a group is to focus more on what they are going to say when it is their turn than on what the speaker is currently saying. This is especially true if one is nervous about making a good impression. Often listeners cannot even remember another's name because of this preoccupation. To foster concentration, leaders will sometimes ask people to share in twos, with each partner then asked to share the other's information with the whole group. Others will stimulate focused listening by suggesting listeners listen for something specific such as things they have in common with the speaker. Sometimes a summary statement enables individuals to be heard and understood. "So you are struggling with a job that tends to undermine how you feel about your value as a person?" Helping another get into a conversation and share what is inside of them is a ministry. In groups it is called "gatekeeping" or "door opening." Typical door openers include:

- Describing what you see. "You look like you identify with that experience." "A frown just creased your forehead."
- Tentatively describing what you hear. "It sounds like you may have some regret over that."
- Inviting another to share. "Would you care to elaborate on that?" "Do go on." "Umm."
- Providing relaxed silence so the person can make a decision to share. Silence tends to seem longer and unnerving to the leader or questioner more so than to those thinking about the question or preparing to share.
- A posture of attending with eye contact and demonstrated interest.

Of particular benefit in self-disclosure is listening for the feelings being expressed. Reflecting back those feelings can enable the speaker to know understanding has taken place. Reflecting feelings is of greater importance than reflecting facts. New facts that affect a situation may only be heard after the listener has accurately reflected the feelings shared. More will be discussed on this in chapter 8 on communication.

Self-disclosure is absolutely vital to the building of Christian community. Being known, accepted, and cared about is the seedbed for growth and transformation. Remaining hidden may seem safe, but it also conveys the doubt of acceptance and the possibility that no one may care. Small groups can be climates for healthy self-disclosure, relational support, and major growth in understanding and commitment.

> O Lord, you have searched me
>   and you know me.
> You know when I sit and when I
>   rise;
>   you perceive my thoughts from
>   afar.
> You discern my going out and my
>   lying down;
>   you are familiar with all my ways. . . .
> Such knowledge is too wonderful for
>   me. . . .

When I awake,
I am still with you.

Ps. 139:1–3, 6, 18

In a Different Voice

What differences between genders will affect community-building? In general women tend to disclose more than men and have more awareness of cues that in turn affect their self-disclosure (Reis, 1998). Likewise the presence of women in mixed-sex groups appears to foster more personal and expressive disclosure in men. However, women appear to prefer other women as constituents of a small group because of the personalness assigned to their conversations when the group is small. In fact, both men and women have been found to self-disclose more to women than to men (Pearson et al., 1985).

One author observes, "the presence of a female has a powerful effect on the social behavior of another; it makes him or her more self-disclosing, more open, and less lonely" (Winstead, 1984, p. 93). Generally speaking, men tend to reveal cognitive information—facts, while women appear to be more inclined to share affective information—feelings (Pearson et al., 1985). Also as expected, the disclosure of the masculine gender generally concerns the task before them in their focus on achievement.

As mentioned earlier, Pearson (1981) found that men will disclose more about themselves in a dyad than in a small group made up of three or more. Females were the opposite, sharing more in a small group than in the dyad (Pearson et al., 1985). Another observable nonverbal difference that occurs as men and women self-disclose is that in disclosing, women tend to move closer through eye contact and physical proximity while men, as they self-disclose, tend to avoid eye contact, move away from each other, or move from facing one another to a side-by-side position (Pearson et al., 1985). Witness males talking, staring off into space while fishing side by side or looking straight ahead while walking and talking. Women turn toward the recipient of their self-disclosure and move closer, probably to pick up on the nonverbal signs of how the message is being received.

The reasons for women being more oriented toward disclosing and receiving self-disclosure are probably numerous:

1. Women are expected to be more open and expressive in our culture whereas men, being competitive, do not disclose for fear of losing advantage and opening themselves to exploitation.
2. Relationships and accompanying openness to others are more important to women than to men.
3. Women, who are seen as lesser-status people, fulfill their position of disclosing more to superior status persons than vice versa.
4. Disclosure patterns are perpetuated through generations as females—having greater identification with the usual primary caretaker, the mother—are nurtured into disclosing while males in their differentiation from the mother are not (Pearson et al., 1985).

Through Others' Eyes

Levels and appropriateness of disclosure vary from culture to culture. The United States is evaluated as an informal culture (Samovar et al., 1998). This means that Americans usually disclose more about themselves than do people from other cultures. Germany, Japan, and other Asian cultures tend to maintain higher degrees of formality. The invitation to Asian groups to "share something about yourself" may be met with silence and downcast eyes. In their culture they were taught to hide their feelings and personal focus in deference to group harmony. So how does a leader build connection among people in such a culture?

The whole purpose of interacting with one another is seen differently in varied cultures. Interactions with people can be seen as means to other ends or as ends in themselves. In the latter the interactions themselves are important and valued. In the United States, interactions with others usually help us reach some other desired goal. We join groups to make friendships, network, or profit from one another's insights and expertise. We have lunch to do business. Arab and Latin American cultures value friends and conversations for their own sake. American groups are predominantly instrumental, using interactions as a means to another goal (Gudykunst & Kim, 1997). Targeting the focus of group goals the Plueddemanns write that in high-context small groups, the purpose of the group will be to build interpersonal relationships, and the group will be people-oriented. In low-context small groups, the group will be task-oriented. The group will want to cover a specific number of verses or finish particular projects (Plueddemann & Plueddemann, 1990).

Firestarters

Differing Agendas

Divide into groups of four.

Provide each foursome with building materials for junk art. Anything will do—string, rope, ribbon, box, tape, safety pins, ruler, pencils, spools, compass, paper towel roll, clips, paper, kitchen utensils, paper plate, cup, plasticware, magazine, paperback book, crayons, markers, plastic flowerpot, crepe paper streamers, balloons, scissors, computer disk, lightbulb, film negative, etc., so each group has twenty to thirty items.

Explain that each person will receive written directions for what they are to do. These directions are to be read silently, interpreted, and carried out without discussing them with others.

Hand out the following directions, one to each member of the group.

1. You are to read this silently and then follow the directions below to the best of your ability. You will have twenty minutes to accomplish them. There will be a prize for the most artistically constructed junk art. Do your best to help your group create a thing of beauty for the judges.

2. You are to read this silently and then follow the directions below to the best of your ability. You will have twenty minutes to accomplish this. The purpose of this project is to design something practical with your junk art pieces. So come up with that invention you've always needed but never found and work with your group to design it in junk art.

3. You are to read this silently and then follow the directions below to the best of your ability. You will have twenty minutes to accomplish this. The purpose of this project is to build junk art that will impress the judges. You know the secret that nobody else in your group knows and you cannot tell them. The judges are looking for the junk art with the most height so build with balance and help your group come in the tallest.

4. You are to read this silently and then follow the directions below to the best of your ability. You will have twenty minutes to accomplish this. You must design your junk art to include as many items as possible. Try to include most of the items given you in your construction project. Put together anything as long as it contains lots of pieces and looks like an art object.

After twenty minutes ask the judges to make their selections and award prizes—foil trophies or bottle cap badges. Every group should receive some kind of prize—most creative, most confused, most tape, most awful, etc.

Ask groups to reassemble in foursomes to process what has just occurred. The following questions may help them learn from the experience.

- Identify what you did or were trying to do in our group (your instructions).
- What did you experience as you tried to do this?
- What were your feelings about others in the group? about our project?
- What questions or problems came to mind as you were experiencing our construction project?
- Let's move this scenario to a small group setting. What does this experience suggest about multiple agendas in a group?
- What are some of these agendas you've experienced?
- What is your agenda for a group you are in right now—what is the bottom line that you want out of the group?
- What happens when a person comes to a group unclear about what he or she wants to accomplish?
- Having gone through this experience, what guidelines would you construct for heading off problems that occur when multiple agendas are in action in a group?
- What happens if all in a group are made to go with one person's agenda?
- What happens if two members' goals are incompatible?
- How would you help a group that has not thought through what it wants?

8

TERMS OF ENDEARMENT
Communication

The dilemma!
I know you believe you understand what you think I said, but I'm not sure
you realize that what you heard is not what I meant.

Gorman

More books have probably been written on the topic of interpersonal
communication than on any other subject dealt with in small groups.
We can define it, recite rules that govern it, continue to perfect technology that enables it, and yet it remains the number one issue people
grapple with.

We live in an age when the communication of information has been
perfected to a technological degree previously unreached. Yet misunderstandings and inadequate or inaccurate information remain as the
number one cause of marital difficulties, a major factor in employer-
employee conflicts, and a great promoter of international disruptions.

Small group communication is "the process of creating meaning in
the minds of others" (Tubbs, 2001, p. 46). For most beginning small
group leaders, the quality of communication plays a predominant role

in their fears about small group leadership. "What if my group won't talk? What if they talk too much? What if they misunderstand my motives? What if I can't get anything across? What if they don't get anything out of the group? What if they don't get along?"

Actually we cannot *not* communicate. Even silence communicates. What then causes it to be so difficult to correctly ascertain meaning? Much is due to the complexity of the process. Communication has meaning both 1) in its content and 2) in how it is said or intended. The latter is often conditioned by the relationship of the communicators. Communication has verbal and nonverbal components. Interpretation of meaning is filtered by 1) needs or emotions, 2) context, 3) previous history, and 4) patterns of interaction developed over time. For example, consider all the meanings the following sentence could convey depending on which word is emphasized:

"I didn't say you were stupid."

Now consider the same sentence communicated with each of the accompanying nonverbals:

- Said with a teasing smile.
- Said with a frown.
- Said in wide-eyed, eyebrow-lifted surprise.
- Said without looking you in the eye.
- Said with a wave of the hand.

Consider the added meaning if you hear this statement after spending hours trying to solve a frustrating problem. Or after years of competing with a brilliant older sister. Or having lived under a teacher's influential pronouncement that you would never understand arithmetic because you were "slow." Multiply these scenarios by the number of people in a group and the number of interactions possible between those people and the magnitude of the hazards of communication becomes evident.

Another complication that thwarts our gaining an accurate understanding comes from the effort and time required to request and receive adequate feedback for grasping the meaning. Most of us don't have the time or the energy to fine-tune each conversation—life would bog down in the process. However, we often jump to conclusions that the communicator never intended unless we double-check by listening closely and asking questions. Many a "But I thought you said . . ." is the result of a wrong understanding.

Expectations too lead us astray in that they promote selective listening. We tend to hear what will confirm our already formed perceptions. Thus we filter out important variables that convey what a person really said.

Challenge #1: Expectations Distinctively Christian

Christian small groups have even more expectations placed on them—sometimes unrealistic expectations—that hinder communication in the group.

- We expect to be understood by other Christians, and it comes as a shock to realize that they do not understand.
- We believe that conflict is wrong so we often gloss over misunderstandings to maintain the illusion of harmony.
- We often live with the assumption that unity means we will all think alike or agree on everything.
- We live under a strong right and wrong orientation and find it difficult not to label ideas and behaviors rather than seeing differences as left and right.
- Because of a strong "do right" perspective, many find it difficult to be honest in communicating in Christian groups. We find it easier to share what we should do and our success stories rather than our real feelings and struggles.
- "Judge not, that you be not judged" is used to avoid any kind of evaluation that could help the group improve.
- Certain types of personality styles and communications are accepted within the Christian culture while others are rejected. Such restrictions may limit our understanding. A person who appears different from acceptable norms will be "frozen out."

Of course, there are many positives of our faith that enhance small group communication: a climate of genuine love, acceptance, a spirit of grace, allegiance to Jesus as Lord, willingness to forgive, the presence of the Spirit of God, insight from the Word of God, a sense of being accepted by God, and a God-given desire to know and be known by the family of God.

Challenge #2: Levels of Communicating

Communication uses two levels of message sending: the informational level and the metamessage level.

The informational level conveys the meaning of the words used. The metamessage level deals with the interpreted meaning conveyed. Metamessages "frame a conversation, much as a picture frame provides a context for the images in the picture. Metamessages let you know how to interpret what someone is saying" (Tannen, 1990, p. 33). We usually react more to the metamessage than we do to the informational message given in the words. For example, the question, "Why do you bring that up?" could be a simple request for connecting information. The metamessage could be, "You're way off the track. Get with it." Or "You must have some hidden agenda you're trying to work in." The metamessage frames interpretation of the informational message and conditions our response. Check out metamessages to avoid misinterpretation. Don't assume that others mean what you would mean if you said the same thing in the same way.

By reframing we avoid jumping to conclusions and misinterpreting communication. To reframe ask yourself, is there any other way this statement could be interpreted? Don't read into communications things that weren't intended. Reframing by rephrasing and clarifying the message or acting in a different way is a powerful way to change interaction in a group. Conflicts arise when the metamessage is read as, "You are not valuable, loved, or esteemed." The informational level is not the issue, the metamessage is.

Conversation serves two purposes: It gives information and it maintains relationship. What makes metamessages tricky is that they strongly influence relationships. When a person says, "I forgot to send you a birthday card," there are many communications going on. More important than lapse in memory is the why and what that says about the relationship. "Does this mean our relationship is deteriorating? Does it mean I am no longer valuable to you? Does it mean you no longer care?"

Challenge #3: Nonverbal Influence

A major component of the metamessage is the nonverbal communication accompanying the information. Facial clues, body animation, vocal pitch, volume, and rate convey information about feelings, attitude, mood, and intended interpretation. Observe your facial expressions in a mirror as you comment, "We need to get this settled before we move on." Now observe what affects interpretation when you say it with a deliberate, slow declaration of each word. "WE NEED TO GET THIS SETTLED BEFORE WE MOVE ON." Make the statement in a depressed mood. How did you express your feelings? Now say it in a mood of serious concern. Nonverbals tend to convey true meaning. Watch a video with the sound off and see how much is communicated by posture, gestures, eyes, mouth, arm positions, and eyebrows.

Other Factors

Environment determines the communication of meanings. Picture the difference that sitting around a table makes compared to sitting in a living room. Sitting on the floor sets up a different communication tone than sitting in classroom chairs.

Researchers suggest that the contribution of the nonverbal to a message ranges from 55% to 65% while the way a person speaks the words contributes 38% and the words themselves contribute about 7% (Mallison, 1989).

Gender Influence

Gender differences, while not stereotyped, appear to play a part in communication interpretation. In general women are more attuned to metamessages. She will say, "Did you notice the tension between Bill and Susan tonight?" He will answer, "No, I didn't see anything unusual." She mentions that Bill ignored Susan's request for attention. Susan argued for accuracy in his descriptive comments. Also, each of them used *I* a lot more than *we* in their conversation. Metamessages are more apparent to women because they tend to be more aware of how people relate to one another (Tannen, 1986).

Another major difference between women's small groups and men's small groups is the need most women have for talking to maintain relationship. If someone doesn't talk, the metamessage is "Something must be wrong with our relationship." Continual interchange assures a woman that the relationship is intact and that the other is still involved. The content of the conversation is not that important. American men, on the other hand, at times find it difficult to know what to say unless some important information is to be conveyed. Culture has taught them not to waste time talking but to get down to the business at hand. This adaptation dominates the American business culture, but it is a definite disadvantage in cross-cultural exchange with counterparts in countries where establishing relationship is primary for conducting business.

In a mixed gender group, the women will usually want to chat just to keep in touch, while the men will prefer to "do what we came to do," and then go home. This does not mean that women do not want information or that men do not want relationships. But the primary focus and basis for evaluating good communication for women will be, "Did we relate?" and for men, "Did we solve the problem or get the information?" Each gender tends to devalue and make jokes about the style of the other without recognizing the need for both informational messages and relational maintenance.

The Challenge of Individual Personality Styles

Personal styles of gathering and processing information affect communication in major ways. Your individual way of perceiving and evaluating the world around you is a communication freeway providing you quick access to information and assessment. Psychologist Carl Jung categorized people according to four dimensions of paired responses to the world around them. Mother and daughter, Katherine Briggs and Isabel Briggs Myers, developed a personality assessment that identifies preference on a continuum between two polar opposites.

The first is the function of gathering information from one's world: *Sensing* (gleaning from what is apprehended here and now) or *Intuitive* (creating meaning connections from possibilities). The second function relates to how people make decisions: *Thinking* (careful analysis) or *Feeling* (subjective connections). The focus for where and how a person gathers information and makes decisions is the third function: *Extrovert* (outer world focus) versus *Introvert* (inner world focus) perspective. Finally, how a person prefers to organize his or her world is categorized by *Judging* (ordered and deliberate) or *Perceiving* (spontaneous and flexible).

An understanding of these different styles will enable us to see why people perceive a group differently and prize a group for different reasons. It will help explain why individuals respond the way they do, ask the questions they ask, and why what is important to one person seems insignificant to another. Realizing that people process the same information in different ways can reframe an act from seeming irritating to making sense. Such information helps us understand ourselves and our responses in the context of a group setting.

Jung's theory suggests that personality is made up of various composites of the above-mentioned four functions. While people have preferred styles in varied proportions, seldom is one person totally one category or the other. It is also important to realize that these are not concrete, unchanging boundaries, and are not prescriptive but descriptive of the usual response made by an individual. Circumstances and value changes may cause a person to change. A graduate school student who by nature prefers to make decisions as a *Feeler* may by virtue of prescribed academic exercise become more of a *Thinking* decision-maker. Or a natural *Introvert* may learn to enjoy being an *Extrovert* and find that energizing as he or she responds to job demands for success. Neither is one choice bad while the other is good.

Information Gathering: Sensing vs. Intuiting

We are continually taking in information from the world around us. Keirsey and Bates claim this difference in how people gather information is the most basic of the differences (Kroeger & Thuesen, 1988).

Sensors are literalists. They see things realistically and are practical in the way they perceive things. They rely primarily on the five senses for gathering information. Sensors major in facts and details and prefer to learn through organized, sequential, and carefully constructed patterns. Exactness and accuracy are factors important to the Sensor. "There were sixty-five people present who ate lunch in the first forty minutes and then broke into fifteen groups of four and one group of five."

Intuitors see meaning in the facts, and in contrast to the literalism of the Sensor, are figurative in their information gathering. They look for meaning and relationships between and within the facts. A yawn is not just a yawn—it has significance. Exactness in information is not nearly as important for them, but they like to see the whole picture and gather information in terms of a holistic framework. The Intuitor puts together the yawn with a previous statement made by the yawner and the way the yawner is sitting.

While samples vary somewhat, a number of researchers estimate that Sensors outnumber Intuitors about seven to three (Kroeger & Thuesen, 1988). These two types often see things in entirely opposite ways. Recall the report of the twelve spies Moses sent to check out the land of promise. Some saw and reported in detail the size of the people, the barricades and fortifications built around the cities, and what peoples lived in which terrain. Others saw the size of the grapes and claimed it was a "land flowing with milk and honey." All saw the same land but picked up different information. On the whole, Intuitors tend to be more optimistic than do Sensors, who collect hard facts and are inclined to see things more objectively.

This literal-figurative conflict in perception has provided laughs for great comedy routines. Gracie Allen was a deadpan literalist who took off on George Burns's comments. Among many others, Jean Stapleton as Edith Bunker, and Jimmy Stewart developed comedy routines that were based on this word-for-word exactness. Intuitors, also, can become sources of humor when they absentmindedly drive miles in an opposite direction, can't remember where they put the keys, or walk the parking lot looking for their car because they failed to note with exactness the important details.

Such communication is not always funny in real life when these two information seekers interact in a group.

Sensor: "What time is it now?"

Intuitor: "Oh, it's getting late!"

Sensor: "Well, what time is it?"

Intuitor: "It's time we should be starting!"

Sensor (impatiently): "But I asked you what time it was."

Intuitor (also impatient): "It's after six."

Sensor (exasperatedly): "Can you tell me the exact time, please!"

Intuitor (frustrated): "I told you already. It's time we were beginning. It's already past six o'clock and we have to be through by 7:30."

And so the conversations go. She says, "Did you notice the new couch the Andersons have in their living room?" He says, "No, I didn't even see it." Or one member says, "Were you aware of the resistance the new members had when you brought up the idea of time?" And another says, "Nonsense, they asked those two questions and after that they didn't say a word."

Implications

- Consider how these personality types will approach contracting for a group differently. Who will probably want it in writing?
- How would they learn in a different fashion?
- What kinds of questions will sensors ask? intuitors?
- How would each respond to a proposed new format before accepting it?
- What aspects of the one might "bug" the other as they work together in a group?
- What could each do to let the other know he or she is heard and valued as a person who is different but valuable?

Of course, most of us exhibit some sensor and some intuitor aspects while selecting one as our primary type and the other as secondary. It's easy to believe our own information gathering is right and to distrust other people's way of processing data.

Decision-Making: Thinking vs. Feeling

Gathering information is only the first step. Then comes our preferred process of making decisions. Thinkers are analytical, logical, and can remain objective and detached. Feelers are much more subjective, being able to identify with others, and become personally involved with the information collected. Thinkers tend to be result driven and can remain uninvolved and firm. Actually the terms objective and subjective would be better descriptors for Jung's classification than Thinking and Feeling because Thinkers also feel and Feelers also think.

A Thinking decision-maker contributes clarity and objectivity to a dilemma and holds to a single standard. A Feeling decision-maker cultivates awareness of what happens to people in the process of making that decision and adjusts to individual circumstances. Both may agree on the decision but contribute different perspectives in deciding. Thinkers base decisions on principles and objective criteria. Feelers ask, "How would I feel if I were the recipient of this decision?" This function of decision-making is the only one that falls along gender lines with two-thirds of American females selecting the more subjective Feeling for making decisions while two-thirds of American males select Thinking. The remaining one-third who go counter to their gender often are ridiculed or rejected (Kroeger & Thuesen, 1988).

Implications

This decision-making function affects personal relationships in many ways. In terms of intimacy, Feelers want to experience it while Thinkers want to understand it (Kroeger & Thuesen, 1988). Each senses the other is out of sync and doesn't understand the other's perspective. In making group decisions Thinkers, after examining the facts, may be irritated by the Feeler's comment, "I just don't feel good about the way we've handled this." In response, most Thinkers will go over the facts and principles "one more time," not realizing that Feelers are asking to explore more than just facts.

Feelers often identify with the subject so much that they personalize decisions. And they may feel that the Thinkers with their brutal analysis of facts and detached mode of operating are insensitive and uncaring. This can lead them to feel that the group devalues them and their way of operation. A more subjective group can frustrate Thinkers as they endlessly explore subjective areas and seek to have everyone on board and harmonious in the decision-making. Neither is actually seeking to thwart the other. But the paradoxical focus, unless valued for being right and left not right or wrong, can become a major battleground with the stronger members winning over the weaker.

Personality choice in decision-making affects the climate and goals of the group. Feelers want to be in harmony with self and with everyone else in the group. Thinkers may challenge another and jeopardize relations in order to get the facts. This decision-making process also impacts self-disclosure by establishing what each thinks and/or feels is important to contribute in order to know and be known.

Focus: Introvert vs. Extrovert

Extroverts are stimulated by people and action outside themselves, talking out their ideas in order to find out what they think. Introverts are drained by these same elements. They would prefer to think through issues on their own, listening and working out decisions internally. The Extrovert becomes impatient with solitude, introspection, and reflection, which seems to recharge the Introvert. Introverts want time to concentrate. Extroverts crave intense interaction to help them work through facts and feelings. Introverts guard their space carefully, resenting intrusions from the phone or people who break into their protected thoughts and time. Extroverts will talk to anyone at any time and never cease to amaze their counterparts with the amount of time they spend in useless chatter. Introverts may think they have communicated their thoughts when in actuality they have rehearsed them only in their minds. Introverts feel uncomfortable with praise while the Extroverts thoroughly enjoy it and need such responses from others to keep them going.

Implications

While Introverts will join groups, they prefer to process internally and will often contribute only when asked. After giving him or her time to work through ideas privately, it is important to ask for input from the introverted member. The person who doesn't show visible stimulation caused by active verbal interchange may be intensely involved on the inside and be able to contribute insight that more open members have overlooked.

Lifestyle Orientation: Judging vs. Perceiving

The final function deals with which organizational pattern a person most prefers as he or she receives information from the world outside of self. Judgers lean toward decision-making while Perceivers prefer to collect information and withhold making a decision on it. Because they bring facts to conclusion, Judgers come across as structured, scheduled, controlled, and doing everything in an ordered and planned way. They make decisions fairly easily and set up choices as right and wrong. Perceivers, on the other hand, appear to be in a holding pattern as they continue to collect new information. This creates the impression of being flexible, spontaneous, and open-minded but indecisive.

Judgers want a sense of closure—an opinion formed, a plan made, a definite time schedule, yes and no answers. Such definiteness disturbs those who prefer to keep open on a subject and they tend to view Judgers as close-minded. New input could change their plan and they don't want to be locked into a time frame or way of thinking. Creativity is at home in the Perceiver but closure is hard. Judgers are often bugged by the Perceivers getting sidetracked or expressing fluidity in thinking. Perceivers may be late because of encountering some new phenomena, or because they get wrapped up in a conversation and forget commitments. Judgers need the freedom to explore alternatives that Perceivers provide. Perceivers need the focused attention that leads to the conclusions that Judgers naturally offer when they take charge.

This conflict between structure and spontaneity, between resolution and remaining open can lead to small group conflicts and tension among members. Some want straight, decisive answers while others don't want to be bound by predetermined structures. The stronger the preference for one of these alternatives, the greater the irritation at the opposite preference (Kroeger & Thuesen, 1988).

Implications

When leading group sessions, Judgers will have structure and time frames with fixed goals while Perceivers will probably work off of several general statements that point out topics and suggest the method will be to follow the flow of conversation. Judgers will give a sense of control in the questions they ask and will move from one organized point to the next. Perceivers will pose open-ended questions of a broad general nature. "How do you feel about the church?"

In wrapping up a group session, the Judgers will want to come to at least one definite conclusion, with an issue resolved or a plan of action decided on, and with a deadline established before the group ends. Perceivers will prefer a tentative conclusion or leave with no decision made but with lots of information and pending possibilities available. There will be an openness for people to take what is important to them or to remain unchanged and undecided.

What differences in response would you get from a group of Extroverts and a group of Introverts if you asked the question, "How do you know that you are loved and cared for by this group?" Extroverts will probably point out their freedom to share openly and to talk through their most radical ideas with a group that listens carefully. Introverts will value the freedom to be different and to be included whether they say something or not, the freedom to "pass" when their ideas aren't worked through sufficiently to be expressed.

How would Thinkers and Feelers respond differently to the above question? Thinkers will probably list facts about what the group does for all its members. Feelers will identify specific circumstances that took place in the group in which they personally experienced love and care.

Suppose a leader wanted to sell a group on participating in a specific project. How would a Sensor present this project differently from an Intuitor? Sensors would list actual facts about the number of people needed, practical goals accomplished by participating or competencies gained, and realistic amount of time or money required. Intuitors would give purposes in theory and possibilities inherent in being involved. They would aim at inspiring members to commit to the cause per se without necessarily being aware of what was involved.

Of course, most people are a mix of the preferences and exhibit characteristics of both preferences while leaning to one as primary. The preferences of the other functions in Jung's theory will color how a specific function displays its preference. A Sensing Perceiver will respond differently than a Sensing Judger. A wise leader who wishes to involve individuals of both preferences cultivates awareness and characteristics of each so as to communicate and challenge group members. A good leader also accepts the perspectives of both styles and enables each to express his or her primary style while cultivating understanding of the other style as different—not wrong—and the person as adding to group understanding and balance, not thwarting or stalemating the members of the differing preference.

So how do we respond in a group? How can we bridge to incorporate these preferences?

WITH EXTROVERTS

- Allow them to think aloud by talking
- Communicate verbally
- Vary topics
- Anticipate immediate action
- Keep the group moving

WITH SENSORS

- Give information clearly
- Be ready with facts and figures
- Emphasize practical application

- Move from one step to the next
- Use real experiences

WITH JUDGERS

- Start on time and always be prepared
- Bring closure—no loose ends
- Be efficient and organized
- Follow through
- Decide and define

WITH THINKERS

- Be logical and organized
- Spell out consequences
- Ask what they think, not feel
- Don't repeat
- Stress fairness and equanimity
- Identify cause and effect

WITH INTROVERTS

- Ask and then listen carefully
- Focus on one dimension at a time
- Allow time to reflect
- Don't complete their sentences
- Use writing to communicate

WITH FEELERS

- Show appreciation
- Talk about people and their concerns
- Be open, sensitive, and considerate
- Affirm legitimacy of feelings
- Ask how they feel

WITH INTUITIVES

- Focus on the big picture and implications
- Allow creativity and engage imaginative potential
- Cultivate possibilities
- Use metaphors, analogies, and experience
- Avoid overwhelming with details

- Brainstorm possibilities

WITH PERCEIVERS

- Expect a lot of questions
- Provide choices
- Keep flexible, provide options
- Take time for deciding, being open to new data
- Emphasize process not just product

adapted from Tubbs, 2001, pp. 136–38

One of the merits of community is the exposure to those who are different, forcing one to grow and recognize the need for others with different perceptions. Building Christian community gives group members opportunity to practice the realities of what it means to claim allegiance to Jesus as Lord, not to self as the only right perspective. It calls for a broadening of insight and acceptance, and reveals our need of one another, because no one has a monopoly on truth. It provides a setting for being together with others whom we might not naturally select as friends.

Individual differences, while constantly changing, are esteemed in constructing the whole of community. Both sameness and variety are of worth. The individual and the community offer valuable unique qualities not available to the other. But the recognizing of those unique qualities enhances their worth rather than rejecting them as being unnecessary or wrong. To fully be an individual, one must be in community. To be in community, one must retain individuality; otherwise there is a sameness that destroys the very possibility of genuine unity. Community is the harmonizing of variety. God reflects both individuality and community, and created us to exist as both in his image.

Communication throughout Group Life

Communication is an ongoing concern in small group encounters. We never reach the point when it is automatic and perfect. New challenges are constantly arising. At the beginning of a group, as already discussed, communication is threatened by awareness of self and what others will think, by a preoccupation to impress with the right thing, and to present our best face only. We tend not to listen to others because of overwhelming sensitivity to how we are being perceived.

Being together longer or becoming closer in relationship can cause the communication to be more fragile than ever.

1. When we feel we are loved, we expect to be understood.
2. The longer you have been with people, the more you expect to be understood. "If you don't understand me, who will?" As the relationship grows, so do unrealistic expectations and thus the misunderstanding becomes more painful.
3. The closer you are to someone, and the longer you have been close, the more you have to lose when you open your mouth. When a relationship has been formed, you don't want to lose it by saying things the other won't like.
4. Misunderstandings are often seen as signs of a failing relationship. "We don't understand each other in this. Maybe this group is falling apart." In getting acquainted whatever prompted understanding or togetherness was seen as building the group. Now, however, any sign of misunderstanding or difference is registered as moving people away from each other.
5. Because relationships have been built, much is at stake so information is now framed in the metamessage question, "Do you still love me enough?"
6. The more time people spend together, the more their differences will surface and be misunderstood. These differences may threaten the group that wants to hang on to the unrealistic relationship that was.

adapted from Tannen, 1986, pp. 121–26

We will never have perfect understanding. One of the acts that binds us together as a community is having to work out understandings and absorb differences. Being in community is a call to commit oneself to the work and time required to develop healthy interpersonal communication, not to enter a community where there is no miscommunication. Talking about communication hazards, checking in, and reframing with redirected actions are all gracious, caring responses to sharing the truth framed in love. Helping people grow in communication skills within a group is helping them grow in reflecting Christ.

In a Different Voice

Who talks the most: men or women? Tannen found "it is men who talk more—at meetings, in mixed-group discussions, and in classrooms. . . . The men's turns ranged from 10.66 to 17.07 seconds, while the women's turns ranged from 3–10 seconds" (Tannen, 1990, p. 75).

When a person enters a group and sees all men or that it is made up entirely of women or that both genders are represented, the individual begins to operate out of largely automatic but unconscious assumptions and expectations. Previous experience, values that the individual has learned, and popular categorizations come into play.

Check your awareness of some of these stereotypical assumptions about men and women in groups. Complete the Through Others' Eyes section by finishing the statements.

Through Others' Eyes

Earlier cultures were identified as individualistic or collectivistic. They may also be grouped into low-context communication (often individualistic cultures) or high-context communication (used predominantly by high-context cultures). "*Low-context communication* is communication in which information is (1) embedded mainly in the messages transmitted and (2) presented directly. . . . *High-context communication* is communication in which people (1) expect others to know how they're thinking and feeling and (2) present messages indirectly" (Verderber & Verderber, 2001, p. 122). The former operates by saying what you mean, getting to the point, while the latter hints and talks around the meaning without expressing an opinion clearly. This makes "certainty" a major dimension. *Low uncertainty avoidance cultures* can live with lack of clarity, tolerating differing ideas and behaviors. *High uncertainty avoidance cultures* work to reduce risk, to secure control, and they tolerate little deviance in opinions and behaviors. Both of these variables will affect communication systems within groups.

Confusion is born when messages mean different things in different cultures. For example, a member of a high-context culture may say *yes* not because he or she is agreeing but because he or she does not want to cause the speaker to lose face. Silence also may be taken as a sign of agreement, or it may be a way of avoiding having to disagree, bringing disapproval or embarrassment to the other. Silence is seldom considered comfortable in low-context cultures.

In high-context small groups communication will be indirect, with emphasis on nonverbal messages. Tone of voice, posture, and facial features will have group meaning. In low-context small groups communication will be direct, either spoken or written. The concept being discussed will be more important than the feelings behind the statement (Plueddemann & Plueddemann, 1990).

The *purpose* of communication is also seen differently in diverse cultures: it can be seen as a means to other ends or as an end in itself. In the latter the interactions themselves are important and valued. In the United States, interactions with others usually help us reach some other desired goal. We join groups to make friendships, network, or profit from one another's insights and expertise. We have lunch to do business. Arab and Latin American cultures value friends and conversations for their own sake. American groups are predominantly instrumental, using interactions as a means to another goal (Gudykunst & Kim, 1997).

Targeting the focus of group goals the Plueddemanns write: "In high-context small groups, the purpose of the group will be to build interpersonal relationships. The group will be people-oriented. In low-context small groups, the group will be task-oriented and will want to cover a specific number of verses or finish particular projects" (Plueddemann & Plueddemann, 1990, p. 121).

Complete the following with your own assumptions.

In a small group:

Men	Women
men act	women act
men speak	women speak
men tend to	women tend to
men avoid	women avoid
men enjoy	women enjoy
men are expected to	women are expected to
men	more than women
women	more than men

One thing I would like the opposite gender to know about what it's like to be a man/woman in a group is

Groups consisting of the same gender usually

Mixed gender groups usually

Look over your answers to the above. Which do you think are actually true? Place an asterisk (*) by them. What is your overall reaction to the picture of gender in groups that you have described? Can you recall specific incidents that have conditioned your response to any of the above?

Our preconceived notions about gender actions condition our behavior and succeeding evaluations. Our identity also becomes tied in with gender roles—we must behave as dictated by appropriateness for our gender. Thus a man's identity may prevent him from being responsive and tender in a painful situation. "Be a man" exhorts him to toughness and moving on as though untouched by the dynamics of a relationship. A double-bind situation for women is set up when showing emotion is seen as "acting just like a woman," but also viewed negatively in being unstable and weak as a leader.

Perhaps one of the reasons women are labeled as talking more is due to the difference in purpose and style of that talk. Most women talk as a primary way to establish and maintain relatedness to others. "Conversation is a way to be with another person—to affirm and enhance closeness" (Wood, 2001, pp. 125, 133). Masculine speech tends to use talk to demonstrate control, maintain independence, entertain, and enhance status. They primarily see talk as a means of achieving a goal or fixing a problem. Thus "Women learn to use talk to build and sustain connections with others. Men learn that talk is to convey information and establish status" (Wood, 2001, p. 133).

No wonder there is the problem of misunderstanding. She brings up an issue or problem to get support and to feel that he understands (rapport talk), and he gives her information or advice (report talk). Such different purposes help to explain, "How can you spend so much time talking on the phone!" "Can we talk about us?" sounds like trouble to the male. Generally males talk about relationships only if there are problems to be addressed. Females, however, need to talk about a relationship to feel that it is okay (Wood, 2001).

General rules of gender tendencies engendered by the dominant U.S. culture include the following:

- Women's talk tends to be supportive (Wood, 2001).
- Men give commands (Tannen, 1990).

- Women speak indirectly, fearing conflict (Tannen, 1990).
- Men fear manipulation where intent isn't clear (Wood, 2001).
- Women use more "fillers." "You know." "Let me see." "Ah." "Well."
- Men interrupt women more than other men (Brilhart et al., 2001).
- Women interrupt usually to show interest (Wood, 2001).
- Men's speech is direct, succinct, personal (heavy use of "I"), and task-oriented (Brilhart et al., 2001).
- Women's talk is indirect, elaborate, contextual, and affective (Brilhart et al., 2001).
- Women use more "tag questions" ("Don't you think?") and qualifiers ("I may be wrong . . . but").
- Women ask more questions than men (Verderber & Verderber, 2001).

Of course not all people follow the tendencies of their gender but in general the above observations fit the intent and rules for interpretation that follow the distinctive styles of communication inbred by our culture.

"A woman expects behavior to be influenced by others and sees herself as requesting cooperation from others, not demanding it. . . . Insofar as men perceive that someone is trying to get them to do something without coming right out and saying so, they feel manipulated and threatened by an enemy who is all the more sinister for refusing to come out in the open" (Tannen, 1990, p. 155).

Nonverbals

"A number of studies have shown that women are better than men at decoding nonverbal vocal and facial cues" (Verderber & Verderber, 2001, p. 145). Women tend to maintain more sustained eye contact, which increases as the conversation increases in personalness. Women and children seem to need the visual gaze and nonverbal affirmations (nodding head) of a listener to feel really heard. While men may be more assertive verbally, women express assertiveness in approaching others more closely than men do. Women express more affiliative behaviors, smiling and nodding at a latecomer or showing empathy and concern for a participant sharing some significant personal material (Grove, 1991).

9

TOO CLOSE FOR COMFORT
Conflict in Groups

To live above with saints we love,
O, that will be glory.
But to live below with the saints we know,
Now that's a different story!

Source unknown

How was conflict handled in your home? Did you or your family members withdraw into silence? Yell and slam doors? Hold a family council? What has experience taught you?

1. "Let sleeping dogs lie."
2. "It pays to speak your mind."
3. "Don't get mad. Get even."
4. "Keep the peace at all cost."

Authentic intimacy comes only through struggle.

Halverson, 1980, p. 63

Our culture gives mixed messages in this area. We are taught to view anger as unladylike, not gentlemanly, and immature. Conflict is viewed as uncomfortable and embarrassing. At the same time we are taught to speak up for what we believe, that we are responsible for our own happiness, that people won't respect you if you don't stand up for what you are thinking, that our idea is as good as another's, and that we shouldn't gunnysack grievances. Generally, it is not the conflict itself that causes a fracturing of relationships but an inadequate way of dealing with that conflict. Conflict is usually seen as negative, and we learn few strategies for dealing with it in a positive way. Most people see conflict as a win-lose situation. We want friends who are unassuming, don't put restrictions on us, don't cross us, never raise their voices, aren't pushy, and don't contradict us.

In some situations, however, conflict and being personally aggressive are acceptable. On the athletic field, in contests, as an entrepreneur, in debates, and in games, these qualities are valued in a teammate and opponent. "Although anger and aggressiveness are officially taboo, as a society we apparently admire and are fascinated by aggressive people" (R. Weaver, 1990, p. 324).

We are taught many dysfunctional generalizations that shape and reinforce our feelings about conflict. For example:

- *Harmony is normal; conflict is abnormal.* Such a statement suggests that to be in conflict is unusual, temporary. "Observation of people in relationships shows that conflict is not a temporary aberration. It alternates with harmony in an ebb and flow pattern. But common expressions such as 'I'm glad things are back to normal around here' or 'Let's get back on track' express the assumption that conflict is not the norm" (Hocker & Wilmot, 1998, p. 7).

- *Conflict is always a win-lose situation.* Such belief results in dysfunctional behavior where one competes to apply enough power to come out on top, lives with the mixed feelings of giving in so the other can feel good, or feels devalued by personalizing the loss.

- *Conflict is the natural result of personality clashes.* This belief is based on the premise that some people just can't get along because one of them is an "Irregular Person." Many Christians find this an affirmation of something they want to believe—some people are impossible to get along with. Now they have confirmation of this suspicion and it justifies their being irritated by certain people. Grove points out the lack of substantiation in this dysfunctional excuse.

> Sometimes we are said to "clash" because our personalities are "so different." Other times, it is because we are "so much alike." Not a lot of information there. Yet many people seem to cling to the idea that we carry little valences around in our bodies which outside of our control, set us up for conflict conversations with certain others who house valences of the opposite sign.
>
> Grove, 1991, p. 291

Personality clashes result from learned human behavior that is under our control and can be changed. "Personalities don't conflict—behaviors that people do conflict" (Fisher, 1974, p. 104).

Christianity has added to these misconceptions generalizations of a moral nature. For example:

- *All conflict is wrong.* It is true there are dysfunctional responses to conflict. James writes, "What causes fights and quarrels among you? Don't they come from your desires that battle within you? You want something but don't get it. You kill and covet, but you cannot have what you want. You quarrel and fight" (James 4:1–2). Note the four dysfunctional ways of handling conflict: fight, quarrel, kill, and covet. However, in Acts 6 the conflict that arose because the Grecian widows were being overlooked prompted improved organization and resulted in the involvement of others in ministering to alleviate this conflict situation (Acts 6:1–7). Conflict between two major missionaries who saw Mark differently resulted in two teams being sent out and may have "saved" Mark for the ministry. Though they conflicted in their point of view, neither Paul nor Barnabas is depicted as being in the wrong. They simply had different values and perspectives (Acts 15:36–41). Jesus himself aroused conflict: "Do not suppose that I have come to bring peace to the earth. I did not come to bring peace, but a sword. For I have come to turn 'a man against his father, a daughter against her mother, a daughter-in-law against her mother-in-law— a man's enemies will be the members of his own household'" (Matt. 10:34).
- *Christians must never conflict but are commanded to live in conformity.* As Christians we are urged, "Live in harmony with one another.... If it is possible, as far as it depends on you, live at peace with everyone" (Rom. 12:16, 18). But harmony and peace speak of living positively with differences, not being uniform in thinking. When harmony is interpreted as everyone being alike, groups cul-

tivate a pseudoharmony, which gives the impression of peace and togetherness but which in actuality declares that Christians cannot be honest and real in their differences. The gospel is thus removed from real life, and hypocrisy and guardedness sets in. True harmony comes from different notes played at the same time in an enriching, not discordant, manner.

- *The Christian way to handle conflict is to give in.* Again we have only one side of the coin. In the Sermon on the Mount, Jesus advocates not only giving in but giving *more* than asked for. "If someone wants to sue you and take your tunic, let him have your cloak as well" (Matt. 5:40). But he also teaches, "If your brother sins against you, go and show him his fault. . . . If he listens to you, you have won your brother over" (Matt. 18:15). Paul illustrates this way of handling conflicting values in reporting his opposition to Peter.

When Peter came to Antioch, I opposed him to his face, because he was clearly in the wrong. Before certain men came from James, he used to eat with the Gentiles. But when they arrived, he began to draw back and separate himself from the Gentiles because he was afraid of those who belonged to the circumcision group. . . . When I saw that they were not acting in line with the truth of the gospel, I said to Peter in front of them all, "You are a Jew, yet you live like a Gentile and not like a Jew. How is it, then, that you force Gentiles to follow Jewish customs?"

Galatians 2:11–12, 14

In reference to the above there are different kinds of conflicts that occur and different ways of handling conflict. Conflict can result in negative reactions or it can produce positive responses that lead to improved conditions and relationships.

Generally speaking, conflict is inevitable in every group. Crabb writes, "Conflict is latent in every human relationship at every moment. It simply awaits a trigger to get it going. Self-occupied passions, the kind that when released generate conflict, are in each of us, simmering beneath our sociable exteriors" (Crabb, 1999, p. 40). But he also offers hope:

Conflict is a problem only spiritual community can handle. . . . The difference between spiritual and unspiritual community is not whether conflict exists, but is rather in our attitude toward it and our approach to handling it. When conflict is seen as an opportunity to draw more fully on spiritual resources, we have the makings of a spiritual community.

Crabb, 1999, pp. 40, 49

Functions of Conflict

Conflict can lead to improved conditions and growth. It can bring to our attention hidden values and assumptions that need to be examined, verified, modified, or discarded. A group that experiences conflict can be a healthier group. People feel that they can express both negative and positive feelings without fear of being rejected. New levels of understanding grow out of the revelation of differences. Where those differences are not allowed out, tension builds that will eventually affect group relationships and group goals. For example, a group that must always be conciliatory in spirit may never develop a level of trust that leads to high commitment and investment because they realize they are only dealing with half-truths. Witness the polite but strained conditions in beginning groups where each person is trying to put his or her best foot forward. Conflict is absent in these early stages but so is depth of commitment. This is natural during this beginning period, but groups that are still experiencing this situation four weeks later are probably stuck in pseudocommunity.

Paradoxically, conflict increases involvement and involvement increases conflict. When members care, they get involved, risking greater investment of themselves in the group. Likewise, the greater the investment a person has in what is happening, the more likely that person is to come into conflict with another. High commitment means greater risk, which translates into increased self-disclosure and involvement because "I have a vested interest in the issue." A group that cares deeply about its members is torn between being agreeable and being honest with one another (which could disrupt harmony temporarily). People in this tension will often test the waters with statements such as, "Can I tell you how I really feel?" or "Please don't misunderstand me. I really like this group but. . . ."

think about this:

- How have you seen conflict propel a person into active participation in a group where otherwise he or she would have remained a spectator?

> If you're going to fight . . .
> Fight for the relationship—not against it!
> Fight for reconciliation—not for alienation.
> Fight to preserve the friendship—not to destroy it.
> Fight to win your spouse—not to lose him/her.
> Fight to save your marriage—not to cash it in.

Fight to solve the problem—not to salve your ego!
If you're going to fight, fight to win . . . not to lose!

Halverson, 1980, p. 63

Conflict also has the potential for promoting a sense of cohesion. Cohesion is defined as "the degree of intensity with which group members are bonded together and motivated to work as a unit toward the achievement of group goals" (Palazzolo, 1981, p. 256). Sometimes called morale, cohesion keeps people a part of the group and is a result of members' satisfaction with what the group is becoming and what they are becoming in the group. On the surface, most would see conflict as destructive to group morale. In actuality, a lack of conflict can be more destructive because of what its absence represents. Working through difficulties together binds members to one another. Just knowing that they like each other and the group enough to reveal and work through issues of deep emotional ownership develops a feeling of commitment to others who shared in that revelation and process. "Not running away" says "while I am committed to this issue, opinion, perspective, I am also committed to you and our relationship." As Fisher and Ellis paraphrase, "The group that fights together stays together" (Fisher & Ellis, 1990, p. 264).

Group conflict also can cause a group to become creative and more productive. Challenging the status quo or working through a dilemma means that members must look for new or improved conditions and the result will probably be a better group. Groups with differing members push the boundaries that often limit and restrict solutions. New paradigms emerge out of conflict. Effort is increased as members clash over alternatives. Increased effort can mean higher productivity. Of course, mismanaged conflict can result in unhealthy deteriorating relationships that will definitely undermine work on the task (Wilson & Hanna, 1986). Both of the conflicts cited earlier in this chapter (conflict over ministry to Grecian widows, and Paul and Barnabas's conflict over John Mark) led to increased productivity in quality and quantity.

All of this sounds paradoxical: Conflict is healthy but it isn't, undermines but builds up. To resolve the paradox we need to look at two different types of conflict.

Sources of Conflict

Wilmot and Hocker define conflict as "an expressed struggle between at least two interdependent parties who perceive incompatible goals, scarce resources, and interference from others in achieving their goals" (Wilmot & Hocker, 1998, p. 34). Incompatible actions and attitudes and aims create stress between people. But that conflict may be in the realm of ideas or in the realm of feelings (personality conflict).

EXAMPLE 1:

Sam: Let's make our next group meeting breakfast at the coffee shop.

Harry: I think it might be easier to talk if we met in my kitchen. I'll put on coffee if one of you will pick up donuts.

EXAMPLE 2:

Sam: Let's make our next group meeting breakfast at the coffee shop.

Harry: No way. I can't believe you'd suggest that for a group meeting. It's so noisy and the service is lousy. We wouldn't get anything done.

Example 1 shows conflict of ideas while Example 2 could easily become a conflict that becomes personal. It could lead to demeaning another's judgment, struggle to win, reaction to a slight, criticism, etc. It is this kind of conflict that James refers to when he says fights grow out of self-centered responses within us (James 4:1, 3) and that Crabb sees as evidence of unspiritual community.

Differences in ideas—ways of doing things—can be beneficial especially during the early stages of idea formulation. Opposing ideas can enrich a group and cause it to search deeper into why it chooses to do what it does. When the conflict moves into the personal realm (my trying to prove I'm more powerful, my seeking to have my ego stroked, my focusing on my wounds and getting even), conflict becomes a tool that harms the community. Hidden agendas house personal, unspoken objectives that are often of a personal nature. The behavior of the group as a whole or as individuals irritates us because it cuts across agendas counter to ours. It is then that our behavior causes conflict.

Conflicting ideas can provide many desirable outcomes. A major key is the level of trust that the group members have in each other and confidence each has that he or she belongs and is valued. Conflict of ideas can prevent stagnation, stimulate involvement and interest, prompt change, help groups move to deeper levels, provoke creative new measures, allow members to be honest, develop thoughtfulness, broaden awareness of perspective, show valuing of difference and uniqueness. Conflict of ideas too early in a group's formation can be taken as personal rejection and turn into personal conflict that comes out later in negative behaviors. Valuing the person is more important than evaluating the idea. Some ideas, while not accepted become helpful steps in the process of finding the acceptable.

think about this:

- How have you seen the benefits of conflict of ideas in a group? How do we deal with conflict when it has arisen? Each type must be dealt with differently.

Conflict Strategies

Personal Conflict (Feelings)

Interpersonal conflict is bound to arise even in Christian communities because while we have been redeemed, we are not yet freed from our sinful nature. The potential is there for change. The presence of the Spirit within us and in our group makes this kind of conflict one that only spiritual community can resolve. Conflict actually becomes a venue for exhibiting the uniqueness of spiritual community.

Regrettably Christian community often has a difficult time facing up to this self-centered trait that distorts and fools us into thinking that we are not at fault, at least not much. We cover up our own wrong attitudes and motivations with pride and manners and alternatives that still allow us to have our own way while protecting the self. Here are five of these false strategies that lead to counterfeit community: congeniality, cooperation, consolation, assigning blame, try harder.

CONGENIALITY

We hide from conflict. "No big deal." "Just forget it." We distance ourselves from any possible clash of opposing agendas. We become Mr. Nice Guy who keeps it light and safe and never gets close enough to risk conflict. Congeniality doesn't deal with conflict so we never own up to its source in us.

COOPERATION

This technique avoids coming to grips with our self-centeredness by channeling the focus elsewhere. It's the old shell game. When conflict might arise in one sphere we move to an alternative realm that allows us to do what we wanted in the first place. Once again we avoid growth by not facing up to areas where God intends for us to change.

CONSOLATION

"You have the right to feel like you do." In consolation we look for others who feel the way we do and thus confirm our "rightness," which in actuality is dodging the "beam" in our own eye. We seek out people who will tell us what we want to hear. And we avoid those whose presence calls us to acknowledge our own role in personal conflict.

ASSIGNING BLAME

"Why" gets us off the hook. If we can come up with a cause, we are excused from accepting responsibility for our ungodly responses. "It's not my fault." Did you ever notice how much easier it is to say, "I was tired (frustrated, stressed, nervous, afraid)" than to say "I was wrong"? Only in spiritual community is there a safety net for admitting what everyone already knows—we are sinners whom God has made winners solely on the basis of his grace. We do not develop ourselves into people skilled in avoiding conflict. We can confess our brokenness to other broken people and find God sufficient to heal us.

TRY HARDER

This is the Avis syndrome and many good Christians pursue it with vigor. We simply increase our efforts to be better so conflict won't happen. We redouble our efforts to put biblical principles into practice in our lives so we don't keep doing the same wrong things. The problem with this practice is that we don't earn our sanctification. The Spirit perfects his fruit in us—and usually through the life situations and conflicts that show us our need for him. Knowing him in increasing connectedness results in our being holy. It does not result from someone urging us to "try harder" or "do better" (adapted from Crabb, 1999).

BEING SPIRITUAL FRIENDS

So what does work in dealing with personal conflict? "If the church is to develop pockets of spiritual community among its people, a necessary process is to regard conflict in two ways: first, as an opportunity for spiritual friendship to flourish and to do its vital work of soul care. Second, as a reason for spiritual directors to rise up and do their equally vital work of soul cure" (Crabb, 1999, p. 42). Spiritual friends are people who remind us of God's role in our lives. They ask the question, "Where is God in this? What is God saying by this realization?" They put us in touch with our hunger for God. They help us gain perspective and recognize our blind spots by focusing on God's perspective. They call us to relate to God, not just to learn relational skills. They are members of our group who long to know God better and who cultivate vul-

nerability and authenticity in the group. They call the group to face
issues boldly in the awareness of the presence of the Spirit.

SEEKING SPIRITUAL DIRECTORS/COUNSELORS

When the pain is too deep, the confusion too thick, the pattern too
difficult to discern, the process too involved for a group member to carry
out, we seek out a spiritual director. Spiritual directors discern the dark-
ness of our deceits and defenses and help us know what to do. They are
fluent in the ways of God, and they can envision those ways in us. They
are wise, experienced saints through whom God addresses us and our
growth into what God wants, thus enabling our soul cure.

BECOMING A SPIRITUAL COMMUNITY

The response to conflict that involves personal issues is centered in
recognizing God in the individuals and the group and knowing that this
experience of conflicting agendas can be used to discover his plan of
growth for individuals and for the group as a whole. Differences drive
us to seek and submit to the One who has love for and designs us all.
Our mutual inadequacies and inabilities to get along turn us toward him
and toward each other in openness and caring postures. It is the means
of our salvation in conflict occasions. "When conflict is seen as an opportunity to draw more fully on spiritual resources, we have the makings
of a spiritual community" (Crabb, 1999, p. 40).

Conflict of Ideas

What strategies help resolve issues in the conflict of ideas realm—
differences in principles, priorities, and process? Our view of conflict
affects how we approach it. Attorney, mediator Diane Yale proposes
metaphors that suggest three different approaches: 1) competitive,
adversarial metaphor; 2) problem-solving orientation; 3) creative perspective. In the first, conflict is seen as a battle with winners and losers
and divisive results. The second view deals with the issue by raising
doubts, by encouraging debate, and by viewing each proposed solution
as containing complexities that raise further problems. Number three
opens up innovative possibilities (Yale, 1988).

Another strategy, useful for resolution of idea issues, is one developed at Harvard called Principled Negotiation. This plan highlights four
principles to manage conflict of ideas (Tubbs, 2001).

1. Separate the people from the problem or the idea. Value and
   respect the people even if you disagree with the idea. Never label

an idea as personal: "John's idea is better than Lisa's" brings personal rejection to Lisa.

2. Focus on interests, not positions. Look for the bottom line or common interest. Look for interests behind positions. A small group was assigned the task of making a presentation that would cause the class to be fluent with K groups. Member A, a technology wizard, wanted to develop a Power Point synopsis of K group purpose, elements, hurdles, etc. Member B, who worked better with people than with computers, felt a better idea would be to try out an actual experience of the K group in class. As the group explored its common interests it found a variety of expertise with each person wanting to contribute to the presentation for the sake of their grade and to maintain interest in the group. The common interest was that all wanted their classmates to develop confidence and knowledge of the designated type of group and wanted to do it by using the skills of everyone in their assigned group. With this common goal, the group used Power Point to quickly help students gain access to facts, and then the presenting group developed responsive actions that class members could take after each presentation to experience those facts or to give evidence that the facts were understood and could be implemented. Each member led a few classmates in processing the information as small groups.

3. Create options for mutual benefit. Try to come up with solutions that include pluses for each side. The above scenario allowed each member to do what he or she did well.

4. Seek objective criteria for evaluating ideas. Draw up a scale of goals important to the group and then rate each plan according to that scale. For years, real estate has used selling prices of "comps" of similar factors and location to set the asking price for a house up for sale. The "Blue Book" establishes a fair market price for cars. Students feel better about papers graded by objective criteria (Brilhart, Galanes, & Adams, 2001).

Awareness Wheel

Miller, Wackman, Nunnally, and Miller have developed a useful tool that enables people and groups to get in touch with roots of conflict. Their Awareness Wheel is made up of the following segments: Sensations, Thoughts, Feelings, Wants, and Actions. When a person senses anger, uneasiness, or general anxiety over another's behavior or comments, checking out the Awareness Wheel can reveal the place where the conflict arises and thus open possibilities for working through it.

Sensations

Each of us is constantly monitoring what goes on around us. We observe facts through seeing, hearing, smelling, tasting, touching, and intuiting. In a brief and wonderful way, the mind integrates all of these together to provide us with sensory data. Amazingly, we are often not consciously aware of many of these messages. Thus in an instant we hear loud words, see flashing eyes and furrowed brow, and sense pressure from another. Our memories flash sensations from the past and our hunches feed us information. Contexts and the actions of others provide us with raw material for answering, "Who? What did I hear? See? Where? When?"

Thoughts

Thinking interprets the above collected facts to make meaning out of them. "What do I think is going on here?" Thoughts come in many forms: expectations, assumptions, judgments, beliefs, reasons, conclusions, impressions, and principles. Thoughts incorporate memories from the past, interpretations in the present, and possibilities of the future. Such thoughts become filters by which we perceive and interpret what is happening. For example, if a person believes that conflict is wrong, he or she will judge strong differences between people as undermining their relationship and will shape his or her actions to eliminate that conflict. If his or her expectation is that good relationships don't experience conflict, he or she may feel that its presence is a sign of deteriorating intimacy when in actuality it may be the opposite. That is one reason why it is important to view interpretations and the perspectives we hold as working hypotheses.

Because most conflicts stem from interpretation, it is extremely helpful to ask, "Is there any other interpretation possible from this data?" Reframing, reinterpretation, or alternate possibilities may eliminate the cause of conflict.

Feelings

Our emotions are often the first indicators that conflict is going on. When what we experience does not measure up to our beliefs and expectations, our feelings spontaneously erupt. You have a great idea and share it with the group, which you expect will treat it and you as brilliant. The group, however, is slow to accept your insight and even subjects you to numerous penetrating interrogations. Hurt and anger accompany a feeling of rejection and disappointment, and these quickly move into insecurity and sensitivity. To cover those vulnerabilities you manifest forcefulness and stubbornness. The issue has moved from your idea to your standing in the group and your value as a person.

An important question to ask when you experience such stressful signs is "What am I feeling?" This will then probably lead to "What am I thinking?" which grows out of "What am I picking up that leads me to that interpretation?" Becoming aware of what you are feeling is a primary step in changing behavior and managing conflict. It can lead to allowing the Spirit of God to reveal to you areas of your life that need to change.

Wants

Each of us has desires and intentions that drive us to do what we do. Conflicts can grow out of competition with or a thwarting of reaching these priorities. Your objective was to lead the group to accomplish a certain level of trust-building in the group session. By the end of the session, you felt angry at them and ready to turn in your leader's badge because they seemed so uncooperative and self-centered. Their actions and joking around left you uptight and in conflict over minor issues.

Becoming aware of your wants—not just for yourself but for them as a group—may be the source of strong feelings of conflict that seem the opposite of what you felt going into the group session. Clarifying what you want can be a first step in managing conflict that exists between you and them.

Motives that are very clear to us may not be clear to another. "What do you want?" may reveal your unrealistic or self-centered expectation and can allow the Spirit to evaluate this want in God's perspective.

Actions

Behavior incorporates what we have done, what we are presently doing, and what we will do in the future—plans and promises that we intend.

Patterns of behavior are interesting insights into how we think and feel. Is there any action that you use in a conflict situation that causes reaction, either negatively or positively in others? "What have I done? What am I doing? What will I do?" are questions that help put us in touch with our actions and the part they play in managing conflict (S. Miller et al., 1988, pp. 103–5).

Stuckness

Speaking of the small group as site for potential conflict, Smith and Berg advise,

> When groups stop "holding" the opposites and move instead toward extruding or subjugating one "side" of a conflictful issue, they often get "stuck," because the balance in the group so necessary for member involvement and participation is threatened. It is indeed a paradox that while the existence of conflict and opposition threatens a group's life, the *absence* of these same forces is also a serious threat. Emotionally, a group that does not provide room for the conflicting and ambivalent reactions evoked by group life is not a place where either the individuals or the group as a whole can thrive.
>
> Smith & Berg, 1987, pp. 82–83

By looking at the conflict through a paradoxical lens, we learn to live with it productively.

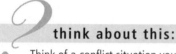

think about this:

- Think of a conflict situation you've experienced in a small group setting. What were the opposing sides? What was your emotional reaction to the conflict? How did this help or hinder your response? How was the group affected? If you could replay the experience, what would you change?

Apathy

The opposite of conflict may not be harmony but apathy. Conflict speaks of vested interest, the will to be involved, and stand up for concerns. Apathy represents indifference, lack of enthusiasm, refusal to invest self, and satisfaction with less than adequate results. In many respects it is easier to deal with a group in conflict than an apathetic group. A common assumption is that a leader can overcome apathy by being inspirational. "An outgrowth of this belief is the prescription of pep talks which, unfortunately, have only momentary effects, if any, and become less and less effective the more often they are used" (Bradford, 1978, p. 67). Dealing with apathy requires identifying and treating the cause rather than the symptoms.

Apathy—withholding interest and involvement—may be due to one or more of the following causes:

1. People feel powerless to influence. Authoritarian leaders who make all the decisions and hold all the control can create apathetic groups who simply follow the leader in meaningless motion. Group sessions become ritualistic without involvement or investment.
2. The purpose of the group—why they are together—does not seem to be important to persons in the group. Being assigned to a group where they have little choice in the goals, direction, and outcome undermines commitment. The existence of the group seems meaningless because the goals and activities are not related to the existing needs of the members. Overcommitment to a printed curriculum that exists to promote denominational goals but is unrelated to present member needs can result in a spirit of apathy when it's time to do the study.
3. Fear of results also leads to apathetic response. When a person is asked to do something that he or she knows could be detrimental, that person will avoid becoming involved. A group that has experienced a crisis such as divisional conflict or betrayal after complying with instructions where these crises have never been dealt with and worked through becomes a group that fears to be real. It is easier to go through the motions with no intention of reaching conclusion or congruency. No one wants to be open to ridicule, attack, or judgment.
4. Likewise a group where hostility exists between members but is treated as though it doesn't is a candidate for apathy. Where a power struggle exists between one part of a group and another, or between a portion of the group and the leader, people may withdraw their participation and support to undermine the opposition.

Bradford, 1978, pp. 67–68

Such causes produce unhealthy, diseased groups with no loyalty and in which usually little is accomplished. Some may be salvageable if the cause is faced and structures changed. Often new blood is needed to give a sense of hope and energy to change behavior. Changed attitudes and probably confession of sinful attitudes and actions will be necessary.

Apathy-prone groups need a new vision of their calling to community and of the Creator of community. The church in Laodicea, charged with being neither "cold nor hot," was threatened with being "spit out of my mouth" because of their apathy. They were called to take it seriously, repent, and renew their relationship with the One who stood at the door knocking (Rev. 3:14–20).

> Lasting relationships are not negotiated. . . . They are forged. That means heat and pressure. It is commitment to a relationship which sustains it . . . not pleasant feelings.
> Treat a relationship as negotiable—it is easily lost.
> Consider it nonnegotiable—a way is found to make it work.
>
> Halverson, 1980, p. 63

Scripture suggests and describes various means of living with conflict that leads to the growth of people and the building of relationships. Going through conflict, while being committed to one another and to living out the principles of our faith, can be a tremendous enabler of community. In conflict we also can refine and expand our understanding of life together as God intended.

Due to the complex nature of us as persons and of the multifaceted aspects of conflict, principles for exploring and processing conflictual issues are extremely difficult to put into practice, especially in an emotion-charged situation. Thus we must continually be humble before each other and admit our need of one another and of the One called alongside to help us in our inadequacies as we live life in community.

In a Different Voice

Attitude toward and behavior in conflict situations reveal variation that falls along gender lines. How would you expect that the typical masculine approach to conflict would differ from the feminine approach? How would you expect behaviors to differ in the midst of conflict?

Conflict managing has some significant observable phenomena (not necessarily true) along gender and cultural lines.

Here are some gender assumptions: 1) Women are compliant and tentative in their assertions; men make generalizations and sweeping claims; 2) Women's speech lacks power and is hyperpolite; men's speech is forceful and often offensive; 3) Women's voices belie weakness and emotion; men are inexpressive; 4) Women are unable to assert their concerns, and they are often silenced; men dominate conversations and interrupt others; 5) Women listen too much; men listen too little; 6) Women smile a lot to mask their true feelings; men are unable to express their true feelings and emotions; 7) And finally, women can better read the nonverbal behavior of others because they are less powerful than men (Borisoff & Victor, 1989).

The feminine focus on maintaining community and strengthening interpersonal relationships usually causes women to view conflict as a threat to such connectedness. It is therefore to be avoided or, if unavoidable, resolved before it causes separation. Direct confrontation is threatening because it offers the possibility of loss. Attachment is priority. Women typically look for similarities, for ways of promoting togetherness and closeness.

From the masculine perspective conflict is not fatal but exhilarating. Discussion and arguments are but contests in which to prove self. They become chances to spar with another, which enhances the sense of being different and independent.

> To many men, conflict is the necessary means by which status is negotiated, so it is to be accepted and may even be sought, embraced, and enjoyed. . . . Because their imaginations are not captured by ritualized combat, women are inclined to misinterpret and be puzzled by the adversativeness of many men's ways of speaking and miss the ritual nature of friendly aggression.
>
> Tannen, 1990, p. 150

Women tend toward wanting harmonious feelings in conflict situations, identifying states of relational union they want to achieve while the male gender pattern puts more priority on the task outcome or the way it is accomplished. It would be incorrect to stereotype all males and females in these categories.

At times, women may act as if nothing is different or conflictual in order to maintain a form of togetherness on the surface when in actuality there exists profound differences and competition. Power strategies are inclined to favor gender lines although there are always exceptions. Women tend to report more indirect strategies of a collaborative nature whereas men use more directness and unilateral ways of getting what they want. Women may undermine the opposition through subtle maneuvering outside the group or through appearing to join the opposition in certain aspects. In many ways they seek to persuade in nonconfrontive ways. Men, in general, seem to feel greater confidence in revealing their desired outcomes and what needs to take place for that to happen. Both genders need to accept the other's perspective if community is to be developed. Both the voices of forthrightness and sensitivity are needed.

Through Others' Eyes

The issue of conflict deviates broadly between cultures. More individualistic cultures require people to use direct, confrontational responses to disagreements between parties. Members of more collectivistic cultures, especially those who value highly nonverbal data, prefer nonconfrontational, indirect means for handling differences (Ting-Toomey, 1985). People from the first group tend to use facts and principles as they seek to solve or persuade. Those from the latter cultures incorporate more face-saving, relationship-stressing measures. They work at controlling emotions, maintaining friendships, and aim for balance. People in the former low-context cultures incline toward placing more emphasis on the importance of task or issues (Ting-Toomey, 1988).

In high-context small groups indirect resolution is sought through mutual friends. Displeasure is shown through nonverbal, subtle communication and conflict resolution may be avoided for as long as possible. In low-context small groups resolution is sought through direct confrontation. People will meet face-to-face and explain the difficulty verbally. And speaking the truth will be emphasized (Plueddemann & Plueddemann, 1990).

It would be inaccurate to suggest that all people in a given culture stereotypically fall into the same categories. However, by familiarizing yourself with various cultural values, you will be inclined to employ certain strategies more effectively than others. As you view television sitcoms and dramas or movies, observe how different cultures or ethnic groups handle conflict and confrontation. To bring cultural ways home, think through how your own family handled conflict. How has this enculturation affected your relationship with someone who grew up in a family culture where conflict was handled differently?

Firestarters

The Complaint

In the spring of the year, when the ministry of small groups in the church seemed to be going well, a group of younger Baby Busters complained against the older generation in their group that they were being overlooked when it came to handing out responsibilities in the group. They didn't feel they had any say in important things. This group talked it over among themselves and approached the leader with their feelings of having to play second fiddle to the established leaders with everything being shaped by the older generation as though they didn't exist.

What differences do you expect in a Christian small group? Why do you expect these things? Is conflict not a Christian thing? Why do Christians have a hard time with conflict?

Look at the following incident and see what it suggests about conflict:

In those days when the number of disciples was increasing, the Grecian Jews among them complained against the Hebraic Jews because their widows were being overlooked in the daily distribution of food. So the Twelve gathered all the disciples together and said, "It would not be right for us to neglect the ministry of the word of God in order to wait on tables. Brothers, choose seven men from among you who are known to be full of the Spirit and wisdom. We will turn this responsibility over to them and will give our attention to prayer and the ministry of the word" (Acts 6:2).

This proposal pleased the whole group. They chose Stephen, a man full of faith and of the Holy Spirit, also Philip, Procorus, Nicanor, Timon, Parmenas, and Nicolas from Antioch, a convert to Judaism. They presented these men to the apostles, who prayed and laid their hands on them.

So the word of God spread. The number of disciples in Jerusalem increased rapidly, and a large number of priests became obedient to the faith.

What were issues in this incident? How many results can you find? What were helping processes and attitudes? Why is it more difficult to accept misunderstanding and conflict in a Christian organization? What are pluses that Christian small groups can count on that non-Christian groups don't have?

10

TURNING POINTS
Passages and Cycles of Growth

On earth we are wayfarers, always on the go. This means that we have to keep on moving forward. Therefore, be always unhappy about where you are if you want to reach where you are not. If you are pleased with what you are, you have stopped already. If you say, "It is enough," you are lost. Keep on walking, moving forward, trying for the goal.

Augustine

Growth, movement, change is a gift. Philip Yancey writes,

So far I have avoided writing about a most difficult period of my life, a time of serious physical complications when I could not talk or walk. I lay in bed all day, barely able to move my arms and legs. My eyes did not focus. I could not feed myself and was incontinent. I had little comprehension of what was going on around me. Resigned to my state, I could not imagine any improvement. I outgrew that condition and now look back on it as a necessary transition time: human infancy. No one reaches adulthood without undergoing such a period of immaturity.

Yancey, 2000, p. 213

Young children are excited about growing, happily adding half or three quarter years to their age. "I'm five and a half." Aging and changing is valued less as we move into mature years, but that is the fault of our culture. God intended that we age and that the changes afforded by this movement cause us to view and value our relatedness to him in increasing richness. The apostle Paul underscores this value. "When I was a child, I talked like a child, I thought like a child, I reasoned like a child. When I became a man, I put childish ways behind me" (1 Cor. 13:11).

Change within a group is a normal sign. It reflects the dynamic of aliveness and health. Do groups move through predictable developmental stages? Do they face similar challenges during corresponding stages? Is development random and spontaneous? Does behavior differ in each developmental period? Do groups have common characteristics when in the same phase of group life? Yes, to all of these. To not experience such movement is to become a "stuck group," a condition preceding death.

However, there are no clear lines of demarcation as groups pass from one stage to another. A particular phase is identified by the kinds of interactions and behaviors exhibited by the members. These changes do not develop in terms of a single variable but are the result of the integrating of numerous systems. Like the meshing of gears, developing internal forces (confidence, identity, experience) combine with external elements (role, familiarity, group need) to create in the group new patterns of action.

Generally a group will go through these stages in the overall development of the life cycle of the group. These group passages may also occur in the process of moving through a series of meetings that encompass a particular discussion or task accomplishment. Some researchers feel that a group is likely to progress through these varied steps in each meeting.

Orientation/Exploration Stage

The first meeting is conditioned by guardedness. Most participants come with ambivalent feelings, high expectations, and nagging fears. There is a tension between the desire for empathy and closeness and the necessity of distance for protection and survival. People come with expectations, individual histories, previous group experience, and questions. Napier and Gershenfeld liken participants to children on the first day of school who tend to keep our feelings to ourselves until we know the situation: look more secure in our surroundings than we might feel . . . lack a feeling of potency or sense of control over our environment; act superficially and reveal only what is appropriate; scan the environment for clues of what is proper: clothes, tone of voice, vocabulary, who speaks to whom; be nice, certainly not hostile; try to place other participants in pigeonholes so that we can feel comfortable with them.

                                                                    Napier & Gershenfeld, 1989, p. 471

Because fear is the dominant emotion—whether recognized or not—the group will seek to build security in the following ways:

- Create structures and rules that give a fragile sense of stability. Groups often appoint timekeepers or enablers who gingerly exercise their rights of control and decision so there is some sense of order.
- Engage in safe chatter as though it was of extreme interest and importance in your life. Or use delaying tactics such as quibbling over details, semantics, being legalistic, or overly elaborate in the making of plans. All this helps delay entrance into unknown and feared territory.
- Become overly polite and formal to keep people at a distance and to avoid all disagreement, as an attempt to ignore or minimize individual differences. Such well-manneredness is being automatic, even unconscious.
- In pseudocommunity it is as if every individual member is operating according to the same book of etiquette. The rules of this book are: Don't do or say anything that might offend someone else; if someone does or says something that offends, annoys, or irritates you, act as if nothing has happened and pretend you are not bothered in the least; and if some form of disagreement should show signs of appearing, change the subject as quickly and smoothly as possible—rules that any good hostess knows. . . . The members pretend—act as if—they all have the same belief in Jesus Christ, the same understanding of the Russians, even the same life history. One of the characteristics of pseudocommunity is that people tend to speak in generalities. "Divorce is a miserable experience," they will say. Or "One has to trust one's instincts." Or "We need to accept that our parents did the best they could." Or "Once you've found God, then you don't need to be afraid anymore." Another characteristic of pseudocommunity is that the members will let one another get away with such blanket statements. Indi-

viduals will think to themselves, I found God twenty years ago and I'm still scared, but why let the group know that? (Peck, 1987, pp. 88–89)

At times fear in these early stages drives groups to focus on being fanatical about the task. They avoid confrontation and depth by making lists and ritualistically going through routine tasks. At the same time they clearly avoid defining the problem on which they are working (Bradford, 1978).

People want to avoid conflict and will use any available means to keep from allowing it to erupt. At the same time, they paradoxically want to be able to trust others and to know that others find them likable and trustworthy. To do this they need to give a little of themselves away. Too much intimacy too soon frightens people at this stage. Thus the leader who forces intimacy on participants may find they won't be back. But if they don't eventually move in the direction of closeness, neither will they feel satisfied.

Dependency on the leader is central in this stage. The leader builds security, is in control, knows what is going on, and has the power to value or destroy. Giving members opportunity to make choices and to participate in other ways increases their sense of inclusion and at-home-ness. Lots of safe sharing of information, particularly about past experience, creates awareness and opportunity for bonding. Cultural rules will determine what is shared as well as how it is requested. Some Asian cultures prefer to allow group members to pass the power that goes with talking from one to another and to allow anyone to pass before calling on another. At this stage group members look for anything that suggests, "We are alike. You think like I do, so I must be okay."

Power and Control Stage

When members move in the direction of "being real," differences come out. Some resent the authority they have given to the leader and begin to vie for recognition and power with the leader by rebelling and presenting countersuggestions. Others reveal antagonisms and evaluations of group members and a pecking order develops.

While trying to blend into a pseudocommunity there is often a reciprocal attempt to preserve one's own distinctiveness and to react by being an individual. This is displayed by arguing, jockeying, and withdrawing from others. During this time some may seek to overwhelm others with their Bible knowledge or their experience and reputation. People are working through "Who am I in this group?" and "How are we going to work together?" If these issues do not get worked through, it is unlikely the group will ever come to cohesion. Questioning, critiquing, and open expression of feeling is legitimized. There may be more anger revealed as well as more laughter. The tentativeness of the early stage is gone. Members state positions with more definiteness and rigidity. Polarization is evident. It is a lively time with lots of energy displayed, but it is also a draining experience as members struggle over whose norm will prevail.

The leader—so needed in the earlier stage—is no less needed now, but often becomes the object of attack. The leader is blamed for what is going on and is often ignored as people in the group seek to rescue it by proposing leadership remedies such as organization. "Let's divide into groups of four and accomplish something." Or "We're going nowhere—let's set up task forces to study the problems and report. We want to get this done." Each spokesperson feels he or she is the savior of the group and has the solution to the struggle in some form of organization.

The leader must be very secure during this phase, realizing that in moving toward, not running from, the issues, there will come balance. Encouraging self-disclosure, valuing differences, identifying similarities, and demonstrating bendability are behaviors that provide strong, stable leadership during this experience of extremes and realism. Some cultures, bound by their code of conduct, will not allow this resistance to come out in overt ways. Rather the resistance is epitomized by withdrawal or passive aggressiveness.

Trust Stage: Emergence

Stage three is ushered in with a developing feeling of "we-ness," a reopening of communication, a growing acceptance of deviations, and a recognition that personal aims are not being met as a result of competitive actions to gain power and to force others to conform. The group moves into accepting one another as having strengths and weaknesses and into seeing itself as an integrated unit that can be open and harmonious. The leader is recognized as a facilitator and becomes more a member of the group during this period. People in the group, as they contribute strengths, are recognized as contributing to the building up of the group. It is a relief to enjoy the group relationships and any disruption of the harmony is feared. Therefore, group members discuss and work through problems with new flexibility and understanding (Napier & Gershenfeld, 1989). Peck describes the action that propels a group into this phase of growth as an "emptying." It requires the giving up of one's expectations, prejudices, need to control, to "fix people," or to provide solutions, all barriers to communication (Peck, 1987).

The Productive Stage

For most people this is the be-all and end-all of the group. It represents being able to get along with others, enjoying them, and functioning well as a unit incorporating differences. It includes carrying out the task and goals that are a part of the group and feeling good about the group and about self and self's contribution. In a Bible study we no longer have to prove how spiritual we are or who knows the most. We are comfortable with these people and we help each other achieve.

Other Possibilities

Several theorists add two additional stages to complete the life cycle of the group: differentiation and termination. Hestenes inserts differentiation after a happy, productive period of group life. It is a natural realignment and reassessment that takes place after reaching a goal. It usually takes place in groups that stay together with the same people for a long period of time but who want to continue to change and grow with those people. As such it mirrors the sometimes radical change known as "midlife crisis" or the reassessment and development of marriage in what is called the empty-nest phase.

How does this show up in a group? The person who has been the responsible one may wish to assume less responsibility; the clown may want to be taken seriously. Differentiation may also occur in the group's goal and process. They may move from being a Bible study to becoming more involved in social action or from always having potluck sessions to eliminating them. Such radical movement can allow the same people to remain together but to add an element of risk and growth for people who like each other but whose needs are changing. If the group is open to this change taking place, differentiation becomes a period of readjustment and newness (Hestenes & Gorman, class syllabus).

Differentiation is important to maintain momentum. Max De Pree, former chairman of the board of the successful Herman Miller Furniture Company, was asked to identify one of the most difficult things he personally needed to work on. He replied, "The interception of entropy," which means to run down or to become chaotic and disordered. He continued, "From a corporate management point of view, I choose to define it as meaning that everything has a tendency to deteriorate. One of the important things leaders need to learn is to recognize the signals of impending deterioration" (De Pree, 1989, p. 98).

Groups who fail to navigate through differentiation (which allows individuals and the group to continue to become something it isn't and adds a freshness to the mix) move on to termination. This is the phase when the group must cope with its own death, reflecting on the success or failure of time together and preparing for the act of separation from one another. It can become a very positive phase, incorporating relational reaffirmation and bringing closure to group relations. It is a time of reflection and review of the group to evaluate accomplishment and growth.

Sometimes groups move into this stage without being aware of what is happening. The group becomes static and boring. It has lost its purpose. People in the group like each other so much that they cannot be honest anymore. Such honesty would threaten the relationship so they don't push or challenge each other. They settle down to maintenance. Somewhere in this process the group dies, but nobody acknowledges what has happened.

Other groups realize that ending a group is part of group life. They focus on celebrating what has been accomplished and the relationships they have enjoyed. They rejoice over needs that have been met and no longer drive them to be a part of this group. They ask questions such as, "Was all this worth it?" "What have we gained by being together?" "How am I different?" "How are you different?" "What is God calling us to at this point?"

Groups usually encounter ambivalent feelings at this parting: sadness in leaving what was known and excitement over moving on with a sense of accomplishment. *Never force this stage on a group.* It must come here on its own. Questions can stimulate action. "Do you want to renegotiate? To develop a new purpose? To end the group?" Assurance of the naturalness of this closing is important here because some people feel guilty and unfaithful in leaving a group. It may be interpreted as failure or disloyalty to the leader. In actuality, concluding is as vital as beginning and fulfills commitments made in contracting to end by a certain time or when the goals have been reached. Concluding allows for new beginnings. Talking about a group's future is necessary to allow people to voice what God is calling them to, whether it be renewed commitment to this group, renegotiated purpose for continued growth, or closure in group existence. Better to give participants a choice in determining the group's life cycle than to slowly watch them drop out one by one while the remaining ones live with resentment or envy.

Stages of relational disintegration as they appear in personal friendships suggest similar counterparts in a group where commitments are changing. A decision must be made to renew or to conclude with positive review.

Stages of Relational Disintegration

- *Differentiating.* A focus on self, rather than on the other person and the relationship, causes people to put emphasis on differences. Instead of finding joy in shared experiences, greater importance is placed on enhancement of the individual and the differences seen in each other.
- *Circumscribing.* Communication becomes limited to certain "safe subjects." Players begin playing with a new set of rules, often refusing even to talk about something. Personal rights determine what is acceptable and unacceptable. This limits conversation and interactions with frequent topic changes to avoid the personal issues.
- *Stagnating.* Such limited conversations evolve into silence. Farthest from reality is talk about the relationship. Avoidance of confrontation, pain, and facing what is happening is a central motivation.
- *Avoiding.* People in this stage remove themselves from being with the other in relationship. If present, they may act as if the other were not there. They withhold any positive affirmation—an act that tends to lower the other's self-esteem.
- *Terminating.* Distance and disassociation break off talking and the relationship. People are usually left with lowered esteem, hurt feelings, and an abrupt sense of closure with much unfinished business but no opportunity to work through it (R. Weaver, 1990).

Awareness of these progressively deteriorating steps can help people in groups honestly face what is happening and deal with it in a more constructive way than simply letting it happen.

Johnson and Johnson have developed the following exercise to help members finalize unfinished business, reflect on group experiences and on what members have received from the group, and express in a positive way their feelings about this termination. "The theme of the exercise is that although every group ends, the things you as a member have given and received, the ways in which you have grown, the skills you have learned, all continue with you" (Johnson & Johnson, 1991).

1. Discuss the topic: "Is there anything that needs to be resolved, discussed, dealt with, or expressed before the group ends?"

2. Discuss these questions: "What have been the most significant experiences of the group? What have I gotten out of being a member of the group? How has being a part of this group facilitated my growth as a person? What skills have I learned from being in this group?"

3. Discuss how you feel about the group winding up its activities and what feelings you want to express about the termination. The following alternatives may generate a productive discussion:
   a. Each of you in turn says good-bye to the group and leaves. Each of you then spends five minutes thinking about your feelings and returns to express anything you wanted to but did not express before.
   b. Each of you nonverbally shows how you felt when you first joined the group and then shows nonverbally how you feel now.

4. As a closing exercise, stand up in a close circle. You are all to imagine that you have the magical power to give anything you wish to another group member. You are then to give the person on your right a parting gift, each taking your turn so that everyone in the group can hear what the gifts are (Johnson & Johnson, 1991).

Other groups may want to write psalms of praise listing benefits gained from God having been in the midst of and working through members. Another helpful and affirming action is to share changes seen in members as a result of having been together in community and then close by thanking God for what he has done in the group and in individuals.

In whichever manner you choose, *celebrate* the final chapter in your group experience.

Stage Patterns

There are at least two major patterns for experiencing stages in groups. The linear stage model suggests that groups progress consecutively from one stage to another in the direction of completing their task. Resolution of one phase is prerequisite to the solving of the next stage of dilemmas.

The cyclical or pendular model suggests recurring cycles of stages or oscillation between phases. Thus new events could trigger dependency, fight or flight, and pairing as alternatives to working on the task. Such possibilities are always present, never resolved completely, and regularly presenting themselves in new guises and dilemmas. Unlike the linear pattern the cycle comes around again and again, the issues popping up in new forms. For example, the need to belong would continue to arise rather than be solved once and forever after moving on to the influence and affection stages. Individual members are constantly changing so orientation must continually go on, conflictual issues continue to arise, and the group must deal with them in new and deeper ways.

The parallel is seen in our growth as spiritual people, both individually and as a spiritual community. As we age temptation does not cease but becomes even more subtle and relevant to the present period of life. What would no longer tempt a fifty-year-old, may be compelling to a twenty-year-old. Likewise a person in her forties doesn't consider the loves of teenage years a temptation at all but must cope with issues never considered at seventeen. The positives of development are reflected in our growing awareness of God. Through all stages God remains constant in his character, and the many phases of our growth bring out new dimensions of his nature. The God of one group stage is rich for that stage to discover, but the revelations ahead are even greater and add to our picture of who God is.

The Dynamics of Movement

Though many have attempted to describe and label the behavior of groups occurring during different time periods of their existence, few have wrestled with what causes movement *within* a group. Which factors seem to release a group to lurch toward an unexplored state? What causes them to become "unstuck"?

Smith and Berg suggest the answer may lie in the way groups respond when confronted with coexisting opposites. The paradoxes of group life offer many contradictory extremes: preserving one's identity as an individual versus developing one's identity with the group; remaining independent, free, and isolated versus developing interdependence, being obligated, and knowing intimacy. We vacillate between self-disclosing vulnerability and self-protecting withholding, between wanting authority and not wanting it, between being distant and uninvolved and being intensely involved.

As groups confront innumerable paradoxes, they risk moving toward extremes and in so doing create motion. However, we fear intensity, and then move back to the middle. Groups become stuck by refusing to immerse themselves in extremes. They invent coping mechanisms that enable them to live in the midst of tension, or they seek to change the paradoxical conditions so they are nonexistent and the tension is released. Members call on all their skills to keep the boat from rocking and thus capsizing.

1. Groups create compromise—a middle ground—where the frustration of contradictions disappears. Such action sets up a "stuckness" as group energy is used up trying to maintain a balance of emotions by incorporating elements from both perspectives. The resultant mix may keep peace for a time, but it also prevents the group from moving ahead because no one dares venture into territory that is off-limits for fear of upsetting the balance created by reconciling the offsetting forces. The group enjoys a harmonious state on one front, but new frustrations arise.
2. Groups call for a show of force between contrary positions and seek to eliminate one of the troubling forces. "Calling for the vote" is an attempt to get rid of the tension created by opposite reactions. Citing authorities who favor one over the other eliminates the opposition. But such domination can cause defeated ideas and emotional expressions to become appealing so as to keep from going off balance. In subjugating one side, the winner grants power to the loser and groups remain in standoffish stuckness.
3. Some groups attempt to overlook or put aside opposing views to get on with the decision. However, the polarization defining each group is not that easily set aside. The group who wants intimacy continues "doing their thing," while the group that stresses autonomy makes decisions proudly affirming their right to individuality (Smith & Berg, 1987).

Such efforts produce stuckness. Stuckness results from trying to eliminate tensions within groups. Movement, on the other hand, grows out of living within the paradox. In moving toward the paradox, not away from it, by immersing oneself in both of the contradictory forces, it is possible to gain insight into what links them together and thus be released to explore new territory.

Even as beginning groups reflect hyperpoliteness to play it safe, there is a pull toward telling it like it is. By immersing the group in both of these, by daring to explore the highly feared territory of each, there is a regathering of emotions denied and thoughts that had to be subjected to making a good impression only. As groups reclaim this holistic view of contradictory emotions and reactions, formerly discarded as tension producing, they set themselves up for movement. In facing the fear and opposite reaction we open ourselves to the possibility of moving into unexplored territory previously forbidden. When emotions of fear or anxiety arise, these are signals that the concern that provoked them is to be explored, not avoided. Only in engaging will the group move through them (Smith & Berg, 1987).

Maturing in life comes from embracing paradoxical reactions instead of retreating to one polarity or living within the boundaries of compromise. As Christians, we live in the paradox of our humanity and our spiritual natures. We have new life in Christ Jesus with our hearts set on what is above yet are never free from our bodies with the humanity they bring. We live with the paradox of grace and effort, of sovereignty and free will, of brokenness and wholeness, of being in the world but not of it.

Role of Spirituality

Growth in a group is impacted in a major way by the willingness of leader and members to admit their fallibility and dependence on God and each other. In this kind of climate the Spirit of God can move freely and create a likeness of Jesus in our midst. Peck speaks of an emptying being necessary, a willingness to give up the desires and activities of self-centeredness, which often are revealed by coming together with others who challenge those passions. What does this giving up include?

1. Our expectations and preconceptions. Being terrified of the unknown we enter groups with false expectations and seek to shape the group experience to conform to those expectations. This prevents our really listening and seeing people and our relationships for what they are and is destructive to community.
2. Our prejudices. These are the judgments we make about people, locking them into preconceived molds—quick conclusions we draw or pigeonholing people without knowing them.
3. Feeling we have the only right ideology, theology, and solutions while discounting any perspective that is different.
4. Our need to heal, convert, fix, or solve. Our actions in this direction are usually motivated out of a need to make ourselves feel better. "I feel uncomfortable when you are in pain or when you call my convictions into question so I must change you," is our mind-set. Our solutions often stand in the way of coming to know and appreciate the uniqueness of one another.
5. Our need to control. To be out of control is scary. It could lead to failure. It leads to manipulation and hidden agendas and forcing my way on people so I can feel at ease. Control says I am taking more responsibility for this group than I should. If it fails, I fail (Peck, 1987).

Crabb would call this condition "brokenness" and claims it is prerequisite for feeling safe with another and acknowledging our dependence on God who alone is the sufficient One. Speaking of spiritual community, he writes,

> Why is spiritual community so rare? I suspect it has to do with the requirement of brokenness. We'd much rather be impressively intact than broken. But only broken people share spiritual community. . . . It is our weakness, not our competence, that moves others; our sorrows, not our blessings, that break down the barriers of fear and shame that keep us apart; our admitted failures, not our paraded successes, that bind us together in hope. A spiritual community, a church, is full of broken people who turn their chairs toward each other because they know they cannot make it alone.
>
> Crabb, 1999, pp. 27, 32

Brokenness eliminates the need for a self-preserving agenda. We are safe with God if and when we admit our inadequacy and realize all that is good within us is of Christ. We share this condition with one another. As Bonhoeffer wrote, "Our community with one another consists solely in what Christ has done to both of us" (Crabb, 1999, p. 39). Knowing him is our entrance into passages leading toward maturity.

Firestarters

The Sunshine Group: A Parable on Pseudocommunity in Rap

Once upon a time there was a lady named Sunshine Sue, admired by all who knew her. Sue was a born leader. People just naturally looked up to her and wanted to be like her. She was a "take charge" kind of person who seemed unflappable. Sue liked being a leader and helping people.

> "I take control, cause I know what's right,
> But you'll love me for it: I can't stand a fight,
> My continual smile gave me my name.
> No matter what happens, I stay the same."
>
> Sunshine Sue

And so it happened that Sunshine Sue came upon women in need of a group. Naturally she organized them and offered to lead them to new heights if only they would follow. Of course, the lonesome women, longing for a place where they could belong, rallied to her call.

The sun shone brightly on Sue's Sunshine Group as they began with excitement and some trepidation this great community journey. But their hopes were high. And to lift their spirits they began by singing "Climb, Climb up Sunshine Mountain," "Heavenly Sunshine," and "Now Let the Sunshine In" as a group expression of their purpose in being. And Sunshine Sue was smiling as always. She thought it best that they start with sharing if ever they were going to end up caring.

> "You all know me: my name is Sue;
> We want to love each other,
> So just do what I do. . . . Next."

And so it continued:

> "Hello, folks, they call me Mary Lou;
> I want to be accepted,
> See, I'm just like you."

> "I guess I'm next, my name is Peek-a-boo.
> I tend to be quite shy
> But I'll try to act like you."

> All around the circle
> They identified who was who,
> While Sue kept the sharing moving
> Till everyone was through.

> All agreed upon the topic
> And the schedule Sue proposed.
> After all, she was their leader.
> No objections were exposed.

> As weeks turned into months
> And months turned into years,
> They didn't seem to have much change,
> But no one voiced her fears.

> They learned to nod in unison,
> On any issue due,
> No matter what the question was
> They all had smiles like Sue.

Their manners were extremely good.
"May I sit here?" "Please do."
When it came to knowing who they were
They didn't have a clue.

Sue thought it was wonderful that they got along so well. And they thought if Sue thought that, it must be true. They must now be a community.

"Our group leader's Sue.
We stick together like glue.
To help to keep us true
We keep these rules in view."

- Keep feelings to yourself.
- Don't ever come unglued.
- Pretend it doesn't ever hurt.
- And never start a feud.

- Be very nice to everyone,
- Especially leader Sue,
- Don't ever question, disagree—
- Just stay away if you do.

Once a newcomer asked to join the clan.
"Hi, I'm new. You're few.
What do I do to be one of you?"

"The answer is simple, safe, easy, and true:
We all think alike. We all think like Sue."

It was true that nobody challenged,
Differed or suggested a thought.
This was the price for
The harmony sought.

Yet to those still outside
It was quite plain to see.
All they'd become was
"Sue do Community."

Sue spoke most often of the world and all its mess;
Another "new translation" when we already had the best!
The sad state of our church music,
Working women and their stress,
The great difficulty of being faithful
When under such duress.

To which the Sunshine Group would unite in chorus:

"How awful!
Isn't it sad!
Who would ever dare to think
That things could get this bad?"

Usually the group was boring
Because everybody knew
That even though they wavered
All would follow what Sue would do.

Occasionally a nagging thought would enter a member's consciousness:

"I've been a faithful member,
But sometimes it's been in lieu
Of who I really am inside
A person you never knew.
Oh, I share what I know is kosher,
Some surface stuff will do.
While deep inside I wonder,
'Will I ever be trusting you?'"

And then an event occurred that was to cast a shadow on the Sunshine Group. A stranger came to the group.

And the questions flew.
"Hello, stranger. Just who are you?"
And stranger replied,
"My name's Sally Woo."

"Sally, my dear,
You can be like us too."

"Oh, that I don't know.
I'm different from Sue."

"Well, that's who we are,
We do what Sue do."

"But I like being me,
I don't want to be you."

Then one and another piped up,
"That's me too."

"Stop! How can we be one
If we start being two?"

And that was the end
Of the Sue-doing crew
Adieu!
Boo hoo!

- What are characteristics of pseudocommunity?
- Why does it occur naturally at the beginning of a group?
- How does it "kill" a group if it continues on?
- How have you experienced some aspect of pseudocommunity in a group?
- What does real community look like?
- How do you see real community in Jesus' group of the Twelve?
- What would it take to move to real community? for the leader? for the members?
- Why do you think so few experience it in their groups?
- What's one area where you are conscious of needing real community in your group right now? What hinders it?
- What beginning step would God have you take to begin developing "realness" in your community experience? What will you do?

PART IV

THE MINISTRY
OF GROUPS

11

LEADERSHIP POWER

Give us a king to lead us.

　　1 Samuel 8:5

Nowhere is the radical nature of the Christian perspective more evident than in the conceptualization of leadership. It is a subject often spoken of in Scripture.

　　Julie Gorman

Theories of leadership abound. Books describing them fill bookstores and libraries. Early studies in the 1920s claimed that leaders were born, not made, and we were accordingly told that leaders were taller (Caldwell & Wellman, 1926, as cited in Baird & Weinberg, 1981), larger and healthier (Bellingrath, 1930, as cited in Baird & Weinberg, 1981), neater (Partridge, 1934, as cited in Baird & Weinberg, 1981), more intelligent and self-confident (Gibb, 1947, as cited in Baird & Weinberg, 1981), better adjusted (Holtzman, 1952, as cited in Baird & Weinberg, 1981), more outgoing and dominant (Goodenough, 1930, as cited in Baird & Weinberg, 1981), and more empathetic (Chowdry & Newcomb, 1952, as cited in Baird & Weinberg, 1981). But this trait theory produced such diversity and fragmentation that it lost its credibility (Baird & Weinberg, 1981).

205

Kurt Lewin's studies in the late 1930s revealed the qualitative differences between autocratic, democratic, and laissez-faire styles of leadership. Ten years later Stogdill postulated the situational approach to leadership, suggesting the nature of the task and the situation define which style of leadership will be most profitable. Function theory focused on the things a leader does that can be learned, and it identified the categories of task functions and the maintenance of socioemotional conditions functions.

Capitalizing on this, Fiedler led a team of researchers in developing the contingency theory of leadership. Dividing leaders into task-motivated leaders and relationship-motivated leaders, this theory suggests that the contingencies of the situation determine which kind of leader will be most effective in maximizing performance. One of the most popular theories involving situational determinants was developed by Hersey and Blanchard. This theory is depicted in quadrants representing four combinations of task and relationship factors in the situation. The level of maturity of followers is represented by a bell-shaped curve that passes through each quadrant illustrating growth in the followers matched by a change in style of leadership. The leader thus must adjust both task and relationship behaviors to compensate for the maturity level of the followers. For each of the following theories, there are dozens more representing the complexity and the perplexity of what it means to be a leader. Max De Pree pictures another kind of authority: "Leadership is an art . . . more tribal than scientific, more a weaving of relationships than an amassing of information" (De Pree, 1989, p. 3).

But the question before us as Christians is what is distinctive about the leadership of Christians? In the 1990s Stephen Covey, an avowed Mormon and successful businessman, swept the leadership scene with his principle-centered leadership habits that sought to create a value system to form leaders. As Christians we have usually hitchhiked on the world's way of leading, baptizing a practice by bringing it into the church scene. However, in the beginning, our leader, Jesus Christ, specifically spelled out clearly that the way in which the world saw leadership as a superior position of lording it over others was not to be the way of the Christian leader (Mark 10:42–43).

The world's framework is "power." Leadership theory describes many varieties of this commodity: coercive power, reward power, legitimate power, expert power, referent power. Jesus claims, "All authority . . . has been given to me" (Matt. 28:18), and the Book of Revelation unequivocally states, "salvation and glory and power belong to our God" (Rev. 19:1). Nowhere are believers given power over each other. That authority is God's alone. The body of Christ is to give respect to its leaders, to "obey your leaders and submit to their authority" (Heb. 13:17). But overseers are to shepherd, not lording over but setting examples with their lives. If there is any power resident in what Jesus is calling his followers to exercise, it is servant power.

> The empowering leader will attempt to establish power in another person. Empowering leadership will not, however, merely yield to the wishes of another person, nor give up one's own power to someone else. Rather empowering leadership engages in an active, intentional process of enabling the acquisition of power in others. The person who is empowered has gained power—the ability or resources from which to lead—because of the empowering behavior of the leader. . . . Empowering leadership is the process of helping the other to recognize strengths and potential within, as well as encouraging and guiding the development of these qualities.
>
> Balswick & Wright, 1988, p. 8

Aspiring to Be a Servant

The basic question of leading is "Who do we intend to be?" Do we aspire in our small group role to be a servant, an enabler, one who makes it possible for others to succeed? Servants in Scripture are not usually in the limelight. Often they don't even have names, just a mission to fulfill that puts the spotlight on others. "What we intend to do, what we actually do, will always be a consequence of who we intend to be. I think we find out who we intend to be, first of all, by asking ourselves, 'What do we believe?' and secondly, 'What is my purpose in life?' I think we need to know, 'To what am I, as a leader, devoted?'" (De Pree, 2000, Monograph 5). If we are devoted to becoming servants of the Lord God and thus of his people, what we do will be affected by that purpose.

Servants are dispensable. Leaders who aspire to become servants have a different evaluation of what really counts than those who aspire to personal prestige and power. And they are willing to die for that. The enrichment and enhancement of another is their mission and dying to themselves so that can be accomplished is the fulfillment of what it means to serve. Jesus knew this. Paul learned it. Moses was open to it. John the Baptist announced it. The death of a servant is unnoticed except by those who were served. Leadership as God portrays it requires maturity, a growing up that embraces this perspective and attitude to fully carry out that for which the leadership role was designed. This kind of value shapes the group. And momentum in developing godliness within a group comes from a clear vision of what a group of servants ought to be.

Relational power expresses itself through provision of safety, knowing names, talking about agendas, allowing others to have a hand in shaping what goes on, and developing boundaries of what the group will and will not do. Servant power makes gentle but helpful inquiry that allows new group members to share who they are in a receptive setting. Their story is heard and their contributions affirmed. Authentic self-disclosure is modeled and encouraged. Care is taken to ensure genuine understanding so the one sharing is truly heard. Everyone is included in the conversation, in the decision-making. The group is portrayed as *our* group, not *my* group, and relational power is comfortable allowing the group to develop its own identity.

Honesty is encouraged by asking for feelings and by frequent checking-in questions to be sure all are included. Nonjudgmental attitudes are cultivated so that participants can feel, "It's safe here. You can be yourself." The leader protects those who appear timid, those deviant in comparison to the majority, and those working through their own issues. Inclusion is sometimes questioned when in the course of group life a participant seems out of step or slower to respond. Servant leadership is not only aware of these anxiety producing situations but also takes steps to initiate acceptance and to allow the deviant to be heard. "It's okay to feel differently on this issue. Let's have Tom help us see things from his point of view."

Eager to Empower

> Leaders are responsible for effectiveness. . . . Effectiveness comes about through enabling others to reach their potential—both their personal potential and their corporate . . . potential. . . . The measure of leadership is not the quality of the head, but the tone of the body. The signs of outstanding leadership appear primarily among the followers. Are the followers reaching their potential? Are they learning? Serving? Do they achieve the required results? Do they change with grace? Manage conflict?
>
> De Pree, 1989, pp. 16, 10

O'Toole agrees, "The leader is the 'servant' of his followers in that he removes the obstacles that prevent them from doing their jobs" (De Pree, 1989, p. xix).

Covey writes, "When you fully empower people, your paradigm of yourself changes. You become a servant. You no longer control others; they control themselves. You become a source of help to them" (Covey, 1991, p. 246). Schutz pictures the same in the leader as completer: "The best a leader can do is to observe what functions are not being performed by a segment of the group and enable this part to accomplish them, or if required, do it for them" (Schutz in Cathcart & Samovar, 1979, p. 400).

God places his Spirit in each member of his family. The role of the Spirit is to frame the likeness of Jesus in the uniqueness of that person's life and to fit that life into the composite of the family to allow a more complete perspective of Christ as reflected by the corporate group. A second role that the Spirit plays is to channel gifting through each individual to enhance the growth of the entire group. Working with the Spirit, helping people and the whole group reach their potential in spiritual community is God's way of a leader carrying out his or her mission of service. The power and authority are present in the leader's exaltation of the Spirit of Christ. The leader and the spiritual community call for submission and obedience to him. This priority is empowering, releasing the power that God claims belongs to him.

Ready to Receive and Be Influenced

Empowering means receiving as well as giving. A leader is one who has the capacity for receptivity as well as initiation. Leading well means facilitating the capacity of group members to fulfill their function. Leaders lead for the satisfaction of others. Fulfilled followers affirm the effectiveness of leaders. Leadership is never a one-dimensional, unilateral process (Lee & Cowan, 1986).

In an essay entitled "Two Conceptions of Power," Bernard Loomer identifies relational power as "the ability both to produce and to undergo an effect . . . to influence others and to be influenced by others" (Loomer, 1976, p. 17). He states, "the conception of relational power, in contrast to power conceived as unilateral, has as one of its premises the notion that the capacity to absorb an influence is as truly a mark of power as is the strength involved in exerting an influence" (Loomer, 1976, p. 17). Relational power portrays the strength of being open to the influence of another. Allowing another to have an effect upon us as individuals is as great a sign of personal strength as having an influence on another. Loomer writes,

> Our readiness to take account of the feelings and values of another is a way of including the other within our world of meaning and concern. At its best, receiving is not unresponsive passivity; it is an active openness. Our reception of another indicates that we are or may become large enough to make room for another within ourselves. Our openness to be influenced by another, without losing our identity or sense of self-dependence, is not

only an acknowledgement and affirmation of the other as an end rather
than a means to an end. It is also a measure of our own strength and size,
even and especially when this influence of the other helps to effect a creative transformation of ourselves and our world. The strength of our security may well mean that we do not fear the other, that the other is not an
overpowering threat to our own sense of worth.

The world of the individual who can be influenced by another without losing his or her identity or freedom is larger than the world of the
individual who fears being influenced. The former can include ranges
and depths of complexity and contrast to a degree that is not possible
for the latter. The stature of the individual who can let another exist in
his or her own creative freedom is larger than the size of the individual
who insists that others must conform to his or her own purposes and
understandings.

Loomer, 1976, p. 18

Influencing and being influenced are a part of maturing. Relational
power leaders recognize that they do not have all the influencing potential. In fact, the group becomes unhealthy if only the leader influences
and initiates. Servant leadership knows its boundaries, its strengths
and limitations, and goes about releasing others to fulfill roles as influ-
encers and initiators. Asking for and taking suggestions, allowing others to assume responsibility, and cultivating ownership of the group
purpose by all contribute toward a sense of power and influence as
well as a willingness to be influenced. Willingness to be influenced
creates trust and breeds a like willingness to listen and hear fairly in
the other. The servant leader does not abdicate leadership but seeks
to use it to express the strengths of all, not just the one who is designated leader.

Relational power leaders are lavish in cultivating and creating new
freedoms for people to grow. They serve by doing whatever is necessary
to provide a comfortable and challenging growth climate for group members. In this common area of power, Christian small group leaders have
the opportunity to live a leader lifestyle that is distinctively Christian,
responding counter to the cultural view of leadership that fosters control over the group.

This conception of leadership in no way suggests that one refuse to
exercise influence and initiative. Rather it includes the additional dimension of being responsive to the efforts of others as they also initiate and
influence. Such radical restructuring pictures a leader as one who is so
attentive to followers that he or she acts out leadership as a ministering
to the needs observed in others. There is no ego-building, no feeling of
control or superiority, only a desire to fulfill the other in the relation-

ship. There is an interdependence reflective of the Godhead, each magnifying the ministry of the other.

Relational power focuses on being open and responsive to doing what another needs to have done. The apostle Paul repeats this again and again. "Christ loved the church and gave himself up *for her to make her holy*" (Eph. 5:25–26, italics added). "Husbands, love your wives" (Eph. 5:25), *feeding and caring for them* (Eph. 5:29). Likewise, wives are to be *receptive* and *responsive* to the fact that husbands need respect. Children serve by giving attitudes and acts of *respect to parents* and parents reciprocate by providing for children *consistent* and *reasonable boundaries* so they do not become exasperated. Slaves likewise offer *respectful responses* to masters and they, in turn, are to give *respectful service* to their slaves.

> Leadership is an art, something to be learned over time, not simply by reading books. Leadership is more tribal than scientific, more a weaving of relationships than an amassing of information.
>
> De Pree, 1989, p. 3

As equals regardless of age, social status, or gender, we are absorbed in providing what will build up and enable the other to carry out his or her role as a child of our Father. John pictures Jesus again teaching the disciples by kneeling before them so they could have clean feet. He prefaced this event with "Having loved his own . . . he now showed them the full extent of his love" (John 13:1). This act of awareness and care, a prelude to the theme of the cross, reveals a Christ who was influenced by the need of the disciples without losing his identity as the Son of God. John notes, "Jesus knew that the Father had put all things under his power, and that he had come from God" (John 13:3). His own behavior was transformed by the presence of those he loved who ate with dirty feet. Dramatically he demonstrates the function of power—it is initiating and responding through simple acts that honor others as equals in the bonds of relationship (Lee & Cowan, 1986).

Open to Sharing the Role

Bilezikian adds this dimension to the above-mentioned requirements: "Leadership is a servant ministry, based on spiritual gifts and always plural" (Bilezikian, 1997, p. 130). This highlights the importance of spiritual community. Where two or three come together, focused on the priority of Jesus, he is there in the midst (Matt. 18:19–20). This shared leadership engages heavenly input in corporate decision-making and keeps the servanthood of leadership in its rightful place.

> Under normal circumstances, the purpose of leadership is to enable the group to exercise its own corporate responsibility. Because of checks and balances, a group of leaders is less likely to become corrupted and to usurp the authority of the community than a strong individual leader who might gain ascendance over it.
>
> Bilezikian, 1997, p. 163

In the New Testament leadership is presented as collective. Leadership as individualism is not an option—we can't grow up by ourselves to the full stature of Jesus Christ (Eph. 4:13). Each needs to be spiritually nurtured and cared for by other leaders who serve in this capacity.

God gives ample evidence of operating out of a community focus; we are one body but made up of many parts. The witness as to who he is comes from many, not one alone. He incarnates himself in the midst of believers *together* while distributing his Spirit to each. Discernment of his will and ways requires the counsel of many *witnesses.* He chose a nation, a kingdom, a people to represent who he is, *not one individual.* We are joined by clouds of witnesses from ages past and by the church on many continents and in numerous forms. Therefore it is presumptuous to believe that God would expect one person to personify all that is needed by members of a community.

The research of Katzenbach and Smith, a secular source, "concluded that in every high-performance team they investigated, 'leadership is shared'" (Katzenbach & Smith, 1993, p. 80).

Leadership Teams

Leadership by teams is in. Modern organizations use teams to affect multibillion-dollar decisions in business. A 1993 survey reported more than 4,000 employee teams active in Federal Express. Motorola lists over 2,200 problem-solving teams. Cadillac involves more than 60% of its workforce in teams (Blackburn & Rosen, 1993).

George Claudis cites collaborative community leadership as imperative for the church.

> The most effective churches today are the ones that are developing team-based leadership. . . . Ministry teams that covenant to be in community with one another and have a central purpose are a powerful unit of ministry. Their power comes not from themselves but from the Spirit, who

acts to create their community, gives them a sharp vision for ministry, and binds them one to another.

Claudis, 1999, pp. 1, 11

By covenanting to be in a relationship of God's love and to agree on purpose, plans, and means to achieve such, they (leadership teams) create a standard for identifying behaviors that tend to work against the image of spiritual community and provide a setting that allows for holding each other accountable in love. As they minister together as spiritual communities, the teams (whether pastoral or lay) carry out the vision of divine purpose and intent, not only in what they are doing but in what they are becoming together. There is a significance and a clarity about what each team member's role is in the accomplishment of their objective. It's not just what they do but how they do it. Working collaboratively, instead of competitively, they recognize and call upon the unique gifts of their team members. Individual weaknesses are disabled by pooled strengths.

This culture of trust enables them to empower others to become what God calls them to be, causing the mission of the church to be widely shared. Claudis identifies them as ministering teams being shaped more and more by the work of the Spirit in their midst into the image of God (Claudis, 1999). His book *Leading the Team-Based Church* is a clarion call to practice the leadership ways spelled out in the perichoresis (choreographic equality of support and contribution) of the Godhead as revealed in Scripture.

An excellent work treating committees in a similar vein of developing spiritual community in becoming the people of God before doing the work of God is Charles Olsen's *Transforming Church Boards*.

Evaluating by God's Standards

Servant power serves in leading members in loving the unlovable. It washes the feet of all, offering acceptance even to the "traitor" in the midst. Relational power is not content to accomplish the task at the expense of broken and ignored individuals. The leader's service is influenced by the cries of group members to be loved. Relational power faces issues of conflict, underground prejudice, ostracism, distancing, and pseudocare. Feelings of estrangement do not generate Christlikeness.

The great ones are those who serve. And that kind of leadership is nurtured only as a person is open to a transforming relationship with Christ who is the Servant Leader.

What Kind of Designated Leaders Are Necessary?

While leadership behaviors may be expressed by anyone in the group, some person or persons must be designated as regularly responsible for certain tasks and actions. The types of designated leaders increase with the size of the small group ministry. Following are listed varieties of these leader roles.

Facilitating Ministers

- Plan and guide group meetings.
- Work best within a predetermined structure in which format and materials have been designed for them.
- Serve as process facilitators who plan and lead the discussion, host facilitators who care for logistical and relational details; special events coordinators who initiate outside events; mission coordinators who oversee outside group projects. Other designated roles arise as needed. In larger groups more than one person may fulfill one of these roles.
- Require some form of minimal accountability and equipping.

Group Coordinators or Coaches

- Work with more than one group.
- Provide pastoral care and practical help for group facilitators such as information, problem-solving, and encouragement.
- Facilitate communication.
- Need extensive training and experience in people relations and group skills.

Strategists and Equippers

- Design a church group ministry structure.
- Recruit, train, and channel group facilitators.
- Promote the ministry of small groups.
- Supervise and train coordinators.
- Integrate small group ministry with other church structures.

Job descriptions for two types of facilitators, coaches, and strategists are included on the next page.

Process Leaders

1. Structure the time frame of the meeting, choosing what to include.
2. Keep things moving, deciding when to move on to the next event.
3. Prepare the content of the group time and help it happen by stimulating discussion, introducing new thoughts and questions, and closing the study with satisfactory conclusion.
4. Maintain good group process, protecting the sensitive, pulling in the reticent, controlling the overtalker, and so on.
5. Work with the host leaders in designing the direction and policies of their group.

Host Leaders

1. Arrange the place of meeting and oversee preparation.
2. Cultivate a feeling of warmth among members, caring for their needs.
3. Help social events happen among members.
4. Promote group attendance and make members aware of where and when.
5. Generate care among members when special needs arise such as illness, death, and celebration.
6. Support enthusiastically the study time by encouraging group response.
7. Share with process leaders in designing the direction and policies of their group.

In recruiting group leaders it is important to seek out spiritually mature people who maintain a relationship with God and recognize their part in the Spirit's development of community.

Generally, it works most effectively to allow couples or individuals to select the person or persons who will be a part of their leadership team.

Coaching Leaders

1. Be active as a group leader, member of a group, or regularly visit the groups under your care.
2. Serve as counselor, resource individual, and troubleshooter for your group leaders.
3. Make regular contact with group leaders or members under your charge to assess the health of the group, to minister to them, and to encourage accountability. Occasionally gather leaders in your group division together to encourage them, and to share face-to-face, ascertaining group health.

4. Work with strategist as counselor and adviser to prayerfully evaluate the ministry, to promote the continued development of groups, to set goals for this ministry, to make needed decisions and to establish needed policies, and to aid in recruiting and training of group leaders.
5. Be present and participate in group training events and encourage your leaders to be involved.
6. Once a year, after evaluation, contact present group leaders regarding their commitment to continued ministry and recruit needed new leaders.
7. A coach's commitment to service should be for at least one year, that term going through August to ensure carryover in setting up new groups for the fall.

STRATEGISTS

May be laity or member of pastoral staff.

Responsibilities

1. Promote the building of Christian community within the church structure, coordinating all elements of the program.
2. Spearhead the recruitment and training of leadership.
3. Schedule and monitor small group meetings and training times in the total church calendar.
4. Assess and evaluate the overall small group ministry effectiveness, proposing changes.

Requirements

1. A person with vision, capable of grasping the overall direction and setting goals for growth.
2. Able to design budget, schedule, and maintain accountability from groups.
3. Be familiar with small group process and able to teach such to personnel involved.
4. Skilled in dealing with and motivating people.
5. Be a person who makes his or her relationship to Christ their top priority.

A team of facilitators has the advantage of reflecting community in leadership, sharing responsibilities along strength lines, encouraging the use and valuation of many gifts, giving feedback and insight along with support, and offering variety in styles to a group.

How Can Leaders be Equipped for Ministry?

The following formats provide varied means of enabling people to understand and learn skills in group process.

1. *Emphasis on increasing personal spiritual maturity* is the best way to be equipped to work with small groups.
2. *Training Events* such as a workshop or lab experience, characterized by a presentation followed by opportunity to experience or express what has been learned by trying out the technique or principle taught is another learning format. This learning is affected by the expertise and experience the participants bring to the event, those with more experience will naturally pick up more.
3. *The Conference or Retreat Experience* lasts longer than the above event and usually occurs no more than once a year. It may last a full day or a weekend, may be at home or require participants to travel to a conference center. It has the advantage of concentrated time to develop an idea or skill more fully in the context of relationship building. This type of equipping is often inspirational and motivational and offers opportunity to experience briefly the living out of some changed attitude or behavior. It also can provide a variety of emphases with seminars on several topics from which participants can choose.
4. *A Course* may last over a period of time and require a regular commitment from participants. While it is easy to load a course with information, it is important that participants experience what is being taught as much as possible. The methods of instruction are most effective when they are those that the participants can reproduce in their groups. The course is most effective when the setting replicates the setting in which the leaders will function. When participants can take what is learned and try it out in their own groups between class gatherings, this becomes an effective means of relating new truth to actual situations. Adding this course to group time already committed is a drawback among time-conscious adults.
5. *In-Service Learning* is one of the most effective means of equipping because it deals with live situations in a relational setting. In this model leaders are grown within functioning groups, the discipler being the actual group leader. Equipping comes in planning and evaluating with the leader who walks apprentices through the process of assessing needs and actions and provides explanation for behaviors and questions. The apprentice often participates in

modified leadership functions thus gaining insight under supervision. The strength of this model depends much on the ability of the supervising leader to recognize and teach at teachable moments and to know how to assess and challenge a learner's growth. It has the advantage of one-on-one personalized training within relational and actual experience.

6. *Existing Groups and Committees* can become learning sites when their regular gatherings include some equipping in group leadership skills. This information and experience is usually brief because it is incorporated within another structure. Because there is no overt commitment or perhaps even interest on the part of members to serve as group leaders, the effectiveness of learning is highly varied.

7. *The Leadership Group* model involves a person with group skills equipping others who want to learn such by modeling good group ministry skills and sharing insight into group situations they experience together. This modeling must be done for ten to twelve weeks. After a positive group experience there follows a period of group members sharing leadership of their group and sharpening one another for another eight to ten weeks. The final phase provides a system of support as the participants are released to facilitate their own groups. When the members have experienced a trial group, they are usually able to replicate a similar group experience for others. This model provides the most in-depth, intensive involvement for leadership training. It also requires the availability of a person who can lead such a training group. Because the members of a leadership group have spent more time together and have invested more heavily in their commitment, it is likely that the transformation of group behavior that has occurred in them will last and be reflected in the groups they lead. Facilitators learn by being good group members first.

Changing Leadership Roles

Initiation

A leader's role changes as the group matures. At the beginning of a group, leaders provide a sense of safety and warmth. Their confidence and awareness of where the group is headed breed confidence in members. Someone needs to be in control of the situation, having planned and now executing that plan. By calling people by name and by eliciting a proper degree of sharing, leaders develop caring and set norms of communication. More than any other time in the group this initial period, where members vacillate between anticipation and anxiety, calls for a more directive, authoritative stance to provide boundaries and keep the group moving. The leader serves as a protective fence and nurturing energizer.

Chaos and Adjustment

During that period when the leader seems to come under question as members define their positions and test others, the leader must be flexible and not take these skirmishes personally. The expression of servanthood at this time comes in the form of encouragement and understanding for those who struggle. Staying authoritarian here can provoke increased resistance. People need to be heard and their feelings acknowledged. However, the leader's stance is never to be perceived as abdication or unsure. Needed is a solid strength that can allow members to work through issues without feeling threatened and can encourage honest examination and the commitment needed to work through to a positive resolution. A vital role is to identify issues of concern among members and to look for ways to blend diverse opinions. The leader becomes the glue the group needs to stay together to work through concerns.

Productivity

When the group enjoys productivity and the freedom of acceptance and risk, the leader's role becomes one of switchboard. Service comes from releasing members to carry out their roles in the group, challenging some to take new risks, supporting their efforts, and helping the group receive feedback and evaluation in terms of goals set. During times of production and enjoyment, the leader serves as wise counselor.

Differentiation

In the midst of differentiation where members initiate challenges and changes in terms of themselves or the group as a whole, the leader provides both a steadiness and an openness to explore. As the turbulence of transition is experienced the leader's service is reassuring the anxious while sensitively encouraging an investigation of newness with those impatient for action. The leader's openness to change will be mirrored in the group.

Closure

At termination, leaders are extremely important in their role of "celebrating finisher." By cultivating positive review and reflection, leaders develop members' attitudes toward future groups. They bring a sense of closure and appreciation. Leaders recognize the sadness and distancing that take place when a group dissolves. They also become key in preserving the steps taken and growth achieved within the group and within individual members. When members begin to pull away in preparation for dissolution, the leader needs to continue strong in confidence and warmth as exhibited when the group was in initial formation.

With the exception of initiation and termination the leader roles described above will probably recycle several times within a group's life. Service to Christ is expressed by enabling each member at every stage to be all that he or she can be as fulfilling his or her contributions to the body of Christ. When a person by inexperience or inability lacks something necessary to the fulfillment of wholeness possible at that stage, the leader devotes his or her time and energy to build up the person and the group. This may be in the form of direction, support, confrontation, challenge, or comfort. It may involve doing for, coming alongside, or releasing and stepping back. Servanthood comes in doing what is best for the other as a leader in relationship. "Even the Son of Man did not come to be served, but to serve" (Mark 10:45).

"To be a leader is to enjoy the special privileges of complexity, of ambiguity, of diversity. But to be a leader means, especially, having the opportunity to make a meaningful difference in the lives of those who permit leaders to lead" (De Pree, 1989, pp. 18–19).

In a Different Voice

Do men become better leaders than women? Many judge male and female leaders to be equally effective. In mixed-sex groups leaders are men more often than women. This appears to be the case even though women appear to be equally as capable as men when it comes to serving as leaders. The major issue seems to be perception: Men are perceived to be more successful in leadership. (This perception may be due in part to the preponderance of men in authority positions in our society.) Masculine attributes that are readily associated with leadership are verbal initiation, dominance, confidence in their ideas, aggressiveness, and independence (Pearson et al., 1985).

Instrumental skills that lead to the accomplishing of a task are often valued over socioemotional skills that create relational harmony in a group. Women are more frequently associated with the expressive acts that build relationships than with accomplishing direction and developing plans. (For female small group leaders, the major hurdle may be the negative attitude that perceives them to be less desirable as leaders. As our culture changes, small group studies may reveal reversals in this perspective.) Already some studies are showing males using the more socially oriented styles (Winter & Green, 1987).

Women are more likely to choose a collaborative, interactive style of leadership while men lean toward the command and control leadership style. The situation largely determines the kind of style that will be most effective. "Interactive style is particularly effective in flexible nonhierarchical organizations of the kind that perform best in a climate of rapid change" (Rosener, 1995, p. 11). "Women encourage participation, share power and information, enhance other people's self-worth, and get others excited about their work" (Rosener, 1990, p. 120). Women seem to naturally share resources and demonstrate more cooperative behaviors than men (Pearson et al., 1985).

Consistently, research studies demonstrate that while both are effective, women, more than men, tend to help others, employing more caring, personal styles (Eagly & Johnson, 1990; O'Leary, 1988; Lunneborg, 1990, as cited in Wood, 2001). Likewise in relationship building both genders have an equal number of relationships with colleagues, but women tend toward building peer relationships for emotional support while men build the same for the furnishing of information (Wood, 2001).

A balanced approach to small group work appears advantageous. Both instrumental and socioemotional skills are needed in a group. Task achievement and good group relations are interdependent. Consulting others and seeking agreement has advantages in building community, but not being afraid of conflict is also a strength in groups. Tannen notes, "Many women could learn from men to accept some conflict and difference without seeing it as a threat to intimacy, and many men could learn from women to accept interdependence without seeing it as a threat to their freedom" (Tannen, 1990, p. 294).

Think of a time you have been under the small group leadership of a male. What were the satisfying elements? Under the small group leadership of a woman. What were fulfilling aspects? Do you associate any of these satisfying factors with gender-related leadership style as mentioned above?

Through Others' Eyes

Two cultural dimensions that affect leadership norms in other cultures are identification of masculine versus feminine cultures and high versus low power-distance cultures.

Masculine cultures require people to maintain rigid gender roles, usually women assuming caring and service-directed roles while men assume the more assertive and dominant roles. Feminine cultures permit both women and men to take varied roles, emphasizing quality of life, care for others, and relationships.

The term "power distance" refers to the unequal distribution of power in organizations and institutions. High power-distance people demonstrate respect for authority, assigning rank and status to them and submitting obediently to their rule. Low power-distance societies minimize inequalities, recognizing authority but not hesitating to question, redefine, or challenge such authority should the occasion warrant it (Verderber & Verderber, 2001). Such cultural perspective explains why some people stand in awe of a leader, expecting that person to tell them what to do and what to believe. That kind of leader can set the agenda, control the group, determine the outcomes, and is expected to be responsible for the group. Members feel they do not have the right to participate, question, change, or initiate.

A very helpful illustration of this power-distance factor at work in cultural groups is found in a work by Eric Law, which he aptly named *The Wolf Shall Dwell with the Lamb*. He writes, "The definition of a leader is not the same in different cultures because how a person is expected to manage a group is dependent on the group members' perceptions of their own power." Leading a group that sees itself as powerless and defers to you for all decision-making is quite different from leading a group that sees itself as equal to you (Law, 1993, p. 30).

An apt leader image in a Caucasian low power-distance group is a traffic cop who keeps all the self-moving autonomous people from colliding with one another. In a group where members have a fragile sense of their power as individuals, unless someone takes on the role of authority, nothing will be accomplished. The image here is of an octopus with tentacles touching varied parts of the group. The octopus leader has a network of trustworthy connections who communicate what the group wants, who wants to be involved, and who is gifted to accomplish the tasks. The leader's information is gathered before the meeting. This allows the leader to invite individuals directly to participate knowing that no one will volunteer (Law, 1993).

In a mixed group, Caucasians, by behaving naturally in their assertiveness and aggressiveness, are viewed as superior by people of color and thus are given power over them. Assuming that such people have considerable power as exhibited by their actions, people of high-context cultures let them talk and do not challenge. The continual interchange and lack of direct invitation to them confirms this assumption. Likewise they are unaware of being perceived by Caucasians as equals in the group. This, Law claims, "is like putting wolves and lambs together in one room." He suggests a process called "Mutual Invitation." The leader shares first, not as expert but as initiator, and then invites another (not directly beside him or her) to share. That one is privileged to invite another to share. Each has the option to pass, while still being given opportunity to invite another to share. This process decentralizes power. For Caucasians, the waiting to be invited is a way of putting into practice the spirituality of the cross (Law, 1993, pp. 31–34, 82–84).

The theology of the cross and the theology of the empty tomb suggest the growing edge for each cultural perspective. The practice of the spirituality of the cross—a submission of power—is the challenge to people of power while the practice of the spirituality of the empty tomb—an empowering that changes perspective on who I am—must be embraced by those who find themselves in powerless positions in relationship to others (Law, 1993).

A summary of positioning of the dominant culture of the United States follows:

Individualism—highest of all countries
Uncertainty avoidance—well below average
Masculinity—well above average
Power distance—below average
        Verderber & Verderber, 2001, p. 123

What assumptions about leadership do you draw in regard to small groups in the United States from this rating? What is most likely to occur? Be difficult to enable? Become a challenge for members from other cultures?

Firestarters

The Monopolizer

The new members gathered in small groups of seven for a ten-week period, each led by a church member enabler. This ten-week group involvement was part of the requirements for their becoming members of Sanford Street Church. In preparation for the seventh session new member prospects were asked to write their testimonies, which would then be shared. The facilitator reminded participants that each was limited to fifteen minutes. This was prompted in part by the presence of one person who tended to monopolize the conversation whenever she was given opportunity to speak. Her life had been very difficult and she continually would go into detail about all that God had taught her and brought her through. Lucy (the monopolizer), Kate, and two men were scheduled to share during the seventh session. The two men spoke first and then Lucy began. Kate was to be the last to share.

The Scene: Kate's Description

"Lucy began sharing at 8:00 P.M. I knew we were in for a difficult time when I saw that she had brought six pages of typewritten notes. I remembered that at the second session we had discussed the problem of people not allowing time for others to share. We had agreed to give one another freedom to hold each other to this. However, this rule never seemed to apply to Lucy. People would make a joke about her continual talking, but no one ever came out and addressed it.

"This evening Lucy showered us with her usual display of detail. At 8:20 I checked my watch, wondering how long she had been talking. During the next twenty-five minutes I became increasingly frustrated and angry. I knew we had some things to go over even after I shared my story. I was also aware that some in the group had people waiting for them, expecting them to be finished by 8:30.

"I kept looking at the facilitator to see if she was going to take action. I could read her struggle over what to do. I watched the others fidgeting in their chairs and staring at the floor. Perhaps I should say something. I hesitated. . . ."

What would you do at this point?
(Continued)

"I tried to get my emotions under control. Then I took three deep breaths and spoke. In the most caring way I could, I began by telling Lucy that I cared about her, but that I was feeling uncomfortable with the amount of time she was taking to share her story. I told her how hard this was to say because I knew she was sharing something very important about herself. I affirmed again that she was an important member of the group but that I felt uptight because we were violating the agreed-upon time frame and I knew others were waiting. As other members gave evidence of their agreement I found myself speaking in the plural 'we.' I finished with the assertion that we would like to know her but that we just couldn't do it in one evening.

"Tracy (the facilitator) jumped in, saying that we would be glad to pray with her about her situation after the group. Lucy became very quiet and appeared to be hurt. I shared my testimony quickly and everyone made a mad dash for the door. The only person staying with Lucy was Tracy. She tried to listen and to pray with Lucy, but Lucy kept insisting that people really don't want to know about another person's life. She left angry."

The Analysis

What are the central issues found in this scenario? Are they different from each person's perspective?

- Should we place limits on the way we care about people?
- Should Christians speak up for time commitment when caring for another is at stake?
- Do we allow others to violate known boundaries when addressing them may cause hurt and misunderstanding?
- How do we enable others to take responsibility for themselves?
- Does speaking up mean that I don't love or accept?
- Can I love and speak confrontingly at the same time?
- Where does loving the group come in?
- How would you respond if you were Tracy?

Evaluation and Postscript by Kate

"I feel the facilitator should have spoken up before I did. Because she didn't I did and felt like hero and heel. The group agenda should have been secondary to what was happening. Time was a major factor. I am convinced that Lucy did not believe she was cared for because no one else spoke up, because the facilitator didn't seem to become her advocate, and because we all left right after the group. I can understand how she would feel.

"The next week the issue was addressed briefly before getting back to the agenda. From that point on we seemed to have sacrificed being real with one another and just endured the last few sessions. Lucy shared only briefly and then in a curt manner. Again this tension was not addressed. I tried to talk to Lucy privately but found she treated the issue as past. She had made up her mind that people don't care. At this point there was nothing left to do. We went on to become members. To this day I try to avoid having to say anything to the members of that group. That one incident seemed to have soured our relationship."

Solution

- How would you respond at this point?
- What needs to happen?
- Who is responsible for helping this happen?
- How could this be done?
- What first steps should be taken?

12

TRANSFORMING THE CHURCH
The Ministry of Small Groups

There is nothing so powerful as an idea whose time has come.

Victor Hugo

Faxes are the rage today. A facsimile is not the real thing. It is a copy. The entrepreneurial spirit of our age causes us to fabricate designer products (from clothing to artistic masterpieces) so people can look like they possess the real thing without having to pay the price. Eugene Peterson warns against turning "community into a commodity." He asks a probing question:

> Community as commodity is one of the more spectacular growth industries in North American religion today. How does it happen that what originates as a creation of the Holy Spirit so frequently (and so lucratively!) gets packaged as a technique or a product? . . . Americans are good at forming clubs and gathering crowds. But clubs and crowds, even when—especially when—they are religious clubs and crowds, are not communities. The formation of community is the intricate, patient, painful work of the Holy Spirit. We cannot buy or make community; we can only offer ourselves to become community.

> Peterson in Crabb, 1999, p. viii

227

In the race to survive, many churches have rushed to set up small group programs that they hoped would bring renewal or resurrection to the congregation. Because these generic groups were often quickly added to the church's marketable menu without an awareness of what true community is and therefore not focused on the role of the Spirit, they became facsimiles that sought to use groups for ulterior motives. Members felt disillusioned and found that the people in their groups were as self-focused as they were and the techniques that promised so much were ineffective in satisfying their need. Leaders, who didn't get the accolades expected, burned out and the groups died as quickly as they had arisen. Community is not one more self-help technique. Spiritual togetherness cannot be programmed nor developed by curriculum alone. It is not simply one more piece in the ecclesiastical pie.

For any approach to remain in long-term practice it must be rooted in and consistent with Christian theology and identity. This text is not promoting some new innovative tool as the real thing. The only way to implement the insights of this book within the church is to frame each aspect of a group with God's desired priority: "How will this enable God's people to know God and be open to community among the people of God?"

Community must be integral to our experience of ministry. It is not achieved by learning self-help skills or by becoming better people. It is a work of God. Our role is to remain open to what God is calling us to be as we commit ourselves to the practice of the Word of God through disciplines that embrace our convictions.

Disciplines Needing to Be Embraced

Discipline: Committing Ourselves to the Centrality of God in Our Lives

Who is God in our midst and what does he want? This discipline keeps us listening to him. The focus is not on "my needs" or "our agenda" but on "what does God desire and declare." This discipline recognizes that God put us together as his body and uses that togetherness to express and display what his character is like. The people who seek first the reign of God and his righteousness (Matt. 6:33) find lesser concerns cared for. As *The Message* states, "Steep your life in God-reality, God-initiative, God-provisions." This is an intentionality that keeps us open to the One who authors community.

How does your life currently proclaim this centrality?

Discipline: Proclaiming God's Vision for Community

This is a second discipline—to commit ourselves to proclaiming that joining together in spiritual community is what God wants and what he intends to bring about among his people. Community is not optional. We will not mature into the fullness God intends without it. The corporate connection enhances every doctrine, every possibility, every goal for growth. People must come to see that individual accomplishment, solo recognition, achievement of our best interests are not what God emphasizes. Looking out for others and doing what enables their growth and fosters our corporate growing together puts us in a place where God can exhibit the fulfillment of his Word in our midst.

What is one way you are currently proclaiming this "vision"?

Discipline: Becoming Spiritual Friends to One Another

Spiritual friends help others get godly perspectives on themselves and circumstances. Developing this intentional discipline saves us from having to "fix" another who is different or in need. We don't have to play God and rescue a situation. We simply fulfill our role as "friend of the bridegroom" (as John the Baptist did) by pointing others to him. He therefore increases while we remain a reflector of the One who is the source of light. This is the highest calling we can have as members of his body.

Think of a situation in your group. What posture would a spiritual friend take to fulfill that calling in your life? How can you become a spiritual friend to the group?

Discipline: Maintaining a Relationship with Him as Priority

This relationship affects all others. It forms our identity, our contentment to allow him to work in another's life, our response to circumstances that occur, our confidence in his ability to resolve any challenge. It is this connection that gives us a love for his church, which provides a patience for the long haul and a pattern for how we are to be and act among people. Any unresolved issue, hurt or mistreatment, confusion over what to do, gratitude for growth shown, joy over accomplishment recognized—all are marked or reframed by this relationship. Like a person in love sees everything differently, so this increasing grasp of who he is affects our response to everything else.

Try looking at each person or circumstance in your group through the eyes of Christ and see what questions and observations transform you as God responds.

Discipline: Letting God Live Community through You

Intentionally putting yourself in a place where you are together with other believers in a committed relationship is a discipline that allows you to live out the reality of his ways and remain open to the transforming work of the Spirit. Being with others will bring out areas needing transformation in us and give us opportunity to live the truth that God reveals to us. Even as you read this you are aware of cutting edge challenges that come to you from being in a group. This openness to living "on the firing line" keeps us aware of our continual dependence on God and provides a setting where his Spirit and his body remind us of what he wants built into our lives.

Consider the group you are currently in. What opportunities does it give you to discover what God is building into your life right now?

Structuring a Small Group Ministry

In a church where many groups exist or are envisioned, there needs to be an overall plan or organizing design. As such, this plan affects how groups fit in with the rest of the adult ministries, how groups carry out the purpose of the church, and it establishes what guidelines help in the origination of new groups.

McBride refers to three types of churches that tend to determine and be influenced by a small group ministry. These three are the Traditional Church, the Transitional Church, and the Transformational Church.

- The Traditional Church offers groups as "one programmatic option; groups must compete for resources and participants; groups are not viewed as essential to the nature or functioning of a local church; group membership is purely optional; none to moderate pastoral support for groups" is available.
- The Transitional Church sees groups as "an integral part of the church; group membership is highly encouraged, if not expected; groups are viewed as being essential to the nature and functioning of the church; strong pastoral support for groups" is evident.
- The Transformational Church causes church identity to be "focused in groups or house churches; group membership is equated with

church membership; groups are the nature of and how the church functions; pastoral leadership focused on group facilitation" (McBride, 1995, p. 46).

Choices to Be Made

In organizing a ministry of small groups there are many alternatives and variations from which choices must be made. Some of those are listed below.

Role of the Staff

The choice here is between Central Control, which provides total supervision and centralized decision-making, and Central Motivation, which stimulates toward community-building in preaching and teaching while encouraging grassroots ownership of the ministry. In the first there is often professional staff to lead the ministry and decisions are passed through official church structures. The second model gives the power to the congregation to form groups, to determine their structure, and to maintain this ministry while professional staff serve as support.

CENTRAL CONTROL

- Designs goals and groups after assessing needs
- Recruits leadership
- Sets up specific number and kinds of groups
- Assigns or enables group members to enter groups
- Groups by contract/age level usually
- Aware of curriculum—often supplied, often uniform, often sequential/thematic
- Guides and supports group leadership and members
- Organizes groups around church year

CENTRAL MOTIVATION

- Pastor models/calls people to construct and become involved in community
- Allows people to design groups according to their motivation/ interests
- Provides minimal enablement

- May group by contract (task/purpose oriented) or by time available (emphasis on being in group for community sake)
- Minimally aware or unaware of specific curriculum used
- Curriculum usually highly varied
- Staff aware of purposes—often unaware of groups' number, etc.
- Groups function primarily on their own
- Groups are organized spontaneously

Membership Formation

Group members may be assigned to groups according to geographical location or as part of a division of the total congregation into cells. This is often the responsibility of the Central Control person or group.

When desirous of keeping members together in manageable locations so they can be attended to by an elder, deacon, or other, some churches assign people to groups according to where they live. Because location is the common denominator, interest and commitment may be less in these groups with the level of sharing often not as intimate as when the members can select the people with whom to associate. Advantages include saving travel time, getting to know your neighbors, and identification with the area. Or members may randomly place themselves in available groups or form new groups of their choice, growing out of the motivation provided by the professional staff.

Group Structure: Sequence or Random

The Predetermined Menu organizes groups around developmentally sequenced goals to provide balance and growth. This incremental strategy is usually designed to be experienced in a definite order with the goal in mind of experiencing growth or transformation by moving through the stages of groups. Some choose to include certain tracks or segments of predetermined group emphases within their small group ministry offerings (e.g., from basic to advanced, from exposure to understanding to implementation).

The A La Carte model offers a plethora of offerings from which any member may select according to interest or need.

Elements Included in Groups

When structuring individual groups you can require every group to contain the same elements to ensure balance. An example of generic elements is the inclusion of Loving, Learning, Doing, Deciding. Some groups follow the exact same patterns; others allow for each group to determine its own expression (George, 1991). Even greater freedom exists in groups that determine which elements and structures best accomplish their purposes and fit their content.

Groups Attached or on Their Own

Forming groups under the umbrellas of established ministries such as Sunday school classes or missionary association is a good way to ease into a small group ministry structure. Because these parent ministries are already ongoing and have credibility, they have great power to motivate their participants to become a part of the small group structure. However, this model limits acquaintance to those already known (though probably not in-depth) to the parameters of the group whether age, gender, marital status, etc., and often results in cloning rather than variety. The Groups Across or Apart from Existing Structures Model brings together people who often do not associate with or know each other. This may mean they take longer to bond. On the other hand, because they are formed on mutual interest and because the participants have deliberately chosen to associate, they may blend more quickly and with higher enthusiasm over involvement.

Varieties of Purpose

The categories of purpose for which small groups may be designed are numerous. Several major agendas are noted below with representative types of groups that carry out the primary goal.

Groups for Belonging	Groups for Knowing	Groups for Healing
Outreach	New Believer	Support
New Member	Study	Recovery Awareness
House Church	Discipleship	Self-help Recovery
		Group Counseling
Groups for Serving	Groups for Enriching	
Leadership Training	Covenant	
Mission/Ministry	Affinity	
Task/Project	Worship	
Advocacy		

Let's move several types of groups into the spotlight for a closer look: Support and Recovery; Intergenerational; House Churches; Spiritual Direction Groups; Alpha Groups.

Support and Recovery Groups

Support groups are probably one of the most popular types in the United States today as people seek an understanding, caring community with which to share the variety of circumstances they experience in common. Defining a Christian support group Morris writes, "we are a fellowship of people who come together to share our common experience, strength, and hope with one another so that we can identify in our struggles, learn about life and relationships, and grow in the ability to trust God and become all that He created us to be" (Morris, 1993, p. 70). Emphasis on God's truth as authority and the Spirit of Christ as enabler in responding to that truth separate Christian from secular support groups.

Recovery groups, while not therapy groups, incorporate information about and mutual help in finding healing in regard to an issue that is a problem in members' lives. Many lean toward self-help, mutual accountability but change depends on a relationship with One who is greater and able to do what the person cannot do for self. Other members cannot become that Higher Power but can only point the way to him. The church must become a safe place for this process of finding acceptance, admitting need, discovering God's strength and the corporate support of his people in a spirit of hope. When this happens people are led from brokenness to the reality of God with redemption, reconciliation, and wholeness.

The wide variety of subjects targeted by these groups adds to their popularity. These subjects include alcoholism, codependent relationships, addictions, abuse, all of which fall under the heading of recovery groups. Support groups include engaged couples, blended families, aging parents, single parents, etc.

Intergenerational Groups

Groups that include the family may be one of the most promising arenas of outreach and growth in the future of small group ministry. God designed the family to exist as community and the impact of modern day living has all but wiped out that experience. Intergenerational groups can model what it means to nurture faith within the family. It also allows people from different generations to share their experiences and perspectives, a feat that enhances understanding and promotes transformation in the people connecting.

What it takes to work across age lines, which create broad diversity in purpose, process, and valuations, can be a challenge but this reconciliation and receiving of other generations is essential and dear to the heart of God. The one who was to precede that arrival of the Messiah was charged with turning "the hearts of the fathers to their children, and the hearts of the children to their fathers" (Mal. 4:6).

House Churches

House churches are small cell groups that meet in homes to worship, fellowship together in a meal, and carry out active ministry as highly involved, committed people. Some are attracted to this unit because it allows them to be personally involved (an involvement often disenchanted with an impersonal institution). For others it avoids the overly heavy organizational load or gives opportunity to know belonging and to have a sense of family. The importance of each person in these basic communities causes each to feel like he or she is known, can make significant impact, and is needed. The requirements of commitment are high with each person (including children) as they're expected to contribute to the health of the group. Members celebrate each other's victories, pour out care in times of need, and are there for one another's growth in Christ. In countries where oppression has forced the church to go underground, the essential community of house groups has kept the church alive and allowed it to grow. Note: for further information see Banks and Banks, *The Church Comes Home* (1998).

Spiritual Direction Groups

Spiritual Direction Groups offer opportunity for people to meet others who want to be intentional about their spiritual life and choose to do that through contemplation. Some people, going through difficult seasons of life, need one-on-one direction. Group direction limits the amount of time focused on each person. A group facilitator "helps the group maintain an open, prayerful environment and invites the group to prayerful attentiveness toward God and away from offering advice" (Bakke, 2000, p. 143). Sometimes the group serves as director with each member taking turn as directee.

Three or four people are maximum for this type of group as they ask questions such as, "How does God appear to be a part of this circumstance?" Or, "What might be God's perspective on this issue?" This is accompanied by silent prayer and listening to the Spirit. Three conditions are noted as essential to this type of group: People must agree to 1) maintain an honest relationship with God; 2) wholeheartedly participate in the group by prayerfully listening and responding; 3) open their spiritual journeys for the consideration of others (Dougherty, 1995).

Alpha Groups

Taking its name from a course designed to help new Christians under-stand their faith, this popular group has become an effective evangelistic outreach for the local church. Alpha is friendship based, consists of talks on the Christian faith, eating together, and experiencing open discussion of that faith and questions about it in small groups. Pastoral care is one-to-one so each person is loved into knowing Christ and then nurtured in spiritual maturity through that care. It is the exercise of believers practicing community in a natural way as designed by God for his church. As such it reflects Christ and attracts people to him. For further information see Gumbel, *Telling Others.*

Criteria for Making Choices in the Areas Above

The following questions can serve to point out factors that could lead to selection of one model as priority over another.

1. What convictions, experience, vision, and goals do I have?
2. What is our church's philosophy of ministry? What priorities are emphasized? Not seen as priority?
3. What is the role of the laity in our church? What role is expected of the clergy?
4. Where is the church in the life cycle of small group ministry?
5. What are people ready for? Cautious beginnings? Risk to change? Conserving the current norms? How does timing of other major emphases or events affect small group plans? (Looking for a senior pastor? Entering a building program? Responding to a financial crisis?)
6. Are many people at the same stage of growth? Many new believers? Primarily young couples? Is the church in a new area so that outreach is prime? The presence of many homogeneous units can suggest a small group emphasis focused on that area as "ripe" for community building. What is the history of groups in our congregation? Anything to avoid? To embrace and enlist?
7. What are congregational needs at this time? Do we require open groups so people can get acquainted with us as a church? Or an interchurch focus to build security and depth? Or an equipping

focus to send members out to live their faith in the marketplace? Or all three in balance?

8. What are the leadership's stated goals? Congregational stated goals? A life of discipleship? Building in new people?

9. What is the role of groups in conjunction with other agencies in the church? A substitute for adult classes? An extension of congregational worship?

10. What leaders of groups are available? What equipping have they had? Do we have leadership available for different types of groups?

11. What kind of support and development system is available for groups and leaders? From the clergy? From the congregation? From the boards and committees? Any support from existing agencies in the church?

12. What has God clearly called us to be and do? What is he motivating in our midst at this time? What is it we simply must do to keep faith with what has been revealed to us?

Steps to Take in Implementing a Ministry of Small Groups

Prepare Personnel and Purchase Resources

After securing approval and sharing your strategy with key people, preach and teach the priority of community to the congregation at large. As people respond to this vision, begin recruiting and training for leadership. It may be that you will simply recruit members for your model group where they will experience community and you will share the leadership process in a life setting of group experiences. If you expect others to lead groups, offer informational and experiential sessions to give them security and a sense of purpose and competence. Teach team concepts and actions within existing boards and committees. Prepare any other needed leaders such as coordinators. All of this preparation is best accomplished with the involvement and guidance of the ministry team, which early on caught the spirit of community and bought into the vision.

When using a printed curriculum, purchase copies far enough ahead to allow leaders time to familiarize themselves with the material. If people are new to the curriculum or to leadership, offer an informational seminar on how to use the material to the greatest advantage. Give an overview of the series and suggest ways to personalize the curriculum to your church's needs. If you allow leaders to choose their own curriculum, make available several series from which to choose. Having material available early gives a feeling of security especially to those who like to plan ahead. There are numerous types of curriculum on the market for all kinds of groups. As strategist you are better able to review and select possible curriculum series. Do not expect lay leaders untrained in knowing what to look for to do this task.

Good PR: Publicize, Recognize

Community as expressed in small group ministry must be kept before the congregation not only so they realize what is available but also to highlight the priority of community in the congregation. Pulpit interviews, brochures describing the ministry, and newsletters describing who is involved and what is happening make this relational emphasis visible. Of course the best publicity is the enthusiastic group participants who tell others of the benefits.

Honor those in the church family who serve as ministers in this vital area. The church in general is often known for using people and then forgetting them. Those who invest their lives and gifts need to be received as those serving God in this capacity. Gratitude is a quality of the Christian that God frequently extols. How have churches done this? Commission group personnel at some period in the church year. Regularly mention them in prayer in public. Publish the names of those who are giving themselves to this ministry. Reward faithfulness with certificates and a dinner for those who lead. Care for their needs and enable them to grow through regularly planned support and training events.

Recycle, Reevaluate, Readjust the Plan with the Ministry Team

Regular evaluations of the ministry plan give opportunity for reflecting on what is taking place within the small group ministry, for adjusting in areas where the fit isn't quite right, and for adding new dimensions. This team becomes invaluable in developing operational policies, setting new goals, and helping to implement the plan through recruiting new leadership, caring for present leadership, sharing in the training of leadership, and publicizing community. They grow because you are investing community insights in them and giving them responsibility for the ministry. These people are the energizers and implementers. They also become the strategists and equippers. Eventually they will be able to carry the primary responsibility for the small group ministry, enabling you to become consultant and to move into new and creative forms of community development.

> We are not human beings having a spiritual experience. We are spiritual beings having a human experience.
>
> Teilhard de Chardin

Continually Restate Priorities

Put emphasis on people not programs. Focus on God more than techniques. Be passionate about community not just small groups. Evaluate by transformation into likeness not just numbers. Small groups do not transform the church—God does and he may choose to do it through communities that make him a priority and open themselves to his Spirit and to each other. "The main social structure through which God's redeeming work is effected in the world is the Christian community. . . . Our responsibility to the world is always first to be the church: to embody what God wants to say to the whole world, to live and demonstrate what salvation means" (Gish, 1979, p. 293).

Community is God's gift. It gives us another opportunity to reflect his character and to fulfill his desires. In so doing, we give God pleasure.

Firestarters

The Question Is . . . Focus: Designing a Small Group Ministry

Paul/Paula (Pastor P), C.E. Board representative Edna/Ed, and Group Leader Lynn settled into the chairs in Pastor P's office. They had agreed to meet tonight to talk about the idea of increasing the small group emphasis at their church. In addition to the three of them they had invited Bible Study Fellowship Veteran Val who now enters the office and plops herself in the empty chair.

Val: Sorry I'm late. I was on the phone with a group leader solving a problem she's been having with people coming late.

Pastor P: Oh, you haven't missed anything. We just got started. I really appreciate your carving out time for this think tank session. I know all of you are interested in this subject of groups and I thought it would be good for us to do some spadework on that issue. It's no secret that I've been giving this idea a lot of thought because I think we need something to give our church more connectedness. We need something to hang on to the people who've been attending since we opened the new sanctuary.

C.E. Board—Ed/Edna: Well, I agree with you there, pastor. Since I represent the adults on the board, I'm interested in this concept because I think we need to provide a full service program for our adults just like we do for our children and youth. How 'bout you, Lynn?

Leader Lynn: Well, I was in a group in my InterVarsity days and I remember how much I grew. I'd like for our people to have that kind of experience.

Val: You talk about growth! You should see what's going on in our ladies Bible study groups. Why, my ladies wouldn't miss a meeting. I'm overseeing six groups now. You know, I think those groups are more important to them than anything else going on in the church right now—no offense meant, Pastor P.

Pastor P: I'm glad you're investing in those women, Val. I guess I'll have to concede that I wish we had that kind of commitment in our other ministries.

Ed/Edna: Well, now you've brought up something that several people in our adult classes have talked to me about. A lot of our adult class leadership is concerned that if we move ahead in this group area, we will undermine commitment to adult classes. I mean, there's bound to be a drain on leadership. We only have so many leaders to go around. And time—only so much time for church meetings. And what if people start getting what they want in a small group? What will happen to our adult classes?

Pastor P: You're right that our people don't seem to be eager to assume leadership. We do have to have enough to fill the slots on the boards and committees. Plus we don't want to sabotage our adult classes.

Ed/Edna: Yeah, how would all this fit in with the other ministries we've already got going? Sometimes people just jump ship from one ministry to get on board the latest fad.

Lynn: Oh, I don't think this is a fad. And what about people who aren't involved in our present ministries? We need to work this adult issue through. I think there ought to be some way to design it so we're not competing. Maybe some way to fit in groups with what we're already doing.

Val: And my Bible study groups have actually produced some new leaders—people who gained confidence and training in the group. They learned how to care by being cared for. I'd like to see Bible studies for the whole church.

Pastor P: Well, it wouldn't hurt, I'm sure. But actually I was thinking of assigning people to neighborhood groups so they could sort of keep track of one another. Maybe we could get an elder to be in charge. I think that would help people become more involved and there would be somebody to care for them who is already a leader. It would be a good way to control what goes on.

Ed/Edna: I still want to lobby for our adult classes. To me the best way to keep control of groups is to have 'em grow out of adult classes. It just seems natural that we could break classes down into small units and assign them a leader.

Lynn: Besides the fact that not everybody goes to an adult class, where are you going to get these leaders? And what kind of leaders do we want? Who's going to find them? And who's going to train them? Most people don't know what to do in a group.

Pastor P: And whom do they report to? How will we keep groups under control?

Val: Maybe we'll end up hiring staff for this. Isn't that what most churches do? Then that person could run training classes for leaders.

Ed/Edna: Oh, boy. Just what we need another couple of meetings every month. Isn't there another way to do it? Can't we just give them a test or something. And don't expect the adult teachers to lead a group. Their job is teaching their class.

Lynn: Maybe we'll get some new members who have had experience in groups.

Val: I think we should grow our own.

Ed/Edna: Well, what do we do—just advertise for group leaders?

Pastor P: I think we better figure out what we want first. I've jotted down some things you've said. What would we want in a group leader? And who's going to make that decision? Who's going to recruit them? Who will be accountable? Who will supervise them? And how will leaders know what to do? And who will supervise them? We need to break this down into manageable pieces.

Ed/Edna: Maybe we should be thinking of ways we can get more adults into our adult classes.

Lynn: I think we need to talk to somebody who knows more about a small group ministry. Surely these questions have been asked before.

Assign each person in a group to be one of the above characters and ask them to read their part in each group. Gather all people representing one character (all Lynns) in new groups and discuss what each one's agenda was and how each saw the ministry of groups.

What will be possible areas of conflict posed by this viewpoint? Areas of strength this person brings to the ministry of groups? If you were serving as "consultant" to this church, what issues would you want to discuss further, clarify, or reformat?

What other "expertise" would you want represented in the strategizing group? What "first step" would you take in designing this ministry of small groups?

CONCLUSION
We Are Destined for Community!

A certain credit card company, when urging the imperative for owning their card, advises, "Don't leave home without it." The implication is, "You won't survive if you don't have this item." This sentiment applies to the importance of community. In essence, as God launches us on our journey, he urges us to a like-minded attitude toward community.

Community is essential to life. "Community matters. That's about like saying oxygen matters. As our lungs require air, so our souls require what only community provides. We were designed by our Trinitarian God . . . to live in relationship. Without it, we die. It's that simple" (Crabb, 1999, in Frazee, 2001, p. 13). Community is part of our DNA. We were made to crave relational connections. They enable us to survive.

Community Is Inherent in Being Christian

Community is a major part of the "abundance" in the promised "abundant living" that comes from knowing Christ. The Christ connection draws us to one another, and our connection to one another will draw the world to him. "All roads lead to Rome" expresses the total supremacy of that location. All community begins and ends in God. The concept is his; the purpose is his; the power to actualize is his; the resulting benefits are his. Nouwen wisely advises:

In the Christian community we say to each other, "We are together, but we cannot fulfill each other . . . we help each other, but we also have to remind each other that our destiny is beyond our togetherness." . . . The basis of the Christian community is not the family tie, or social or economic equality, or shared oppression or complain, or mutual attraction . . . but the divine call. The Christian community is not the result of human efforts. God has made us into chosen people by calling us out of "Egypt" to the "New Land," out of the desert to fertile ground, out of slavery to freedom, out of our sin to salvation, out of captivity to liberation. All these words and images give expression to the fact that the initiative belongs to God and that God is the source of our new life together. By our common call to the New Jerusalem, we recognize each other on the road as brothers and sisters.

Nouwen, 1986, p. 153

Community Is Intrinsic to Our Evolving Christlikeness

What distinctively identifies the followers of Jesus is their treatment of one another. Community is distinctively Christian.

Sainthood is perfected in communion with others, never apart from it. . . . The purpose of Christian formation is not developing a better self-image, achieving self-fulfillment or finding self-affirmation; nor is it the development of individualistic qualities that make singularly outstanding saints. Rather, it is developing certain qualities that enable us to live responsibly within the community that we have been baptized into. . . . The theological virtues of faith, hope and charity make the best sense (if not the only sense) for Christians when they are lived out in the Christian community as the "peaceable kingdom."

Chan, 1998, pp. 102–3

Community Is God's Gift to His Own, Now and Forever

"In my Father's house are many rooms . . . I go to prepare a place for you." Think of it, not only will we be living in someone else's house— we will be living there together! Forever! And the consummation of our earthly community will be sharing the marriage supper of the Lamb. Until then we can celebrate the previews as we gather together with the Groom in our midst.

REFERENCES

Adler, R. B., & Towne, N. (1990). *Looking out, looking in* (6th ed.). Fort Worth, TX: Holt, Rinehart and Winston.

Adler, R., & Rodman, G. (1991). *Understanding human communication* (4th ed.). Fort Worth, TX: Holt, Rinehart and Winston.

Anderson, R. S. (1982). *On being human: Essays in anthropology.* Pasadena, CA: Fuller Seminary Press.

Anthony, M. J. (Ed.). (2001). *Introducing Christian education: Foundations for the twenty-first century.* Grand Rapids, MI: Baker Book House.

Argyris, C. (1990). Interpersonal barriers to decision making. In *People: Managing your most important asset.* Boston: Harvard Business Review.

Augsburger, D. (1986). *Pastoral counseling across cultures.* Philadelphia: Westminster Press.

Axtell, R. E. (1991). *Gestures: The do's and taboos of body language around the world.* New York: Wiley.

Baird, J., Jr., & Weinberg, S. B. (1981). *Group communication: The essence of synergy* (2nd ed.). Dubuque, IA: William C. Brown Company.

Bakke, J. A. (2000). *Holy invitations.* Grand Rapids, MI: Baker Book House.

Balswick, Jack, & Wright, Walter (1988). A complementary empowering model of ministerial leadership. *Pastoral Psychology,* 7.

Banks, R. (1988). *Paul's idea of community.* Grand Rapids, MI: Eerdmans.

Banks, R., & Banks, J. (1998). *The church comes home.* Peabody, MA: Hendrickson Publishers, Inc. [orig. pub. (1989). Australia: Albatross Books].

Barker, L. L., Wahlers, K. J., Watson, K. W., & Kibler, R. J. (1991). *Groups in process* (4th ed.). Englewood Cliffs, NJ: Prentice-Hall.

——— (2001). *Groups in process* (6th ed.). Boston: Allyn & Bacon.

Barker, S., Johnson, J., Long, J., Malone, R., & Nicholas, R. (1982). *Small group leaders' handbook.* Downers Grove, IL: InterVarsity Press.

Barna, G. (1988). Seven trends facing the church in 1988 and beyond. *Nation and International Religion Report.*

——— (1990). *The frog in the kettle.* Ventura, CA: Regal Books.

Barrett, L. (1986). *Building the house church.* Scottsdale, PA: Herald Press.

Baxter, L. A. (1982 Summer). Strategies for ending relationships: Two studies. *Western Journal of Speech Communication, 46,* 223–41.

Beaudoin, T. (1998). *Virtual faith.* San Francisco: Jossey-Bass.

Beebe, S. A., & Masterson, J. T. (1990). *Communicating in small groups: Principles and practices* (3rd ed.). Glenview, IL.: Scott/Foresman/Little, Brown Higher Education.

——— (2000). *Communicating in small groups: Principles and practices.* New York: Addison-Wesley.

Bellah, R., Madsen, R., Sullivan, W., Swidler, A., & Tipton, S. (1985). *Habits of the heart: Individualism and commitment in American life.* Berkeley, CA: University of California Press.

Bennis, W. G., & Shepard, H. A. (1956). A theory of group development. *Human Relations, 9,* 415–37. [Reprinted in G. S. Gibbard, J. J. Hartman, & R. D. Mann, (Eds.). (1974). *Analysis of groups.* San Francisco: Jossey-Bass.]

Berkowitz, L. Group standards, cohesiveness, and productivity. *Human Relations.*

Bertelson, D. (1986). *Snowflakes and snowdrifts: Individualism and sexuality in America.* Lanham, MD: University Press of America.

Bilezikian, G. (1997). *Community 101.* Grand Rapids, MI: Zondervan.

Birkey, D. (1988). *The house church.* Scottsdale, PA: Herald Press.

Bittner, J. R. (1983). *Understanding each other.* Englewood Cliffs, NJ: Prentice-Hall.

Blackburn, R., & Rosen, B. (1993). Total quality and human resource management: Lessons learned from baldridge award-winning companies. *Academy of Management Executive, 7,* 49–66.

Bloom, A. (1987). *The closing of the American mind.* New York: Simon & Schuster.

Blumberg, H. H., Hare, P. A., Kent, V., & Davies, M. F. (Eds.). (1983). *Small groups and social interaction* (Vol. 2). New York: John Wiley and Sons.

Boff, L. (1986). *Ecclesiogenesis: The base communities reinvent the church.* Maryknoll, NY: Orbis Books.

Bolton, R. (1986). Listening is more than merely hearing. In J. Stewart (Ed.), *Bridges not walls* (4th ed.). New York: Random House.

Bonhoeffer, D. (1954). *Life together.* New York: Harper & Row.

———(1963). *Sanctorum communio.* St. James Place, London: Collins.

Booth-Butterfield, M., & Jordan, F. (1989). Communication adaptation among racially homogeneous and heterogeneous groups. *Southern Communication Journal,* 4, 253–72.

Borisoff, D., & Victor, D. A. (1989). *Conflict management.* Englewood Cliffs, NJ: Prentice-Hall.

Bormann, E. G., & Bormann, N. C. (1988). *Effective small group communication* (4th ed.). Edina, MN: Burgess.

Bradford, L. P. (Ed.). (1978). *Group development* (2nd ed.). San Diego: University Associates, Inc.

Bradshaw, J. (1988a). *Bradshaw on: The family.* Deerfield Beach, FL: Health Communications, Inc.

———(1988b). *Healing the shame that binds you.* Deerfield Beach, FL: Health Communications, Inc.

Brilhart, J. K., & Galanes, G. J. (1989). *Effective group discussion* (6th ed.). Dubuque, IA: William C. Brown Company.

———(1995). *Effective group discussion* (8th ed.). Madison, WI: Brown and Benchmark.

Brilhart, J. K., Galanes, G. J., Adams, K. (2001). *Effective group discussion* (10th ed.). Boston: McGraw-Hill.

Bruce, A. B. (1971). *The training of the twelve.* Grand Rapids, MI: Kregel.

Bryce, J. (1914). *The American commonwealth* (Vol. 3. Repr. of 1888 ed.). New York: Macmillan.

Buchanan, M. (2000, January/February). We're all syncretists now. *Books and Culture,* 9.

Butterfield, H. (1979). The role of the individual in history. In C. T. McIntire (Ed.), *Herbert butterfield: Writings on Christianity and history.* New York: Oxford University Press.

Carli, L. L. (1990). Gender, language, and influence. *Journal of Personality and Social Psychology,* 59, 941–51.

Carpenter, A. (1996). *Facts about cities* (2nd ed.). New York: H. W. Wilson.

Carr, J. B. (1984). *Communicating and relating* (3rd ed.). Dubuque, IA: William C. Brown Company.

Cathcart, C., & Cathcart, R. (1988). Japanese social experience and concept of groups. In L. A. Samovar & R. E. Porter (Eds.), *Intercultural communication: A reader* (5th ed.). Belmont, CA: Wadsworth.

Cathcart, R., Samovar, L. A., & Henman, L. D. (1996). *Small group communication: Theory and practice* (7th ed.). Madison, WI: Brown and Benchmark.

Chan, S. (1998). *Spiritual theology.* Downers Grove, IL: InterVarsity Press.

Cho, P. Y., & Hostetler, H. (1981). *Successful home small groups.* Plainfield, NJ: Logos International.

Chronicle of higher education. (1999, August 27).

Clapp, R. (1996). *A peculiar people.* Downers Grove, IL: InterVarsity Press.

Clark, R. E., Johnson, L., & Sloat, A. K. (Eds.). (1991). *Christian education: Foundations for the future.* Chicago: Moody Press.

Claudis, G. (1999). *Leading the team-based church.* San Francisco: Jossey-Bass.

Coleman, L., & Scales, M. (1989). *Serendipity training manual for groups.* Littleton, CO: Serendipity House.

Condon, J. C., & Yousef, F. (1975). *An introduction to intercultural communication.* New York: Macmillan.

Corey, G., & Corey, M. S. (1987). *Groups: Process and practice* (3rd ed.). Monterey, CA: Brooks/Cole Publishing Company.

Corey, G., Corey, M. S., Callahan, P. J., & Russell, J. M. (1988). *Group techniques* (Rev. ed.). Pacific Grove, CA: Brooks/Cole Publishing Company.

Covey, S. R. (1989). *The seven habits of highly effective people: Restoring the character ethic.* New York: Simon & Schuster.

——— (1991). *Principle-centered leadership.* New York: Simon & Schuster.

Crabb, L. (1991). *Men and women, enjoying the differences.* Grand Rapids, MI: Zondervan.

——— (1999). *The safest place on earth.* Nashville, TN: Word.

Cushman, P. (1995). *Constructing the self, constructing America.* Reading, MA: Addison-Wesley.

Cyprian. *On the unity of the catholic church.*

Defoe, D. (1990). *Robinson crusoe.* Philadelphia: Running Press.

De Pree, M. (1989). *Leadership is an art.* New York: Doubleday.

——— (2000). *Does leadership have a future?* Pasadena, CA: De Pree Leadership Center.

Dodd, C. H. (1997). *Dynamics of intercultural communication.* Dubuque, IA: William C. Brown Company.

Donahue, B., & Robinson, R. (2001). *Building a church of small groups.* Grand Rapids, MI: Zondervan.

Dougherty, R. M. (1995). *Group spiritual direction: Community for discernment.* New York: Paulist Press.

Doyle, J. A., & Paludi, M. A. (1991). *Sex and gender* (2nd ed.). Dubuque, IA: William C. Brown Company.

Duerst-Lahti, G. (1990, August). But women play the game too: Communication control and influence in administrative decision making. *Administration and Society, 22,* 182–205.

Dyrness, W. A. (1989). *How does America hear the gospel?* Grand Rapids, MI: Eerdmans.

Edwards, T. (1997). *Spiritual friend: Reclaiming the gift of spiritual direction.* New York: Paulist Press.

Eliot, T. S. (1952). *Choruses from "the rock," complete poems and plays.* New York: Harcourt and Brace.

Fablo, T., & Peplau, L. A. (1980). Power strategies in intimate relationships. *Journal of Personality and Social Psychology, 38,* 4, 618–28.

——— (1990, February 12). Finding friends—for a fee. *Newsweek.*

Fisher, B. A. (1974). *Small group decision making: Communication and the group process*. New York: McGraw-Hill.

Fisher, B. A., & Ellis, D. G. (1990). *Small group decision making: Communication and the group process* (3rd ed.). New York: McGraw-Hill.

Fiske, E. (1990 March 5). Of learning and college: How small groups thrive. *New York Times*, p. A1, 3.

Fitzpatrick, M., & Winke, J. (1979). You always hurt the one you love: Strategies and tactics in interpersonal conflict. *Communication Quarterly*, 27, 1, 3–11.

Forsyth, D. R. (1999). *Group dynamics*. Belmont, CA: Wadsworth. [2nd ed. Pacific Grove, CA: Brooks/Cole Publishing Company, 1990].

Frank, A. & Brownell, J. (1989). *Organizational communication and behavior*. New York: Holt, Rinehart and Winston.

Frazee, R. (2001). *The connecting church*. Grand Rapids, MI: Zondervan.

Gaede, S. D. (1985). *Belonging*. Grand Rapids, MI: Zondervan.

George, C. (1991). *Prepare your church for the future*. Old Tappan, NJ: Revell.

Gibb, J. R. (1986). Defensive communication. In John Stewart (Ed.), *Bridges not walls* (4th ed.). New York: Random House.

Gillette, J., & McCollom, M. (Eds.). (1990). *Groups in context: A new perspective on group dynamics*. Reading, MA: Addison-Wesley.

Gilligan, C. (1983). *In a different voice*. Harvard: Harvard University Press.

Gish, A. (1979). *Living in Christian community*. Scottsdale, PA: Herald Press.

Goodall, H. L., Jr. (1990). *Small group communication in organizations* (2nd ed.). Dubuque, IA: William C. Brown Company.

Gorman, J. A. (1993). *Community that is Christian*. Wheaton, IL: Victor Books.

Grayson, C., & Johnson, J. (1991). *Creating a safe place*. San Francisco: Harper Collins.

Griffin, E. (1982). *Getting together: A guide for good groups*. Downers Grove, IL: InterVarsity Press.

Grove, T. G. (1991). *Dyadic interaction: Choice and change in conversations and relationships*. Dubuque, IA: William C. Brown Company.

Gudykunst, W. B., & Kim, Y. Y. (1997). *Communicating with strangers: An approach to intercultural communication* (3rd ed.). Boston: Allyn & Bacon [1984 ed. New York: Random House].

Gudykunst, W., & Ting-Toomey, S. (1988). *Culture and interpersonal communication*. Newbury Park, CA: Sage Publications.

Gumbel, N. (1994). *Telling others*. Colorado Springs, CO: Cook Ministry Resources.

Hackman, M. Z., & Johnson, C. E. (1991). *Leadership: A communication perspective*. Prospect Heights, IL: Waveland Press.

Hadaway, C. K., Wright, S., & DuBose, F. M. (1987). *Home cell groups and house churches*. Nashville, TN: Broadman Press.

Haleblian, J., & Finkelstein, S. (1993). Top management team size, ceo

dominance, and firm performance: The moderating roles of
environmental turbulence and discretion. *Academy of Management
Journal,* 36, 844–63.

Hall, E. T. (1959). *The silent language.*
Garden City, NY: Doubleday.

——— (1976). *Beyond culture.*
Garden City, NY: Doubleday.

——— (1983). *The dance of life.*
Garden City, NY: Doubleday.

Hall, J. A. (1984). *Nonverbal sex differences: Communicating accuracy
and expressive style.* Baltimore,
MD: The Johns Hopkins
University Press.

Halverson, R. C. (1972). *How I
changed my thinking about the
church.* Grand Rapids, MI:
Zondervan.

——— (1980). *Somehow inside of
eternity.* Portland, OR: Multnomah
Press.

——— *Perspective.*

Hansan, P. D. (1987). *The people
called: The growth of community in
the Bible.* San Francisco: Harper
and Row.

Hare, P. A. (1976). *Handbook of small
group research* (2nd ed.). New
York: The Free Press.

Hauerwas, S. (1981). *A community of
character.* South Bend, IN:
University of Notre Dame Press.

Hawkins, K. W. (1995, May). Effects
of gender and communication
content on leadership emergence
in small task-oriented groups.
Small Group Research, 26.

Hemphill, J. K. (1950). Relations
between the size of the group and
the behavior of the "superior"
leaders. *Journal of Social
Psychology,* 32, 11–22.

Heshka, S., & Nelson, Y. (1952).
Interpersonal speaking distance as
a function of age, sex, and relationship. *Sociometry,* 35, 481–98.

Hestenes, R., & Gorman, J. (1992).
*Syllabus: Building Christian com-
munity in small groups.* Pasadena,
CA: Fuller Theological Seminary.

Hirokawa, R. Y., Ice, R., & Cook, J.
(1988). Preference for procedural
order, discussion structure, and
group decision performance.
Communication Quarterly, 36,
217–26.

Hocker, J. L., & Wilmot, W. W.
(1985). *Interpersonal conflict* (2nd
ed.). Dubuque, IA: William C.
Brown Company.

Hoopes, M. H., Fisher, B. L., &
Barlow, S. H. (1984). *Structured
family facilitation programs:
Enrichment, education, and treat-
ment.* Rockville, MD: Aspen
Publishing.

Horton, M. S. (1991). *Made in
America: The shaping of modern
American evangelism.* Grand
Rapids, MI: Baker Book House.

Houston, J. (1996). *The heart's desire.*
Colorado Springs, CO: NavPress.

Howe, N., & Strauss, W. (2000).
*Millennials rising: The next great
generation.* New York: Vintage
Books.

Huszczo, G. E. (1996). *Tools for team
excellence.* Palo Alto, CA: Davies-
Black.

Iacocca, L. with Novak, W. (1984).
Iacocca: An autobiography. New
York: Bantam Books.

Icenogle, G. W. (1994). *Biblical foun-
dations for small group ministry.*
Downers Grove, IL: InterVarsity
Press.

Johnson, D. W. (1972). *Reaching out: Interpersonal effectiveness and self-actualization.* Englewood Cliffs, NJ: Prentice-Hall.

Johnson, D. W., & Johnson, F. P. (1991). *Joining together* (4th ed.). Englewood Cliffs, NJ: Prentice-Hall.

Katzenbach, J. R., & Smith, D. K. (1993). *The wisdom of teams: Creating the high-performance organization.* Boston: Harvard Business School Press.

Keirsey, D., & Bates, M. (1984). *Please understand me.* Del Mar, CA: Prometheus Nemesis Book Company.

Kenneson, P. D. (1999). *Life on the vine.* Downers Grove, IL: InterVarsity Press.

Kinlaw, D. C. (1991). *Developing superior work teams: Building quality and the competitive edge.* Lexington, MA: Lexington Books.

Kirchmeyer, C. (1993, February). Multicultural task groups: An account of the low contribution level of minorities. *Small Group Research,* 24.

Kirchmeyer, C., & Cohen, A. (1992). Multicultural groups: Their performance and reactions with constructive conflict. *Group and organization management,* 17, 153–70.

Kleisser, T. A., LeBert, M. A., & McGuinness; M. C. (1991). *Small Christian communities: A vision of hope.* New York: Paulist Press.

Kolb, J. A. (1997). Are we still stereotyping leadership? A look at gender and other predictors of leader emergence. *Small Group Research,* 28, 370–93.

Kraus, C. N. (1979). *The authentic witness.* Grand Rapids, MI: Eerdmans.

Kroeger, O., & Thuesen, J. M. (1988). *Type talk.* New York: Dell Publishing.

Law, E. H. F. (1993). *The wolf shall dwell with the lamb.* St. Louis, MO: Chalice Press.

Lawrenz, M. (2000). *The dynamics of spiritual formation.* Grand Rapids, MI: Baker Book House.

Lee, B. J., & Cowan, M. A. (1986). *Dangerous memories.* Kansas City: Sheed and Ward.

LeFever, M. D. (1985). *Creative teaching methods.* Elgin, IL: Cook.

L'Engle, M., & Shaw, L. (1997). *Friends for the journey.* Ann Arbor, MI: Servant Publications.

Lohfink, G. (1984). *Jesus and community.* Philadelphia: Fortress Press.

Loomer, B. (1976, Winter). Two kinds of power. *Criterion.*

Louv, R. (1990). *Childhood's future: Listening to the American family.* Boston: Houghton Mifflin.

Luft, J. (1984). *Group processes: An introduction to group dynamics* (3rd ed.). Mountain View, CA: Mayfield Publishing Company.

Lukes, S. (1973). *Individualism.* New York: Harper & Row.

Lumsden, G., & Lumsden, D. (2000). *Communicating in groups and teams.* Belmont, CA: Wadsworth.

MacIntyre, A. (1984). *After virtue. A study in moral theory* (2nd ed). South Bend, IN: University of Notre Dame Press.

Mallison, J. (1989). *Growing Christians in small groups.* Sydney, Australia/London: Scripture Union.

Mayers, M. K. (1974). *Christianity confronts culture: A strategy for cross-cultural evangelism.* Grand Rapids, MI: Zondervan.

McBride, N. F. (1990). *How to lead small groups.* Colorado Springs, CO: NavPress.

——— (1995). *How to build a small groups ministry.* Colorado Springs, CO: NavPress.

McKnight, J. (1995). *The careless society.* New York: Basic Books.

Meisels, M., & Guardo, C. J. (1969). Development of personal space schematas. *Child Development,* 40, 1167–78.

Miles, M. S. (1990). *Families growing together.* Wheaton, IL: Victor.

Miller, H. (1979). *Christian community biblical or optimal?* Ann Arbor, MI: Servant Books.

Miller, P. M. (1958). *Group dynamics in evangelism.* Scottdale, PA: Herald Press.

Miller, S., Wackman, D., Nunnally, E., & Miller, P. (1988). *Connecting with self and others.* Littleton, CO: Interpersonal Communication Programs, Inc.

Moltmann-Wendel, E., & Moltmann, J. (1983). *Humanity in God.* New York: Pilgrim.

Morris, B. (1993). *The complete handbook for recovery ministry in the church.* Nashville, TN: Thomas Nelson, Inc.

Morton, T. R. (1954). *Community of faith: The changing pattern of the church's life.* New York: Association Press.

——— *The twelve together.* Glasgow, Scotland: The Iona Community.

Naisbitt, J., & Aburdene, P. (1990). *Megatrends 2000.* New York: William Morrow & Co.

Napier, R. W., & Gershenfeld, M. K. (1983). *Making groups work: A guide for group leaders.* Boston: Houghton Mifflin.

——— (1989). *Groups: Theory and experience* (4th ed.). Boston: Houghton Mifflin.

Neighbour, R. W., Jr. (1990). *Where do we go from here?* Houston: Touch Publications, Inc.

Nichols, R. G., & Stevens, L. (1990). Listening to people. In *People: Managing your most important asset.* Boston: Harvard Business Review.

Nouwen, H. J. M. (1986). *Reaching out.* New York: Doubleday.

——— (1998). *Sabbatical journey.* New York: Crossroad.

——— (1987, January/February). The spirituality of waiting. *Weavings* 11, 1.

O'Halloran, J., SDB. (1996). *Small Christian communities.* Maryknoll, NY: Orbis Press.

Olsen, C. M. (1995). *Transforming church boards into communities of spiritual leaders.* Washington, D.C.: The Alban Institute.

Orlick, T. (1978). *The cooperative sports and games book.* New York: Pantheon Books.

Otto, H. A. (Ed.). (1976). *Marriage and family enrichment.* Nashville, TN: Abingdon Press.

Palazzolo, C. S. (1981). *Small groups, an introduction.* New York: D. Van Nostrand Co.

Palmer, P. A. (1997). *A place called community.* Philadelphia: Pendle Hill.

Pearson, J. C. (1981, September). The effects and setting and gender on self-disclosure. *Group and Organization Studies.*

Pearson, J. C., & Spitzberg, B. (1990). *Interpersonal communication* (2nd ed.) Dubuque, IA: William C. Brown Company.

Pearson, J. C., Turner, L. H., & Todd-Mancillas, W. (1985). *Gender and communication* (2nd ed.). Dubuque, IA: William C. Brown Company.

Peck, M. S. (1987). *The different drum.* New York: Simon & Schuster.

Pedersen, P. B., Draguns, J. G., Lonner, W. J., & Trimble, J. E. (1989). *Counseling across cultures.* Honolulu: University of Hawaii Press.

Peterson, J. (1980). *Evangelism as a lifestyle.* Colorado Springs, CO: NavPress.

Phillips, G. M., Pedersen, D. J., & Wood; J. T. (1979). *Group discussion: A practical guide to participation and leadership.* Boston: Houghton Mifflin.

Piper, W. E. (1983). Cohesion as a basic bond in groups. *Human Relations,* 36, 2, 93–108.

Plantinga, C. (1988, March 4). The perfect family. *Christianity Today* (pp. 24–27).

Plueddemann, J., & Plueddemann, C. (1990). *Pilgrims in progress.* Wheaton, IL: Harold Shaw.

Powell, J. (1969). *Why am I afraid to tell you who I am?* Chicago: Argus Communications.

(1999, August 23). Predictions: If the crown fits. . . . *Newsweek,* 8.

Reis, H. T. (1998). Gender differences in intimacy and related behaviors: Context and process. In D. J. Canary & K. Dindia (Eds.), *Sex differences and similarities in communication: Critical essays and empirical investigations of sex and gender in interaction.* Mahwah, NJ: Erlbaum.

Renz, M. A., & Greg, J. B. (2000). *Effective small group communication in theory and practice.* Neidham Heights, MA: Allyn & Bacon.

Robinson, H. W. (1980). *Corporate personality in ancient Israel.* Philadelphia: Fortress Press.

Roof, W. C. (1999). *Spiritual marketplace.* Princeton, NJ: Princeton University Press.

Rosener, J. B. (1990, November/December). Ways women lead. *Harvard Business Review,* 119–25.

———. (1995). *America's competitive secret: Utilizing women as a management strategy.* New York: Oxford University Press.

Rothwell, J. D. (1992). *In mixed company: Small group communication.* Fort Worth, TX: Harcourt Brace Jovanovich College Publishers.

Samovar, L. A., Porter, R. E., & Stefani, L. A. (1998). *Communication between cultures* (2nd ed.). Belmont, CA: Wadsworth.

Schein, E. H. (1991). *Organizational culture and leadership.* San Francisco: Jossey-Bass.

Schutz, W. C. (1958). *FIRO. A three-dimensional theory of interpersonal behavior.* New York: Holt, Rinehart and Winston.

Schultz, W. C. (1979). The leader as completer. In R. S. Cathcart &

L. A. Samovar (Eds.), *Small group communication: A reader* (3rd ed.). Dubuque, IA: William C. Brown Company.

Shimanoff, S., & Jenkins, M. M. (1996). Leadership and gender: Challenging assumptions and recognizing resources. In R. S. Cathcart, L. A. Samovar, & L. Henman (Eds.), *Small group communication: Theory and practice* (7th ed.). Madison, WI: Brown and Benchmark.

Sikora, P. J. (1991). *Small group Bible studies.* Cincinnati, OH: Standard Publishing.

Singer, M. R. (1987). *Intercultural communication.* Englewood Cliffs, NJ: Prentice-Hall.

Smith, D. K. (1992). *Creating understanding: A handbook for Christian communication across cultural landscapes.* Grand Rapids, MI: Zondervan.

Smith, K., & Berg, D. (Eds.). (1987). *Paradoxes of group life: Understanding conflict, paralysis, and movement in group dynamics.* San Francisco: Jossey-Bass.

Snyder, H. A. (1975). *The problem of wineskins.* Downers Grove, IL: InterVarsity Press.

——— (1980). *The radical wesley.* Grand Rapids, MI: Francis Asbury Press.

Sommer, R. (1959). Studies in personal space. *Sociometry, 22,* 247–60.

Stewart, J. (Ed.). (1986). *Bridges not walls* (4th ed.). New York: Random House.

Stewart, L. P., & Ting-Toomey, S. (Eds.). (1987). *Communication, gender, and six roles in diverse interaction contexts.* Norwood, NJ: Ablex Publishing Corporation.

Sussman, V. (1988, August). Smart toys: The little computers that could. *Washington Post.*

Swindoll, C. R. (1983). *Dropping your guard.* Waco, TX: Word.

Tannen, D. (1986). *That's not what I meant.* New York: William Morrow and Company.

——— (1990). *You just don't understand.* New York: William Morrow and Company.

Thelen, H. (1954). *Dynamics of groups at work.* Chicago: The University of Chicago Press.

Thompson, J. (1977). *Our life together.* Austin, TX: Journey Books, SPC Publications.

Ting-Toomey, S. (1985). Toward a theory of conflict and culture. In W. Gudykunst, L. Stewart, & S. Ting-Toomey (Eds.), *Communication, culture, and organizational processes.* Beverly Hills, CA: Sage Publications.

——— (1988). A face-negotiation theory. In Y. Kim & W. Gudykunst (Eds.), *Theory in intercultural communication.* Newbury Park, CA: Sage Publications.

Triandis, H. C., Brislin, R., & Hui, C. H. (1988). Crosscultural training across the individualism-collectivism divide. *International Journal of Intercultural Relations, 12,* 269–98.

Tubbs, S. L. (1984). *A systems approach to small group interaction.* Reading, MA: Addison-Wesley.

——— (2001). *A systems approach to small group interaction* (7th ed.). New York: McGraw-Hill.

Vanier, J. (1989). *Community and growth* (Rev. ed.). Mahwah, NJ: Paulist Press.

Verderber, K. S., & Verderber, R. F. (1986). *Inter-act: Using interpersonal communication skills.* Belmont, CA: Wadsworth.

——— (2001). *Inter-act: Interpersonal communication concepts, skills, and contexts* (9th ed.). Belmont, CA: Wadsworth.

Verderber, R. F. (1984). *Communicate!* (4th ed.). Belmont, CA: Wadsworth.

Verdi, A. F., & Wheelan, S. A. (1992, August). Developmental patterns in same-sex and mixed-sex groups. *Small Group Research, 23,* 356–78.

Voges, K., & Braund, R. (1990). *Understanding how others misunderstand you.* Chicago: Moody Press.

Volf, M. (1996). *Exclusion and embrace.* Nashville, TN: Abingdon Press.

Wakefield, N. (1981). *Listening: A Christian's guide to loving relationships.* Waco, TX: Word.

Watson, D. L. (1986). *Accountable discipleship.* Nashville, TN: Discipleship Resources.

Watson, K. W. (1996). Listener preferences: The paradox of small-group interactions. In R. S. Cathcart, L. A. Samovar, & L. Henman (Eds.), *Small group communication: Theory and practice* (7th ed.). Madison, WI: Brown and Benchmark.

Weaver, C. H. (1972). *Human listening: Processes and behaviors.* New York: Bobbs-Merrill.

Weaver, R. L. (1990). *Understanding interpersonal communication* (5th ed.). Glenview, IL: Scott, Foresman/Little, Brown Higher Education.

Wheeless, L., Wheeless, V., & Markman, F. D. (1982). A research note: The relations among social and task perceptions in small groups. *Small Group Behavior, 13,* 373–84.

Whitman, W. (1972). *Complete poetry and collected prose* (J. E. Miller Jr., Ed.). New York: Houghton Mifflin.

Willis, F. N. (1966). Initial speaking distance as a function of the speaker's relationship. *Psychonomic Science, 5,* 221–22.

Wilmot, W., & Hocker, J. (1998). *Interpersonal conflict.* New York: McGraw-Hill.

Wilson, G. L., & Hanna, M. S. (1986). *Groups in context.* New York: Random House.

Winstead, B. A., Derlega, V., & Wong, P. (1984). Effects of sex-role orientation on behavioral self-disclosure. *Journal of Research in Personality, 18,* 541–53.

Winter, D. A., & Green, S. B. (1987). Another look at gender-related differences in leadership behavior. *Sex Roles, 16,* 41–56.

Winthrop, J. (1965). A model of Christian charity. *Puritan political ideas, 1558–1794* (E. S. Morgan, Ed.). Indianapolis: Bobbs-Merrill.

Wolff-Salin, M. (1988). *The shadow side of community and the growth of self.* New York: Crossroad.

Wolvin, A., & Coakely, C. G. (1982). *Listening* (3rd ed.). Dubuque, IA: William C. Brown Company.

——— (1988). *Listening.* Dubuque, IA: William C. Brown Company.

Wood, J. T. (2001). *Gendered lives* (4th ed.). Belmont, CA: Wadsworth.

Woodbridge, J. D., Noll, M. A., & Hatch, N. O. (1979). *The gospel in America: Themes in the story of America's evangelicals.* Grand Rapids, MI: Zondervan.

Wright, G. E. (1954). *The biblical doctrine of man in society.* Philadelphia: Trinity Press.

Wuthnow, R. (1991). Evangelicals, liberals, and the perils of individualism. *Journal of Reformed Thought Perspectives* (pp. 10–13). Grand Rapids, MI: Reformed Church Press.

——— (1994). *Sharing the journey.* New York: The Free Press.

——— (1998). *After heaven: Spirituality in America since the 1950's.* Berkeley, CA: University of California Press.

——— *The restructuring of American religion.* Princeton: Princeton University Press.

Yale, D. (1988). Metaphors in mediating. *Mediation Quarterly, 22,* 15–25.

Yancey, P. (2000). *Reaching for the invisible God.* Grand Rapids, MI: Zondervan.

Yankelovich, D. (1982). *New rules: Searching for self-fulfillment in a world turned upside down.* New York: Bantam.

INDEX

Julie A. Gorman is Professor of Christian Formation and Discipleship at Fuller Theological Seminary in Pasadena, California. She served as an editor for Baker's *Dictionary of Christian Education* and is the author of two small group studies, *Let's Get Together* and *No Strangers to God,* as well as *The Small Group Training Manual.*